METAMORPHOSIS OF A
Young Maiden

Dr. Wm. Patric Leedom

ARPress
ILLUMINATING IDEAS.
EMPOWERING VOICES

ARPress
45 Dan Road Suite 5
Canton MA 02021

Hotline: 1(800) 220-7660
Fax: 1(855) 752-6001

Ordering Information:
Quantity sales. Special discounts are available on quantity purchases by corporations, associations, and others. For details, contact the publisher at the address above.

Printed in the United States of America.

ISBN-13:   Paperback   979-8-89676-204-1
           eBook   979-8-89676-205-8

Library of Congress Control Number: 2024925148

Dedication

July 26, 2019
With drawing grateful inspiration from:
Elizabeth Barrett Browning's poem:

How do I love thee? Let me count the ways.
I love thee to the depth and breadth and height
My soul can reach, when feeling out of sight
For the ends of Being and ideal Grace.
I love thee to the level of everyday's
Most quiet need, by sun and candlelight.
I love thee freely as men strive for Right;
I love thee purely, as they turn from Praise.
I love thee with the passion put to use
In my old griefs, and with my childhood's faith.
I love thee with a love I seemed to lose
With my lost saints—I love thee with the breath,
Smiles, tears, of all my life! —and, if God choose,
I shall but love thee better after death.

From my heart, Metamorphosis of a Young Maiden, is the greatest work of love that I and Shelley ever coauthored. Hopefully it is not approaching pretentiousness to suggest that the thoughts expressed by Elizabeth Barrett Browning's poem can be discerned throughout the letters we exchanged.

I know for myself, and I believe for Shelley, our love filled every waking moment. My strongest desire was to express my deep love for and to Shelley—as defined by 1. A profoundly tender, passionate affection for another person 2. A feeling of warm personal attachment or deep affection, and 3. Sexual passion or desire.

Once we were married, I gave up living in California and my lucrative bank job, and relocated to Our Town, and took an ordinary job to be close to Shelley, support her in her schooling, to attempt to provide any and all of her needs, and provide loving care.

I therefore dedicate this record of our journey through one of life's greatest experiences to all those who are on similar journeys.

PROLOGUE
TO SHELLEY'S AND PATRIC'S LETTERS

I think this Love Story of Shelley's 33 Letters and Patric's 15 Letters was unusual in a number of Dynamics:

The story takes place 1969-1970, at a cultural time when people actually put pen to paper and wrote letters. No electronics of any kind other than the telephone and tape recorder.

The story takes place in a conservative mid-western city.

Because the older sister, SALLY, and PATRIC had dated for about a year in 1959, I, PATRIC, was well acquainted with the family, and they me.

Bryan, older brother, and Theresa, sister-in-law, HAD married in the mid-1960s.

In 1959, I had become aware of Shelley—the much younger pudgy 9-year-old—but she never talked to me because there was no reason to. In later years, Sally occasionally talked to Shelley about me.

Once I reappeared on the scene in September 1969—and Shelley was now 19 and a student in a professional music academy—the family decided I should marry Shelley; for example, every time I came over for dinner, e.g. the September meal, and Thanksgiving, at the end, the mother, Stella, requested that Shelley get out her 12-string guitar and play and sing (her own compositions) for me.

The big change was when her mother, Stella, requested me to escort Shelley downtown to the Men's Christmas Chorale, for she was the guest soloist singing "Ave Maria." At first I "choked" as I was 29 and Shelley was a teenager of

19. I hesitated as I contemplated if it was socially proper for a man of my age to date a teenager. Up until that moment I had not ever considered Shelley, only as Sally's kid sister (9 years apart).

But I did accept the request to escort her. Over the next two days in December, when I spent a lot of time with Shelley, and the "MAGIC WORKED"—I fell madly in love with Shelley—that might be described in a way as "NUCLEAR FUSION." **

We were together every day, sometimes in the daytime and more often evenings when Shelley and I were sitting together in her family's love seat in her living room into the wee hours.

Another dynamic was that I had departed from graduate school in Illinois and had plans to return to California, where I was living before graduate school, and to live with my father in Los Angeles. I was to leave on January 12th, so there were a lot of time pressures.

Within two days of the Christmas Chorale Concert, I was telling Shelley that I loved her, to which she responded, "HOORAY!" Shelley had started to fall in love with me during their September family dinner. Shelley wrote in her diary just before Thanksgiving: "If he asks me to marry him, I would!"

So Shelley was "armed and ready" to go deep into a relationship, thus she wrote "HOORAY" in her diary. A few nights later, I did ask Shelley to "marry me." To which she tentatively said, "YES."

Once we decided we were engaged, our nightly dates went deeper into physical loving—I introduced Shelley to sensual, sexual passions. We very quickly discussed her virginity, and together we took a VOW that Shelley should be a virgin on her wedding night, and we did keep that VOW. Discussions of the VOW show up in many of Shelley's and Patric's letters.

In the early stages we planned to marry after Shelley had graduated from her music academy, so then we began planning for Shelley to come out to my home in California in June for a four-week visit in the summer of 1970. See the January and February letters. But by late February we decided we should get married in June 1970.

A note about Shelley: She was 9 years younger than her siblings so Shelley grew up alone in the house. Also her parents were arguing and fighting a lot in those years; Shelley felt lonely and somewhat abandoned. She did have her dog, Sarabel, to talk to, and provide loving comfort. As a teenager, she grew up reclusive and naïve about dating and sex. She was conservative in her personal values. She wrote in her diary that she had "The World's Biggest Inferiority Complex." This was partly due to her mother, Stella, often telling Shelley, "You are ugly and you are fat!" Shelley certainly did have a weight problem in her teen years. At 11 she weighed 136 pounds, and a few years later she weighed 163 pounds. But then she got active and went on a strict diet, shedding most of that weight.

When we were married, I thought Shelley was beautiful and voluptuous—but not overweight. Shelley, however, went through her whole life feeling and believing that she was "FAT."

Another dynamic was Shelley was naïve about dating and sex—hardly ever considering the topic in relation to her. So when I came along I introduced her to sexual pleasures, it turned her whole world "upside down." Shelley had a group of female friends and they were shocked that in less than two months—her friends exclaimed that Shelley went from being the "recluse and shy person to now being engaged to be married and Happy as Sin."

In a January letter Shelley wrote: "In case you have not noticed it, I like sex!" So you will see sensual and sexual themes running through most of her and his letters.

Nuclear Fusion Atomic interaction in which NUCLEONS are fused together, creating new atomic nuclei and releasing ENERGY In fusion, the light nuclei of hydrogen atoms **are joined together at extraordinary high temperatures **to form a single heavy helium nucleus, ejecting high-speed neutrons in the process."** [Dictionary of SCIENTIFIC LITERACY, Richard P. Brennan, John Wiley & Sons, Inc. New York, Copy: 1992]

So I submit that once Shelley and I both understood the possibilities of our relationship, we were strongly attracted to each other and our relationship did resemble Nuclear Fusion; certainly a "lot of ENERGY and HEAT was generated."

METAMORPHOSIS OF A YOUNG MAIDEN
THEME IN A CAPSULE

"How did I get so lucky? I used to think that reality never would be able to approach my dreams...but my dreams of happiness and love as I saw them before you came along could never hold a candle to the heavenly reality that exists now: the reality that Winston Patric Spencer loves Shelley Lynn Bennington. Wow!! What a wonderful world!

LETTERS FROM SHELLEY AND PATRIC

Climbing Up the Mountain of a Beautiful Life's Dream
    A series of metamorphoses for a young maiden who adventures through revolutionary events, turned herself into a young maturing woman.

CALENDAR OF EVENTS 1959

Most of the year, I dated older sister Sally—took her to her high school prom, etc. Her younger sister by nine years, Shelley Lynn, was a quiet, shy, pudgy nine-year-old, seen mostly in the shadows. Then Sally went off to college in the East and got married; I went off to the West Coast and got married.

Ten years later, in September 1969, Sally coordinated to meet with me and talk as old friends. This developed into "I'll meet you in our old familiar church." So Sally and her husband, Clifford, and Sally's and Shelley's mother, Stella, and I all sat in the same pew together in the congregation. Sally issued an invitation for me to come back to the family home for a Sunday dinner, since everyone in the family knew me and would enjoy seeing me again. So I joined the family for dinner, which was very pleasant. Shelley, now a serious 19-year-old student in a Music Academy, was requested to get out her 12-string guitar and play and sing for us. I thought it was beautiful music.

As I got up to leave, Shelley's mother asked me if I was coming back to our town from my graduate school in Chicago to attend Thanksgiving. "Yes." "Well, you must come and have dinner with us!" "Okay." So, at Thanksgiving I did join Shelley's family. It was very pleasant. Again Shelley was requested to get out her guitar and sing for us. Again, very talented, enjoyable music. As I got up to leave, Shelley's mother asked if I were coming back to our city for Holiday Break? "Yes." "What day?" "16th." "Oh, good, you are just in time to escort Shelley downtown, where she is the guest soloist for a Christmas Chorale program." I choked and hesitated when I was asked to escort a teenager to a music concert. I was 29 years old; would that be proper? Well, Shelley was 19 and seemed interested, so I agreed to do it.

December 16, 1969

Patric arrives in Our-Town from college in Chicago.

December 17 [Wednesday]

Civic All-Male CHRISTMAS Chorale Concert in the Marriot Hotel Ballroom: Shelley Bennington, age 19, is the guest soloist to sing AVE MARIA!! We went to Shelley's house for dinner; to the concert with Shelley and her older brother, Bryan, to a local restaurant; to Bryan and Theresa's house; and ultimately to Shelley's house, where Shelley and Patric spent a quiet hour together in the Benningtons' living room talking.

December 20 [Saturday]

Talk session with Stanwood kids at Hopedale Church; to Shelley's at 4:00 P.M. Out to buy a Xmas Tree for the Benningtons; dinner; decorate the tree; then to [Patric's Cousins Mary and Bob Chamberlain's house to trim their tree with lights]. *FIRST KISS –WOW! wrote Shelley in her diary.*

December 21 [Sunday]

Shelley and Patric went to church; then to the Golden Gate Flower Conservatory—magnificent tree—to Patric's cousins' (for more tree decorating)—to Open House with the Chamberlains. To Shelley's for sandwiches...AND...?

December 22 [Monday]

Cheesecake baking. Catastrophes, disasters; calamities galore...

December 23

To Patric's mother, Elinore, and stepfather, Mark Harrington's apartment to bake cookies with sister Elizabeth; to Kit and George's house for a brief stop; to Shelley's to top-off the evening. A sudden snowstorm came up and: *"**WHAT A SHAME...STRANDED AT SHELLEY'S FOR THE REST OF THE EVENING-(morning?),"** wrote Shelley in her diary.* We went for a walk in the snow together... (beautiful).

December 25th

To Shelley's in the evening; Shelley's older sister, Sally, and her husband, Clifford arrive later; Shelley and Patric go for another walk (earlier). "Lovely talk 'session'...much later into the wee hours—alone in the living room on the Love Seat.

December 26th

Dinner at Shelley's parents' home with Sally and Cliff; Party at Bryan and Theresa Bennington's...dancing etc....beautiful...

Pat tells Shelley "I love you!" Shelley wrote in her diary: !!!!!!!HOORAY!!!!!!!

December 28th (Sunday)

To Shelley's for a rather miserable dinner; Pat says "Mrs. Shelley Spencer." Pat tells Shelley that all his layers of fear and doubt are stripped away.

December 30th

To Bryan and Theresa's home to make a tape of Shelley singing for Pat. Before Pat arrived, he had been downtown to a business luncheon with his surrogate stepfather, Carl Jacob. All men at the table consumed four martinis (which was usual for them). Pat drove out to Shelley's home and…Pat is tipsy from drinking 4 martinis with Carl Jacob. [The last time I saw Carl alive!] Shelley to Pat "Tsk, tsk!" Dinner at Bryan and Theresa's; then to Shelley's home. Stella and Pat have a talk; Shelley and Pat stay up too late (early in the morning?) alone on the couch in the living room…once more…

December 31st

New Year's Eve—dinner at Shelley's party at Chamberlains' …. Happy New Year Patric, Shelley tells Patric, "I love you."

January 1st

New Year's Day…went to listen to Shelley's recorded singing tape at Chamberlains'; look at Andrew Wyeth Album; dinner at Patric's Mother's and Stepfather's home—the Harringtons; (lovely family) … back to Chamberlain's house for Pat to change clothes; back to Shelley's home for another "Quiet Night" [ah hem]—after Bryan and Theresa leave…*Patric asks Shelley to marry him.* Shelley accepts because… because "I love you **Patric and with you I am whole.**"

[Shelley's first letter to Patric]

Dear Pat,

Last night I started a letter to you, but when I read over it this morning it sounded so sticky-sweet that it made me a bit queasy. So, I tore it up & threw it away. I figured that there will be many times in the next 6-7 months when I'll be missing you so much that the letters will be melancholy gushy. But not now. If you left this morning at 8:00 A.M. & travel goes according to schedule, you ought to be about an hour away from the town of Shenandoah Cave. I hope you got a good night's sleep; I dreamed about you & woke up in the night to find that I was hugging Sarabel, not you. Disappointment. Well, the day will come....

But I just am going to put myself into an optimistic frame of mind—the sooner I start the sooner each passing day will go by, bringing the time for us ultimately be together that much closer. What a dream we share.... And the reality that backs up that dream is as rare as the dream itself.

I hope your evening last night was very pleasant at your mother's and that you and she got a chance to talk and relate to one another. I was very happy when you called at my best girl-friend Gayle's house. I told myself all day that you wouldn't call because you wouldn't have a chance. But in the back of my mind, I kept thinking that you would call, and I'm so glad you did....

Usually I have no trouble writing, but now I sit here all tongue-tied, in my brain! I want the letters that I'll be writing, to you to have meaning for you. I want them to convey all that I feel for you...but without destroying the beauty of wordless emotions. As I write I am remembering our hours together. I am hearing your voice—whispering, speaking, resounding in laughter. I am seeing you—walking, sitting in the rocker, stretched out in front of the fireplace. I am feeling your gentle touch, your kisses. And, dammit, I'm missing you like crazy! But time will pass.

Pat, I really don't know what I'd do if something happened between us. Mother asked me if I don't think that perhaps I will change my mind as time goes by. But if I had the slightest doubt—even the tiniest bit—I wouldn't have said I'd marry you. I love you very much, and I know that our love will expand and grow and deepen within the years….

I feel so happy—very privileged & honored to think that you—Patric Spencer actually love me. That's what I call thrilling. I thought I knew what love is, but now after knowing the joy of being in love with you…

Love Shelley

January 11th

Patric's last night before he departs to drive to California. Stella tells Pat to stay overnight at their house [which means up on the second floor, where there are just two bedrooms which have no doors between the two bedrooms]. [**Patric and Shelley are engaged, so they do sleep together lovingly.**]

Monday, January 12, 1970, 6:00 P.M.

Dear Pat,

This is the third time I've started a letter to you in the past 5 minutes or so. It's difficult to describe the tremendous "turmoil" my emotions are going through. The house is so quiet tonight that it made me very lonely, despite the fact that mother and the three animals are right downstairs. So I put four records on...records that I haven't listened to in a long long time, because when I had no one to think of, the music made me very sad. The meaning of the pieces was lost, or incomplete, when they remind one only of the past.

But now I can listen to them again, and *feel lonely sometimes, perhaps,* —more often though, a soothing peace will settle within me, because I'll think of you. "Tender Is the Night" is playing now. They're not masterpieces or anything; they're just romantic, emotional and sentimental pieces with no words to interfere. And now, "Tara's Theme." This album happens to be one of movie themes. Did you see *Gone With The Wind*?

I love Tara's Theme—it's so warm and yet wistful and longing. Sometimes I just sit and cry when I hear it, not because I feel so sad, but because it expresses something within me. Maybe that's why I told you last night that in a way I felt I had no "right" to cry: no right because to me, laughing, crying are definite expressions of feelings inside. By crying last night I would only have confused myself and felt the worse for it because it wouldn't have been a means of expression at all. Today, I cried and didn't bother to think about it...the tears were there so I accepted them. This is the dumbest letter I've ever heard of.

I guess I'm just rambling on because I have so much inside of me that any minute I may burst—and it has nothing to do with the fact that I just ate supper!

Somehow, I feel no fear tonight. I guess it's because I really can believe that we are moving closer to one another. Each hour that I'm with you, I learn more about you. During the week, nagging little terrors kept snapping their fingers at me and warning me— "Hey, dumb-dumb, what makes you think that Patric won't find another love? What makes you think that perhaps another 'casual' affair—just as yours started out to be—won't turn into a deep and even more meaningful relationship to Patric?" And I cringed at the thoughts, but I let the thoughts come anyway, because I wanted to hear myself out. Sometimes I didn't even bother to answer them—I just let them be. Now, I can answer them all, I think. "I believe in Patric, that's why I know we'll marry and make a good life for ourselves." Sometimes I have to sit and say to myself, "Pat loves me." And I sit and listen to myself, and then I turn my mind's tape recording and play back your voice. And I look at you, and hear you, and touch you, and nothing else matters as much as you.

I've never written a letter like this before—usually I have something specific to tell, some thought-form in my mind that will shape the letter. But, here I am a blank! Sometimes when my feelings are at a peak inside, I go blank.

This afternoon I came up here to my room and took the white rug on the floor out; replacing it with the yellow one that was by my bed. And I took **our** rug and laid it down where you wanted it. Then I hung the picture of the two horses that Gayle gave me, and put the flowers on the top of my "Horse Display Case." That's the sacred place in my room—before, only the horse statue could stand there, because of its beauty and elegance (well, I think it's rather elegant.) But now my flowers—your flowers [from Farmers' Market in H.]—sit and smile at me and say "just look at us—we carry a lot of Pat in us." And I put the "cone flower cluster" at the base of the flower vase…. So now my room has more of a Patric atmosphere to it, and it is a great comfort [includes a Farmers' Market Rug] I don't know if I really thanked you for these wonderful gifts…

But it seems to me that words have to be handled very carefully, because they can so easily destroy or distort an image, make it less beautiful, turn its simple purity into something less dignified. Thank you, my darling Pat, for these tangible symbols of the intangible. They are so Beautiful, they are so…well, they're so **YOU.** You put a lot of thought into the selection of these gifts, and I **know** that if I saw identical objects sitting in a mountain store or anyplace else, those rugs and flowers, etc. would not be half as beautiful as these because they wouldn't possess the love that you let flow into these. I really believe that; I'm not trying to sound…well, "poetic" I guess.

Mother [Stella] really gets me sometimes. You know I was _really_ upset with her last night—I haven't felt that kind of anger toward her in quite a while. She never lets me know exactly what she's upset about when she gets into a mood like that.

Well, then today, she's been really nice and she apologized for the way she acted last night. Somehow, in the course of the conversation which was about you, naturally, since you'd just left, we got to talking about your staying here. I told her I was no longer concerned about the sex issue and she agreed. That was good. I casually managed *to say something about how I bet we could go to bed together and not have relations [intercourse]. I wanted to see her reaction, I guess...and she agreed with me. Then she laughingly said,* **"WHY— did you two sleep together last night?"** *And I just laughed and said "I'LL NEVER TELL."* Mother got this expression that perhaps a 5-year-old will when he/she finally yanks that loose tooth out—surprise, a little dismay and delight. **"YOU DID!!!"** she blurted. I just teased her. But she said that was OK as long as we weren't making ourselves unduly "upset" by doing so. I hope you don't mind that mother is fairly certain we did sleep together—I guess I feel pretty good about it because, well for one thing, when you come again I won't have to be nervous about it—and we won't need a clock!

When I was a kid (and I don't need a comment on that statement!!) I used to think that if I ever kissed anybody on the lips—that I'd be so embarrassed I'd never be able to look the boy (man)—in the face again!

Well, I graduated from that to every other stage as I learned about SEX, but when you and I talk about it, I feel no embarrassment. It's something that you and I feel very good about inside—like a secret between just the two of us. It makes me excited & happy and makes me feel wanted. But our relations now, and eventually when we can run the full gamut of physical love, will always be something I will never discuss with anyone else, the way many girls I know talk about what they do with their boyfriends. Everyone knows about sex eventually and the jokes and crude remarks are funny, but no one never need (get that **grammar**— let's try it again!)—but no one ever needs to talk about the special, wonderful...mmmmm...drat it—I so seldom make mistakes that when I do make one such as the "no one never" back there, it shakes me up so that I go into shock and can't remember what I was saying! This letter's getting painful anyway…meaning that my head is killing me. I woke up with a headache this morning and kept it all day. I think it's some of this tension inside causing it.

If I were you, I'd just go back to the beginning of this letter, pretend you haven't read any of it, and then throw it away before you torture yourself. After I become accustomed to writing to you, I'll quit worrying so much about my letters. Now I keep thinking that I have such a limited vocabulary that it's almost impossible to express myself. As I told you, I got out of the habit of expressing myself either in thinking or writing, and it's a little hard to get back into. That's why I've written four pages before this and you can't remember what any of them said. The letter you wrote to me was by far the most beautiful letter I have ever been privileged enough to receive. [Note: It was hand-written with no copy.] To me, it's far greater than any jewel: it is a treasure—my kind of treasure. I'm going to read it again after you write me again. Now I want to think of Saturday and Sunday and this morning.

These past two nights—Saturday and Sunday, and all-day Sunday as well as this morning…oh brother, that's a ridiculous beginning to a sentence. Try again. Ahem... ready? Go! Start over. Saturday night through this morning have brought some of the most meaningful moments to us that we've yet shared. [When we slept together.] You are such a complex person that I feel different each time I see you from day to day, week to week. You gave me TREMENDOUS PLEASURE in a physical sense. And the warmth and love that you expressed by looking at me smiling at me, sharing your feelings and thoughts with me have made me happier than I ever have been before. I hate to sound trite, but I LOVE YOU, I love you very much Winston Patric Spencer.

When we have bad times, we'll work the out through sharing, and suffering together. When you feel angry, just let me know at first how to react. If you want to shout at me, I'll listen; and if you want to be left alone, I won't intrude. If you want to talk about something important and you find me not responding, not in the mood, give me a nudge—say "hey, this is important to me, and I want you to listen." If I know that it means a lot to you, it will also mean that much to me. Sometimes you'll have to help me, because I won't know how to handle a mood, perhaps, or I won't understand what's clicking behind those beautiful blue eyes of yours. You know more about adjusting in marriage than I do, of course, and so I may need your help because it will be a tremendous step for me to move away, etc. And I do so want to make you happy. **I don't like arguments, but sometimes they're a good healthy means of expression. I hope you see my many faults now. Pat, so that there will be no disappointments eventually.** Sometimes I have a tendency to let little things irritate me, and I shrug them off and let them go until I can't take them any longer.

If you irritate me, I'll let you know and you must let me know if I bother you. We can't change things we're unaware of. Well, enough. I'll try to write a letter to every stopover [on your car trip west to Los Angeles]. I enjoy writing to you. Every letter marks more time gone by...and each minute draws us closer toward a lifetime together. I hope you'll write—even if it's only on a postcard. It means a lot to hear from you. It helps me so.

Pat, you've changed my world—and I can't begin to tell you how much you mean to me. Have a good trip [to California] and please be careful. By the way, if something ever would happen to you, I'd want to be notified immediately—I mean that. Somehow, if you needed me, I'd get there, no matter where you may be.

I don't want to sound pessimistic or anything, but it is important to know that if you did get hurt or anything I would want know as quickly as possible. I'll be worried until you get to California—you know how crazy drivers are. Please be careful, take care.

Tonight I'll dream of you; *last night you were real*. I'll hear movement in the bed in there, [other bedroom] and I'll stop and think for a moment. And I'll think of the future then to ease the disappointment. I love you. My darling, Pat.

Today, I started hearing an old old folksong in my head as soon as you left. I'll sing it to you on tape sometime. It says:

"Oh, he's gone; he's gone away for to stay
A little while.
But he's comin' back, if he goes ten thousand miles
Look away,
Look away, look away, over yonder
"Who will tie your shoes?
And who will glove your hand?
And who will kiss your lips when I am gone?
Pappy will tie my shoes.
And Mammy will glove my hand.
And YOU will kiss my lips when you come back."

Well, it made me feel a lot better—made a rather nice arrangement of it. I hope your lunch date with your mother was very meaningful and happy for you and her.

I love you. Please write when you want to…I look forward to hearing. What a lucky girl I am…Patric loves me. Miss you. Love you. Yours always, Shelley [Hearts and flowers drawing.]

Tuesday January 13, 1970, 10:00 P.M.

Dear Patric,

I am all choked up now, after having just talked to you a few minutes ago. I came upstairs and had planned to write in my diary, but then I thought "don't write about him at a time like this—for goodness sakes, write to him." So here I am. I guess I'm just humoring my emotions right now. Thank you for calling me. I needed that and I didn't even know it. As your voice came to me again, I sat with tears in my eyes and I wanted to snap my fingers and find myself by your side. I'm glad you called, Pat. I thought about you all day long, and when my voice teacher expressed some surprise about my state of mind, I told him I had a very good reason. Only you filled my mind today. I was almost afraid to go into the other bedroom today because I knew how it would make me miss you. I did go in and just looked around, remembering, thinking.

You always time things so beautifully. I was heading for a great big depression this evening…I laid on my bed daydreaming about our future. I can't recall at the moment just what the visions were, but it helped to think of our married life. There's a big lump in my throat because I am listening to your voice as it sounded on the phone tonight—so tired and rather sad. Last night I couldn't make myself stop writing to you, so I didn't go to bed until about 11:00 P.M. which is generally rather late on a school night…. Oh, I'm so glad you called. My darling, wonderful Pat. I love you so much—I never really believed that there could ever be a love like ours. The time will pass, so don't be too lonely. Just think of me, and know that I am missing and loving you every minute of the day. When you need to hear from me, don't hesitate to tell me because chances are, I'll be needing reassurance too.

I couldn't resist writing you again—figured there was no reason not to write. Thank you, Pat, for being you. We are going to have such a wonderful life together, and these lonely months will make us treasure togetherness all the more. I love you so. I'm kissing you good night now. Lovingly yours, Shelley

January 16, 1970, 8:00 P.M.

Dear Patric,

This evening I went shopping for a few minutes, and decided to buy some stationery, and some cartridges for my pen. Now what fun is it to buy all these goodies without putting them to use? Naturally, I owe about three people a letter, but alack, alack! Me noble pen refuses to write a single letter unless it is confident that it is writing to you. And who, pray tell, am I to argue? However, there is one slight problem: this pen was meant to be handled by a right-handed person, so it's a bit difficult to manipulate. Oh, the woes and pains that cruel prejudice inflicts upon poor humble innocents!

Oh, I can just tell this letter's going to be a real winner!

Today, I was rather hoping to hear from you but I knew that you probably wouldn't have had any time yet to write. I was feeling pretty blue for a while there today—finally I went for a walk with my friends Agnes & Lyle, but in spite of the gorgeous weather, I couldn't seem to really enjoy myself much—I wasn't very jolly company I guess—I sort of felt half-dazed in a way. But I talked myself out of the melancholy—mother helped when I got home. I couldn't help but think about the last week at this time—the wonderful anticipation of your homecoming. It was sad—especially at the end of the Chorale (my last class.) I could remember my exact thoughts and everything. But then I scolded myself and reminded myself that if it were last week at this time, then I would have to go through this week at this time again. And the sooner the days go by, the sooner we'll be together. And that's enough to shut off the dumps for a while.

I yelled at Agnes today, who started to pick up my depression. She was going up to South Bend after she dropped me off. She is staying up there this weekend with her boyfriend. She got kind of moody and I said "For heaven's sake, don't you get down. You should be all happy and excited—I would be! I wish I were spending the weekend with the person I love. Try going six months without Michael!" I wasn't nasty or anything and it worked: She pulled right out of it. I did too—I thought, "Why, I wouldn't trade places with Agnes for anything, because I've got Patric at the end of all that waiting."

What are you doing now, Pat? Are you eating dinner, or maybe having a nice chat with friends? Are you thinking of me? Missing me? Loving me? I love you so—always remember that in good times and bad. I'll always love you. My darling, Patric.

I have been sort of avoiding the living room and the spare bedroom up here. Last night I decided to read in the living room, and when I first sat down, I just *looked around and was suddenly re-living some of our moments. I saw you sitting on the couch with me. I saw you walking in* from the hallway.

I saw you blowing out the candles; and you picked up the bouquet of flowers from the rocking chair. I saw you with the tray of food gazing at me and telling me that all your doubts and fears were gone. I saw us standing up and holding each other, *and once again you asked me to marry you. Oh boy; I got a big lump in my throat then, and I have one now.*

January 17 [same letter]

Well Patric, you put me into a wonderful cloud and I'm riding high. It makes me feel so strong, emotionally when you express your feelings for me—no matter what *you* do or where you are or how you do it. *How did I get so lucky? I used to think that reality never would be able to approach my dreams…but my dreams of happiness and love as I saw them before you came along could never hold a candle to the heavenly reality that exists now: the reality that Patric loves Shelley Lynne Bennington. Wow!! What a wonderful world!*

When I write to you, it makes me feel less lonely— closer to you…

I love you, Patric—
my wonderful, funny, sweet, gentle, and **SEXY Patric.** What a future we have—what a love we have, what a life we'll have, I couldn't ever love anyone as much as I love you. *I don't think my heart could physically stand the strain!* I never used to think that there was such a thing as "meant for each other" or "one love only" I thought that people fall in & out of love and they lose a love, they find another. I hope I don't sound trite—but there just couldn't be another you…I would never be able to fall in love again after being

in love with you, feeling the tremendous power of your love that makes me tingle so.

…This isn't a letter, it's a book….

…Because at the end of my rainbow…my rainbow that brightens at every month period and that ends at 2 ½ years… at the end of this rainbow is my darling Patric—you and another rainbow shines in your eyes and through your soul. That rainbow never ends and it never begins. It is deeper than infinity and more brilliant than any star; it is warmer than the suns of the entire universe, and softer than any cloud. It is full of passion and love, peace, and beauty. And all of its gentleness whispers and talks to me whenever your eyes meet mine; or when your lips caress mine; or your hands softly sing their love to me. My God, Pat, I love you so much that I don't know what to do with it all. Dream, dream. Be peaceful and calm and know that whatever you do, whenever you go, my heart and my love is with you. Goodnight, my darling. I love you. I'm yours, love Shelley.

Sunday, January 17th

Dear Patric,

Maybe I should be more careful about what I write to you…I don't want each letter to sound like a "carbon copy" of the last one. And I don't want you to become bored with my letters, **or any other part of me either!**

8:30 P.M. I have my record player on and I am listening to a record by the "Journeymen." They're a good group, but they broke up a few years back. They're "Folksingers."

While I was taking my shower a while ago, I was thinking about our first evening at the Chamberlains. Do you remember? That was so beautiful. I was so glad that we didn't go to the party that Agnes wanted you to go to. Sitting there on the Loveseat with you, I remember that my heart started racing and the "Goose Bumps" covered me all over. It was a magical, wonderful evening. And I kept thinking as we spoke *"Why are we trying so hard to run away from each other? Why do you keep talking about fulfilling a relationship? Why can't you? Because you're leaving? Well, I'm not ready to marry yet either. But if you asked me to, I'd wait."* And then I scolded myself for trying to see beyond your words. I told myself I'd better believe what you are saying—and believe what I was saying.

I knew damn well that if things didn't develop, I'd be broken hearted—maybe worse than ever. But I did want to make a lot of memories because I knew that if I got hurt it would not be because you were deceitful or dishonest— only I would be to blame. And so I wanted the experience of having a lovely—even if brief— "affair" with you.

But I couldn't shut out the vibrations that were coming from you. They were there then, Pat. Did you feel them? Were you aware of them? I think that is the reason I felt so comfortable with you—I kept getting these wonderful vibrations. I wanted to be able to say, "I love you" that night, but I didn't want to hurt you. I always assumed that if nothing permanent did come of our relationship, *I would never, never let you know how much I cared.* I meant it too—I can be a hell of an actress, and I cared too much to hurt you, to make you feel regretful for my sake. *Well, something happened—maybe it was those vibrations that told me to please be honest and not be afraid to show that I would be willing to love you. As I look back, I know that I must have unconsciously been showing you a lot more than I intended to.* Does it make you feel funny to have me say these things?

Maybe if it does, you'll want to express what's going through your mind as you look back. The main thing now is that I love you. Your "sad" will always be my "sad," your "happy" my happy. I love you so much, Patric.

[Well, I do know for certain that Shelley definitely had Extra Sensory Perception (ESP); so maybe that included her ability to detect VIBRATIONS. And as I look back now, in 2018, I can say that the vibrations Shelley was giving to me positively led to my falling "madly in love with her." I know that from that December when I was so strongly attracted to Shelley, I NEVER ONCE, for a millesecond—had any doubts or concerns about loving and marrying Shelley. I loved her more and deeply than anyone I have loved before or since. I also would add, that Shelley's strong physical attraction to me, and my strong attraction to her certainly led to my becoming sexually involved quite early in our relationship; and that certainly led on to my last night in town, for us to become sexually involved and sleeping nude together.]

The phone rang as I began that last sentence, and it was Gayle calling from Wisconsin to tell me that a good friend of hers had suddenly become aware that she was pregnant with her boyfriend…

Well, I guess you know why I'm upset. Gayle told me that the two of them had an agreement to sleep together without relations (intercourse). My God, Pat, I'd absolutely die if something happened and I should get pregnant. If we're ever tipsy in California or here, please, let's make sure we're either sobered up by the time we go to bed, or let's not go to bed together at all. I trust you—but I don't know about me with alcohol. **Lord, when I think of how badly I wanted you (that night we slept together in the nude)—well, that's over with.** I love you too much to ever want to spoil it by getting pregnant before we are ready. And I don't know if I told you how much I appreciate you for not trying to talk me into giving in to myself. Thank you. This thing just really shook me up, and I feel better after telling you about it.

If you are wondering what the deal is with (this tiny) writing, I didn't want to start a new page, and I wanted to tell you that stuff, and I wanted to end on a happier note. So, if you can read it, congratulations. Sometimes I write like this in my diary—and it's a mess!

Bless my soul! My heart is going about 1000 r.p.m. I'm sorry for getting so shaken up—I am not apologizing, I'm just sorry that I did. I believe we'll have a wonderful time in California. But I am worried about your father. It's important to me that he doesn't think badly of me, and I wouldn't want to do anything to offend him in his home. I hope he…well, anyway.

Patric, I love you. I'm looking forward to a letter from you; I love the way you wrote the last one…just write what you're thinking…I don't want your letters to me to be a major chore. I love you so. Now I'm going to lie here and think of you and dream of your kisses and California. Take care, my darling. I hope your journey is wonderful and safe. Thank you, Pat. With all my love, Shelley.

Monday, Jan. 19, 1970
5:00 p.m.

Dear Patric,
(Picasso strikes again!)
It's been ages since I've written to you, and you've probably forgotten that I ever exist by now. O.K., o.k., I'm kidding, already! This pen seems to be coming up with awfully thick lines all of the sudden.

I mailed a letter to you this morning – hope it's waiting for you in Colorado. If you're on schedule, you should be leaving Chicago tomorrow. So near, yet so far. It feels as if you're a million miles away sometimes.

Don't worry, I'm not neglecting my studies to write to you. Today I had my voice boards, & it was a nightmare, as usual. The voice teachers sit there like Draps, with expressionless countenances, and very little sheet music. Some of them are really friendly – they'll look up occasionally and blink at you to let you know that it's poor personal obituary they're writing. Guess I shouldn't be so sarcastic – but the boards are such a tremendous strain for such a long time (preparation, etc.). And I know that they won't be very kind in scoring me because they just aren't interested in my voice. Mr. Kockritz, my teacher, was not originally assigned to teach me last year. The teacher I was assigned to told the board after they heard me the first time that it was hopeless to try to do anything with this voice; that it would serve no purpose that he was working it for; that to try to raise and build it would be

---

Monday, January 19, 1970, 5:00 P.M.

Dear Patric (Drawing of flowers: Picasso strikes again!)
It's been ages since I've written to you, and you've probably forgotten that I even exist by now. OK, OK I'm kidding already! So near yet so far. It feels as if you're a million

miles away sometimes. I'm still floating after talking to you on Saturday. That was wonderful of you.

[Shelley had her friends Mary, Charla Anne, and Darby to her house one evening.] ...we talked over old times a bit, but we mostly talked about our love lives. I brought them here to see all the lovely gifts you gave me and they were very impressed. And Mary fell in love as soon as she saw your picture—and Darby fell in love as soon as I told her how tall you are.... The big conversation topic of the evening was a fellow named Patric. **Well, I was always the recluse of the gang** and suddenly here she is as happy as sin and none of the kids could believe it! They had to know all about you— everything (Well—they'll never know ¼ of it!).

Oh, Patric...how you do give me heart fits. When I answered the phone and heard your voice before I said "hello," I couldn't believe in that instant that it really could be you. And I was so excited that I almost cried when it occurred to me that my darling Patric was speaking to me once again... Oi veh...what am I going to do...I'm so thrilled just to have heard your voice again, and to know you're thinking of me as much as I'm thinking of you. Thank you. I'm the happiest, luckiest girl in the world.... You, Patric, are the man whom every romantically-minded girl or woman dreams of in her most enchanting fantasies but in her heart she doesn't believe that such a man could exist in reality. But you do exist; you're not a fairy tale, and I'm deeply in love with you—not a dream. My Pat...such a man as you are could never have been before & never will be again.... The main reason is that I've always gone to a certain point in self-expression and then drawn up the reins and stopped short. You've helped me to ease those reins tremendously...I've never "used" so many of my thoughts in an actual letter. Well, anyway. I don't want to get all sugary and sticky, because that's enough to turn anybody off! My Patric…your Patric…how I love you. I enjoy writing to you because it means so much to know that you look forward to my letters.

I can't believe you called again! I was still in a cloud before…now I'm completely out of the earth's atmosphere! Thank you…Oh, you passed the final true test today without even knowing it. I saw Carmen Miranda today [Conductor of the city's symphony orchestra] I got a mad crush on him sometime last quarter (I think I thought about him three whole times). He's a fantastic musician—that's what I had a crush on. Anyway, he is kind of sexy I guess. I saw him about six times today—till the last few times we just laughed every time we saw one another coming and we haven't even met.

Well, Patric, I thought "I had a crush on that? You're a nice guy Carmen M. but boy, have I got a man!!!" Now aren't you just thoroughly delighted. Yeah…I'll bet….

My eyes are refusing to stay open and alert, but I really didn't want to stop writing. And I don't want to go to sleep because I want to think of you and listen to your voice again. I guess the reason I'm unhappy about all the nightmares I've been having is because they come on so strongly that they block out my dreams of you. Nightmares I'm used to…but nothing will ever make me get used to not thinking about you—never again will I be without your presence within me. And that's so wonderful. Our relationship is unusual, and the people around us will recognize the special quality of our love is lucky, I think. But not nearly as lucky as we….

Tomorrow you leave from Chicago to go to Los Angeles, and I hope you have a good trip, with as little trouble from the weather and car, etc., as possible. I'll be thinking of you.

Tomorrow night is our anniversary—one month ago (December 20th) at Chamberlain's house, we kissed for the first time. Happy Anniversary my darling. I'll be thinking of us and what we did a month ago all day tomorrow. And every time I think of our first kiss, I'll be kissing you now, holding you, knowing your warm body is there when I reach for you. These moments will come, my love. I'm so in love with you. Each "tick" of my clock brings me closer to you, each hour, each day no matter how much alike they may seem, each one is pulling us like a magnet closer, closer. Oh, I'm going to love meeting your father and seeing the house [When Shelley comes for a visit in California] I'm going to love doing things for you both. I'll anticipate your homecoming each day, and I'll be ready for you. And we can have dinner and share our thoughts and many wonderful moments with your father.

And we'll go to bed early when you have to get up, and it will be just lovely.... In the mornings I'll get up and fix your breakfast and I'll send you off to work. Patric, Patric. I know that this summer and all our plans and dreams of it will come true.

I have faith in you. You're the dearest, most precious person in the world to me, and you always will be. I know that, too, because I know me.... Take care. I love you, forever. Shelley.

January 20, 1970 (Tuesday evening), 5:00 P.M.

[20-page letter!] Beautiful flowers

Dear Patric,

I've been thinking about you all day, and so, since I have no studying to do, I thought that it would be fun to write to you again. Believe me, this may not be the most glamorous paper, but the lines are a welcome addition. Hope you don't mind—if you feel the same way about letters as I do, I'm sure you don't really care what it's written upon. Anyway, variety is the spice of life. That's a new phrase that I just made up—do you think it'll catch on? Nothing like a little snitching here and there to keep the soul honest?

I'm going to write on both sides of the page—I hope it won't look too obnoxious…it sure saves paper!

The mailman never came today—naturally he wouldn't on the day that I left the letter to you for him to pick up. I got home later than usual for a Tuesday—about 2:40 P.M.; [my dog] Sarabel and I went to the post office to send the letter. I don't know how long they take to deliver, but if I mail this tomorrow morning when Agnes and I go to school, it ought to reach you by Saturday. Hopefully.

Today has been a big headache—physically and mentally. It snowed again, and with the City Street Maintenance Worker strike on, the roads were just awful. I left here at around 8:10 A.M. and didn't get to school until 20 minutes of 10:00. Missed my piano lesson (which just broke my heart) (yuk, yuk). It was so slick, and I found myself having to stop on long, steep hills because of traffic ahead of me. Starting up again was really hard—I got rather nervous with all the ice underneath the car, and the cars in front of, on the side of, and in the back of me--all coming within inches of me, as they slid uncontrollably at times. And I thought about you, hoping that your trip wouldn't be tedious and difficult. I can't help but worry—I realize that you're a born driver, but there are a lot of nutty drivers on the roads.

I wonder where you are and what you are doing as I sit here writing to you. I wonder what you're thinking now? "Whatcha thinking?" …. Isn't my life just astounding? Well, as a matter of fact, it is, ever since a man named Patric came into it.

I hope these letters manage to make some sort of sense occasionally…. I really don't know whether they do or not. I don't really read them over at all carefully. Achoo! I just sneezed—been doing that all day—sinuses. This letter is so exciting that the suspense must be killing you. ("When will it end, when will it end?") When I write too often, my mental well seems to run dry (and my pen cartridge does too!) That's why I usually don't care to write more than once or twice a week. But since you are little by little travelling (or is it two "l's"?) farther and farther away, I want to be sure that you know that I'll always feel very close to you. And now I think the separation bit is going to start hitting you a little harder, because you'll soon be settling down to a routine, without the travel to occupy your mind so much. And if you enjoy my letters, then I want to follow you and cheer you as you go…. But you called me and brought me up tremendously. I needed those calls, but I never expected them. I needed the reassurance you gave me. Just to have you tell me that you miss me…and to hear you say you love me meant the world to me.

Right now I'm more or less riding on the "high" side— I'm pretty happy under the circumstances. I'd rather be sitting here writing to you—who are so far from me—than to be out on a date with any other boy or man on earth. I'd rather be here waiting for you than keeping company with anyone closer at hand. I'm not shutting myself off, I enjoy having friends to goof around with, but well, I won't say anything more.

I want to make one thing clear to you, if you haven't already figured it. Even so, I want to say it. Pat, I am young: 19 years is young. But I've had reason to make myself grow up before some girls my age, in certain ways. I have a lot of growing to do, I know, and I work at it, just as every young person does. But I will work at it, just as every young person does.

But I know myself rather well in many ways. No amount of time would make me feel any more certain my feelings for you. I've thought and felt and thought some more. And I am stubborn and obstinate—once I make up my mind, that's that (when it is important as this) I don't—didn't fall in love easily, because I knew that if I fell for you it would kill me if it was going to be only a one-sided deal, I wanted to be in love with you so badly…and I wanted you to be in love with me. I knew it was right. And now, I am completely devoted to you. You would never have to worry about my falling for anyone else, because I'm just not like that. You told me to date others and get around so that I can be absolutely sure. Well, my darling I get around as much as I want to—and it doesn't have to be through dating either. I am absolutely sure. And I will have a good time while you're gone—but to me, good times and dating just aren't synonymous. I'll have as much of a social life as I'll care to have. Don't worry about me—I'm just fine.

I never played the kind of games with you people play when dealing with romance. I never played coy, or tried

to "trap" you, believe me—I wouldn't even have known how. I ignored all the little do's and don'ts of romance with you. I never put on a front before you, never teased—lied is the word—with you. I guess the name of the whole courting game is just "dishonesty." Well, I may not have revealed even to myself how much in love with you I am—not for a while there. But I was never dishonest with you...

How I love to write to you, Patric. It gives me such a warm feeling to know that when I come back upstairs, there are some blank pages waiting to...I can't wait to talk to you again. I'm so EXCITED!!!!! Patric, I miss you so much....

Still I can't predict [my periods of creativity... when I write beautiful songs], because my soul has never been so full of happiness and warmth and love. ***And I've never known the meaning of any of this before.*** But you've...well. I love you, Pat, and knowing that you love me is the most unbelievably thrilling exciting joy I ever dreamed could exist. Well, I never even dreamed of it because I'd never be able to even imagine the happiness that I know now. The happiness called Patric.

My thoughts are racing by so quickly that I can't grasp at them, so I'll stop and reflect a moment and come back. There. Now I'm under the covers. I want my mind to slow down a bit. My heart too for that matter. Have you begun your search for a job? I hope you find what you want. And how are you feeling? I worry about you my love, and I do wish I could be with you. I'm still overwhelmed by the tape. And the last letter too [I didn't make a copy]. I can't tell you how much your letters mean to me—especially this week. Anyway, I hope that things are working out for you, and that you're feeling much, much better.

I dreamed about you last night. I had so many dreams that it was very confusing and restless night; but I woke up feeling that I'd been dreaming of you, though I don't recall the dream. Oh—yes I do remember one dream. It was just after I turned off the light. Sometimes you start to dream and don't realize it—you're not awake, but not asleep. Do you know what I mean? Anyway, I dreamed that it was this summer, and we were in bed together. We were sleeping. It's funny—this is one of the few dreams I've ever had where I saw myself. Anyway it was the strangest thing. I was dreaming in my dream. Got that? **And I was having a nightmare—a nightmare that I actually have had many, many times, but not in years.** I'd forgotten all about it. When I was very young, I remember waking up at night just crying away—and many times. Well, anyway. I'll tell you that dream sometime—but I hate it so much that I'd just as soon wait to tell you in person—it terrifies me. Weird, huh? To continue, I was having this dream (and I had it—rather, I saw the dream as I would if I were really sleeping as I was in my dream). I am so damned confused! I hate to think of you trying to decipher this. Well, I saw myself beginning to toss and turn in my sleep, and I saw you there too. You sort of began to wake up because of the commotion. **And suddenly I saw myself start violently and sit up and just scream like crazy.**

Well, you woke up then and were holding me. But I woke myself up in reality—you know how all of the sudden you'll "hit bottom" and wake yourself up? That's what happened. And for a minute there, I thought that I had been screaming and that you were really there. It was the strangest feeling—not really very pleasant. At least in the dream, you were there. Well, now that I've got you completely baffled about what you've just attempted to read, I'll come back to the present.

Well Patric, it's about 1:30 A.M. and I have to get some sleep. Darn it, now I've got that stupid dream—the old nightmare—floating around in my mind. I'm wondering if perhaps I shouldn't have let this letter happen?

I love you so much. Do you know what I dreamed once, a while back? I dreamed that we were ready to start having a family; I'd been off the "pill" for a while. One day, we were out walking together. It was a beautiful spring or summer day. We were way out in the middle of nowhere, with no one around but the trees I guess, and the animals and the wind and Sun and sky.

It was such a beautiful day. We came out of the wood we'd been walking in, and there, before us was the most beautiful hill. Its incline was very gradual, and so smooth that it looked like a painting. The grass was so green, and it was soft & tall. And we could smell the fragrance of the grass and wildflowers on the breeze. There were Daisies here and there. We looked at each other, and went out on the hill, where we found a lovely soft spot—the grass was so thick and cool and inviting. And there, under the open sky with the sun smiling down, and with the birds singing a warm song of love, there we laid down, and ever so gently began to combine our flesh into one. And I felt that I would conceive your child there under that beautiful blue sky. It was a beautiful dream, Pat. It was so beautiful that I wish we could make it come true.

I hope that when I write about our physical relationship, that the love that compels me to express my thoughts is conveyed as completely to you as it is felt by me. I would be heartsick if it ever sounded as if I only love you physically. Such a love in itself—the physical love alone, I mean—does not exist in my soul, Pat. I love you in every way I am capable of loving. And whatever happiness that I am able to help you find, I want to give to you. And whatever strength or stability or peace of mind that I can help you achieve—well, I hope I can help you. For you help me so much.

And whatever pleasure physically that I can give to you, that too, I want to give. If you want me to kiss your breasts, then that's what I want to do. And if you want for me to stroke your legs, and kiss you and hold you, then that is what I want to do. And if you want to lie on top of me, and place yourself between my legs, then I want you to do it. For it makes me happy to do what you desire, too, my love. You give me such pleasure that I can hardly stand to think of it because my heart starts to beat so fast, and I long for you terribly. I am so completely in love with you in every way.

You are the epitome of... *well, you're so much more than the epitome of everything I ever dreamed of. I want to tell you something that may sound sort of...well, I don't know what it'll sound like. But here goes. When you climaxed that night, I can't tell you how happy I was. I guess maybe that's understandable. But I wanted for you to be able to do it the next night too—but I was afraid for you because of the dogs (of all things!)...* but I guess you knew that I was kind of nervous. If this sounds...well...I hope you understand. But I hope that this summer I will be able to give enough to you that you may feel as much pleasure as you did, and many times. I want for you to be as satisfied as possible...I'm just not used to expressing myself yet, believe it or not!

I really don't know what it is within me—and you—that makes me want to keep on writing and writing and writing. Love, I guess.

I hope that the way I expressed myself in here doesn't sound foolish to you. If it does, don't feel funny—I'm sure that there'll be many times when I don't say something right that's really very important in value to one or both of us!

I love you very much, Pat, and I thank you for encouraging me, and not laughing at me when anybody—perhaps everybody else—might be tempted to. There are so many times when laughing at one's self is crucial—I do it all the time!...You understand me very well, you know.

The minutes tick by, and still my pen rushes madly from page to page. *I wish I could be with you tonite. I wish I could see your naked body lying next to mine. I wish I could stroke your stomach and kiss your breasts and stimulate you into nearly overwhelming ecstasy. I wish I could feel your wonderful softness become hard and erect in my hands, and feel your trembling shake the bed. I wish I could cuddle up next to you as you rest, feeling the occasional shiver that grips you afterward. I wish I could feel your arms around me gently petting me. I love you, Pat, and I want you and need you. There are so many corridors for us to explore... the hallways of our minds that are waiting to be entered, each of mine waiting for you, and yours for me. There are so many sensual experiences awaiting us—with or without intercourse. I am not promiscuous, I am not wild, and I am not careless. I am deeply in love with you and you alone, and my respect for you and yours for me is strongly intertwined in our love...*Bless you, my precious darling. Lovingly, devotedly yours.

Xxx-Shelley-xxx.

January 21, 1970, 6:15 P.M. [Family Life drawing]

Dearest Patric,

One month ago this evening you were just leaving me to go to your mother's…We had spent a lovely day together & had ended up here at my house, where we each had a salami sandwich and eggnog. Do you recall it? It was Sunday, and we met at church, and then we went to the Golden Gate Conservatory, and saw the beautiful Christmas tree and the flowers. Then we went to Chamberlain's house, and you helped Mrs. C. [Mary] put up the greens…. It was such a dream-like day. Well anyway, it was a great day, and I remember it all so well. I sat and watched you decorate the tree…and was so amazed when you stopped in the middle of a strand and bent down to ***KISS ME. WOW!*** I have been remembering today…Gee Pat, I miss you. I did manage to tune out my thoughts of you for 3 hours today…. When I start thinking about you, everyone around me disappears, and I find myself lost in my dreams of you—and it's so pleasant to be "lost" like that because I'm with you.

Every day it's so much fun to come home and drag myself upstairs—and see the flowers and cones smile at me and to have the rug comfort my tired feet. I adore the rug, Pat; I think it's the most wonderful rug in the world because you picked it out. Well, they are all so beautiful that I could never take them for granted. Well anyway, when I get a picture of you blown up, I'm going to buy a frame and put it where I can see it from my bed especially so that your handsome face will be the last impression in my mind at night, and the first in the morning. I have a tiny little calendar, and each day I cross off another number, and feel wonderful as I do it because that means I'm one day closer to you….

Would you still love me if I told you that I have a wart??

Patric, have I ever told you I love you? Well, I love you, whether I have told you or not. No joke. I've never in my life written 3 letters in 3 nights…let alone when they're all to the same person. You just do something, Patric. It must be you. I love you so much. In fact, I love you too much to make you suffer anymore with the mood that my mind seems to be in now…so I am going to run downstairs and wash the cobwebs out of my sleepy head. One day, we'll wash the cobwebs out together! Have you ever…

Well, Patric 2 ½ years isn't too long to wait when you really like somebody. And I really like you…. It is important to be friends—good friends—when two people are in love. Friendship can sometimes be a stabilizing factor in a relationship…Love as deep as ours—and I have no doubts that it has just begun to reveal its potential—is so full of emotion and feeling that sometimes it doesn't include thinking.

I keep thinking of you, and wondering about the car and how the driving has been. The moon outside tonight is simply glorious. I looked up at it and wondered if perhaps you were noticing it too. I made a wish on it—guess that's silly. But it was a wish for my love and that's not so silly. Perhaps there will be a lovely full moon when I am with you this summer. And we can look at it, and take a walk in the soft glow from it (the sun, I know, but gee whiz!) And *we can kiss in the silvery light.* I miss you Pat. I love you.

Thank you again for all the wonderful telephone calls. They did me so much good. I really can't believe that you, Patric Spencer, could ever love me so, because you are so much more than I ever dreamed of. It took me a while to resolve myself to the fact that there is such a thing as honesty; that you wouldn't lead me to believe something one day and then deny it all the next. Not because I didn't believe you... I just kept going back in time **and fearing the future.** I wanted to be in love with you so badly. Well and then I thought "I'll bet Pat is a fantastic teacher." Suddenly I was sitting in a classroom, gazing proudly at my husband, Mr. Spencer, who was so involved with his students in a very deep discussion. I was at the back of the room, and I felt so privileged to be wearing your ring—the wife of the man whom all the young people so admired, and upon whom all the girls had a crush...

When we get married... Lordy, I don't even remember what I was going to say because it shook me up to see that "When we get married" staring up at me...Oh Pat, I love you so much. I can't be casual when referring to marriage. Sometimes I sit and wonder if any of my friends will ever have the kind of love for their mates that I have for you.

I was telling my sister Sally at Thanksgiving time that I had a secret: "If he asked me to marry him tomorrow, I would!" But I didn't really think I would be so lucky... at least I was too afraid to think I would be.

Song writer: Ewan MacColl;
Lyricist and composer: Ewan MacColl.
I want you to have the words to the song "The First Time."

The first time ever I saw your face,
I thought the sun rose in your eyes and the Moon
and stars were the gifts you gave to the Dark
and empty skies my love.

"The first time ever I kissed your lips
I felt the earth move in my hand,
Like the trembling heart of a captive dove
That was there at my command, my love.

"The first time ever I lay with you,
And felt your heart beat close to mine,
I felt a joy to fill the earth, and to last
Till the end of time, my love.
And to last till the end of time."

And it fits so beautifully. I love to hear songs that fit us.

Sometimes I wonder about what you'd think about when you were driving away from my house. I wonder sometimes when it was that you felt that you wanted to marry me. Oh, I had such wonderful thoughts to think of. And I missed you so then...Pat, I love you so. You've given me so much. We have such a life to live together. We have so many common bonds to tie us even closer to one another. I feel like crying now, but not for any particular reason. I'm just emotional...I tend to get that way whenever I think of, or write to you. Or, had you noticed that?

I love you very much...in sickness and in health, in sorrow and joy, in pain and happiness. Talk to me Patric...because we both need these letters. I long for you, and miss you...All my love, Shelley.

Saturday, January 24th, 1970, 8:05 P.M.

My darling Patric [Lots of beautiful artwork all around—vines with roses]. As I sit here in the living room with your letter [Hand-written with no copy] beside me on the Love Seat, I'm just reflecting on the events of the past 2 weeks for it was two weeks ago tonight that you came back to me from the town of Shenandoah Cave [Mother and Father Mark's place] It seems as if so much more time should have gone by, by now, but I still look ahead at the many weeks between us with optimism. That was such a "magical" night two weeks ago...I felt like a Queen as I put on my yellow robe, and my perfume: Chanel #5...because I was getting ready for my Precious Patric. I was so excited about your homecoming. I sat in the rocking chair after I had everything finished, such as lighting the candles, etc. Then, when I heard the VW I ran to the window and tried to look out of it without being so obvious as to attract your attention. I had to see my love. Oh my, Patric, I love you so much. I have to stop writing for a few minutes—my eyes are so full of tears that I can barely see....

I just had myself a good cry—the first since you left. Oh, I shed a few tears here and there, but that's not really crying. I think what did it tonight was that little bit of thinking back. What I mean is, I don't particularly want to write a depressing letter because I'm not depressed. And I don't want for you to feel low, Patric. When I think of it, these two weeks actually have gone pretty fast. I set up landmarks for myself to guide me through days and weeks...

If you are wondering why I am printing—it's because I'm in the mood to write a little slower than I usually do, and besides my printing is easier to read when I do write this small. Why am I writing so small? Well, because it takes up less room—and I'm a big cheapskate. You never would have guessed, huh?

Last night I was so thrilled when mother said, "Well, hi Pat." I nearly had a fit when she wouldn't let me talk to you at first. She said I wasn't supposed to hear, so I didn't listen, but let me tell you, I was going crazy; so I didn't, because I want to be surprised. Believe me this is taking willpower!! Thank you, my darling, for calling me. You're so good to me, and I appreciate it more than I can begin to tell you.

Thank you. I was so worried about your long trip.

Bless you, Pat, you're wonderful. You have given me the greatest gifts...love, respect, devotion, strength, and patience. As I observe more and more people and their loves, I become so acutely aware of the sacredness of our relationship, and how rare our love really is.

I love you so much, Patric. Every day I am shown new dimensions, new realms and new depths that we will be able to explore and discover from now until forever, in ourselves and our children...You give me such love—Your devotion is everything to me. Knowing that I have you to turn to makes every dreary day brighter, every problem smaller. I've read your letter 3 times so far, and each time I cried. Such beauty. You are so honest and tender and warm as you write, that by merely touching the paper that you wrote upon radiates that love to me. You caress your words of love, and I feel your caresses as I read. Your letters are so well worth waiting for. I feel us becoming closer and closer to one another with each day that goes by.

I love you, Patric with every bit of my soul. I love you. When your heart sings, my soul hums along, and when your heart cries with sorrow or loneliness or pain, then my heart and soul weep with you. I love you so much.

...And you are very much with me. Your letter is sitting on my night table, and your presence within the letter almost lets me hear you softly breathing, gently whispering to me; I can nearly feel your tender touch... your wonderfully serene hands. Patric, Patric, what you do for me. Tomorrow is the 25th—one month after Christmas. Do you remember

Christmas night? When we are old and grey, I will still put on your favorite perfume for you, fix my hair the way you like it, and wear the garments you like the best. I will write little notes to you and put them under your dinner plate, or inside your napkin.... Whenever you are away for even a few minutes I will miss you and will feel my heart leap when you come home.... I am so lost right now in these happy thoughts that my heart is just a pounding away and there's a lump in my throat.... And I couldn't sleep because I kept thinking of you, and so I didn't even mind my half-awake—half asleep state. And I'd doze off & dream of you....

And so your poor eyes will probably never be the same again after roving through this maze. I do apologize for the writing—I didn't realize how small it really gets at times. Thank you so much for the calls—you do me such a world of good....

My darling, I'm going to read your beautiful letter once more, and then I'm going to sleep. I've enclosed (or rather will do soon) the information you wanted [Clothes sizes top to bottom] but it's rather confusing. Please send me your "vital statistics" too—everything.

Good night my love. I am dreaming & thinking of you constantly and loving and missing you always. Thank you, Patric, You're the most wonderful man in the world, and I love you so. Take care, darling. I miss you. Lovingly yours, Shelley.

[Same letter]: January 25th, 1970, 3:40 P.M.

Surprise, surprise! I just decided to write a little more, because I don't think I'll be able to write again this week & so I thought if this letter was a bit longer, then perhaps you wouldn't miss it too much if I didn't get a letter to California before you get there.... I trust you; I have faith in our future together, and I believe in you. Am I really very young—am I really so ignorant about life and people and men in general? I'm not doubting you for a minute. I'm just wondering, if, like Bryan, you are doubting me? I don't want your reassurance in all this—I really want to know what you're thinking. You are more understanding and mature in many ways than Bryan is. I love you, Pat, and I don't think I'm being foolish and naïve by making plans now...And I realize I have to grow up in many ways—but I do know what I want and need. If I weren't absolutely sure, I never would have told you I'd marry you.

Pat, I love you. I'm willing to work hard in school for you and wait the 2 ½ years to get married because we both need that time. Don't worry about it when I write this way to you—it's important to express our feelings as they come at the moment we are writing. I love you so much. It's amazing—I feel so much better now after getting this out of my system. Do you mind when I get upset & tell you all about it like that? I don't know—I just feel that we really just communicate everything that we can in our letters.

Thank you Patric. Thank you for being strong when I need you. Thank you for communicating your "sads" as well as your "happys." Thank you for your thoughts. Thank you for loving me, physically, spiritually. And thank you for believing in me and our future. We have something beautiful to share...perhaps Bryan will never understand this.

I love you. All night long I kept waking up and thinking of you. And that gave me as much peace as sleep would have. The wind keeps blowing today, and it seems to be carrying your name to me, and your loneliness. Nothing gives me more strength and hope that the knowledge that you love me. I miss you, my darling. The song that I wrote for Kenny in ways fits you too. But there will be more that are just for you too. Every love song will be for you. But the song in my heart will never be put into "singable" music, and there will never be words for it. It belongs to you and only you. Only your heart will hear and know. Because it's my love for you that writes it, and only your love for me will be able to hear. I love you Patric, and I miss you. Take care. All my love forever, Shelley

Monday, January 26, 1970, 9:30 P.M.

My Darling Patric,

To say that I'm a bit confused at the moment would be an understatement. Your letter from Colorado Springs arrived today [Hand-written: no copy], much to my delight, as I wasn't really expecting it. Your funny little "return address" made me laugh—and it also made me curious—do you remember it? Well anyway. First, I want to talk about other things.

You had a terrible trip to Colorado, and I was so worried about you. I wish I'd been with you so that you wouldn't have had such a grueling drive. [When I, Patric, awoke in Iowa, my entire car was frozen—the engine, the transmission, and the wheels. A farmer had to drag me (and the car) about a mile with a log chain just to get all parts working. Then, I decided not to turn off the car again until I reached Colorado Springs—15 hours away!!]

You expected too much of yourself Pat, and I wish you could have had a more enjoyable journey. My poor baby!! Please don't do that anymore…you'll make yourself sick or worse; I'm scared to death of the fact even now that it's over that you could have fallen asleep at the wheel. Yes, I <u>know</u> you're a born driver, and one of the best too. Still. And if anything ever happened to you, Pat, I don't know what I'd do. I love you so much. Well, it's over now, your terrible ordeal. Thank goodness. Perhaps you'll have better luck the rest of the way. Wish I were with you.

I wasn't really planning on writing to you again in Reno and I hope this gets there on time. If I mail it early tomorrow, it ought to reach you Thurs. or Fri. and you told me I could still mail one out tomorrow. Perhaps Mrs. Taylor will forward it if it's too late?

Patric, I'm sure that if I told you that I'm quitting school tomorrow, or that a mysterious admirer sent me $1,000,000.00 for free or that I'd lost 50 pounds in 3 days, that you wouldn't be any more curious, surprised, etc., than I was when I read a particular part of your letter. And if you don't know what I'm referring to, you ought to be spanked! You realize, of course that I'm going absolutely crazy, so I figured I'd write to you, get it out of my system and wait for an explanation from you. If I try to figure it out, I'll only start thinking what I want to think, which may not be too smart.

What in the world is going on in your head? I'm just about to burst! First you were talking about how Mrs. Mineah asked you how you could stand to leave me and be away from me. And you said that it's not easy to be away from me. Then, you said, "TO BE CONTINUED" and said you'd pursue your thoughts etc. What are you thinking, my darling? I'm praying that I get a letter from you tomorrow so that I don't get ulcers!!

Are you thinking of coming back here, perhaps, for a while? Well, I suppose I'd best not speculate. I wish I could see your face—sometimes you tell me just as much by looking at me as by speaking to me.

This isn't going to be a long letter, love. Friday night I got to bed at around 1:00 A.M. (Saturday A.M.) and I woke up early on Saturday, much to my dismay. Saturday I wrote to you and was in bed by 11:00 P.M., but I had a miserable night with very little sleep because I got a pretty violent headache—must have been the weather. But it stayed with me all day Sunday (yesterday) and so last night I took a sleeping pill even 'because I was desperate! Well it was as if I'd taken a pep pill, because I got to bed and was wide awake I know until after 11:00 P.M. and again at 1:00 A.M. and I was thinking about you—you see, you are even stronger than a sleeping pill! So tonight minus the headache finally, I'm rather tired! The weather's been so strange that everybody's sinuses are revolting.

Patric, whatever you are scheming in your mind, I'm not going to influence you. I love you so much that I can endure the 2 ½ years at 6-month intervals. It will be a terrible strain on us both, but I can take it if I set my mind because you're everything to me. So, if you were thinking about coming back here to work or study or something and you've by now changed your mind, don't worry about having built up my hopes. I just won't think any more about it. I never said anything about not wanting you to go to California because it never occurred to me to. It never dawned on me to think that "if he loved me, he'd stay." That's ridiculous. I just thought about things being the way they are because it's necessary. If it should turn out that such a long separation wouldn't be altogether necessary, of course I'd be overjoyed. I'd love to be near you.

But you must decide because you know what's best for you, and for us. I want you to be happy, and if that means that you must stay in California, I certainly understand. I love you, Patric. If I've misinterpreted your letter, don't hesitate to tell me! I may be way off target. But I can't wait to hear from you again. I promise I won't get all excited about the possibility of your coming back here. You might say I don't know what the ^&*@#$' is going on! Perhaps our letters will cross—if I'm lucky. I'm so tired I really can't think clearly (at least I have an excuse this way!) Don't get upset if I've misunderstood you. I love you, my darling. I love you too much to wait forever... but I love you too much NOT to wait for as long as you need. And 2 ½ years certainly isn't forever! Take care of yourself, dear. You're so very precious to me. I hold your letters in my hand and picture you writing them. I love you so. Please drive carefully as usual. My funny, handsome, adorable, and so very wonderful, lovable Patric.

I kiss you, I touch you, I miss you, I love you always, and I'm so lucky to have your love. It's too precious to be tangible, too real to be intangible; it is both. Take care my darling. I hope you get this on time. I'm thinking of you. And I love you so very much, Patric.

Yours forever, xxxx Shelley xxxxx

Tuesday, January 27, 1970, 8:30 P.M.

My Darling Patric,

Tonight you should be in Reno. Was your trip a very difficult one? It couldn't have been too much worse than your journey to Colorado Springs. Perhaps this letter will be waiting for you at your father's house—I hope so. It feels kind of funny to be writing to you in California at last. So many eternities have passed since you left that it seems as if you should have been in California long ago.

Last night I wrote what now seems a very strange letter to you, and this morning I very quickly skimmed over it and almost tore it up. But a little voice told me to just let it stand, and so I mailed it. Unfortunately, it will be the last letter you receive in Reno—if it gets there before you leave. Your letter is here on the bed with me—I like to just glance over and see your handwriting smiling back at me. It looks so warm and loving because it's yours.

At any rate, I hope that last night's letter made some kind of sense somewhere along the line. I was so very tired when I wrote it, and I was having an argument with myself the entire time that I wrote. Your letter from Colorado Springs did confuse me. Well, anyway. I won't say any more about it until I hear from you.

How are you, my darling? I miss you so. **Your presence is within me always. I treasure your letters. They give me just a little more to sit and look at when I'm lonely. If I wanted to count how many times a day I think of you, there'd be no way on earth to count it**. You are constantly on my mind.

Today, I had a piano lesson. My instructor just gets on my nerves. But he is a very good pianist. We were talking just before I left and he wanted to know what I'm going to do after I graduate. Well, I just grinned at him and said, "Oh, well, I'm going to get married that June!" I loved the expression on his face—like maybe he couldn't believe anyone would want me! It was beautiful. Then he got all embarrassed and red—Lord knows why—and he wished me luck.

Pat, I think about you all the time. My life is so wonderfully exciting now, so full of magic and beauty because of you, my love. By the way, what is the time difference between L.A. and Our-Town? Also, when I send a tape, at what speed do I record on? I'm going to get two tapes, so I can have one of you while mailing one. Haven't decided yet whether I am going to tape over your voice. What a terrible thought.

Now Tara's Theme is on again. I just think of us when I hear that. It's so full of hope and pride and love...**and tender loneliness.**

Tuesday, January 27, 1970

It must sound kind of dumb, I guess, but each night my thoughts of you keep me awake. I remember things as I lie in bed. I remember waking up and not realizing what was happening...Pat, I love you so, and I've done an awful lot of thinking in the past 1 ½ months or so. **My entire set of moral standards have been scrutinized, evaluated, re-evaluated and scrutinized some more.** I feel that we made the right decision, and I'm so glad that you go along with me [not to have intercourse until marriage]. I think it is much better this way because...when I walk down that aisle, it will be with honesty. At night in the dark, I miss you most of all, but at the same time, I feel very close to you. You have my love and my heart, Pat.

Sometimes, now for instance, so many thoughts pass through my brain that I can't grasp them all—Forever is a long long time, Patric. And I devote myself, commit myself to you, forever. You have it in writing! No hardships or storms could begin to tear away the tremendous bond that ties me to you. Yes, I will marry you. I will love, honor, and cherish you in sickness and in health. I believe in you. And, My God, I love you so much. Now there is a lump again (in my throat) and my heart is pounding hard enough to shake the bed nearly. Your love means too much for me to express. Yes, I'm an idealist, and so are you. But I know that this is real— you are real, and nothing can change that. Oh, my darling Patric. Your gift of love to me is the greatest reality that I have ever known. And in exchange, I give you all of the love that I am capable of giving in every way. Thank you, Patric. The tear in my eye is not one of sorrow, but of love. Love for you. Goodnight my Patric.

I'm going to mail this in the morning. Perhaps I'll hear from you in the near future. Sweet dreams, my darling. Please give my regards to your father, and tell him he has a very wonderful man for a son. I miss you so. I love you, I love you, and I love you.

All my love xxxxx Shelley xxxxx

29 January 1970, a Card

"I miss you..." on the cover; inside: **...every hour of the day!** My Darling, **Thank** you so much for calling me again…but your bills will be so high that I wish I'd accepted the collect call. I will be calling you on Valentine's Day (evening) so if you have a time that you prefer, please let me know.

I hope that your trip to L.A. was a very enjoyable one, despite the cold bug. My poor darling—you sounded so miserable. I wanted to be able to comfort you, stroke your head, gently and caress you to sleep. Take care of yourself now, Patric. I love you very much, and miss you terribly. Feel better, my love.

All my devoted love to my precious Patric, Yours, Shelley.

January 30 & 31st, 1970, Saturday

Do you remember a month ago at this time? I do. It seems an age since New Year's Eve. And we were only going to have one more day together, because we didn't see each other that Friday, and you left on Saturday for the town of Shenandoah Cave [with your cousins]. As much as I wish I were with you now, I'm glad that it's not a month ago!

I have my picture album out, and I have opened to 2 pictures of you. My darling, I miss you so. I… I thought for a moment—would this separation be more difficult or less, if we were married? Mother mentioned once that perhaps we should just get married and still keep everything else as it is now—our living arrangements and education plans, etc. I'm not suggesting anything, Patric, I'm just, well, I suppose "musing" is the word. In ways, that would be easier—and more enjoyable for us even while apart. But by the same token, it would be very difficult too in ways. Well, I like to daydream and try to play with ideas in my mind. Besides, I like to sit and think about you!

When we are married, I will take very good care of you when you're sick. Perhaps you'll have a cold—nothing serious, but aggravating just the same. You'll have to teach, and how I'll hate to send you off in the morning. I will have a very warm and cheerful house ready to welcome you when you return. Perhaps you'll want to take a hot shower before dinner, and so I'll fix a drink for you and have everything ready to serve you when you want to eat. We'll sit in the living room for a while—maybe you'll want to rest on the couch for a few minutes. You might want to sit quietly, so I'll massage your tired shoulders and neck, and I'll kiss your weary eyes. After a while, we'll eat, and perhaps we'll have only candles to light the table & room. You may go back in and lie down, or read the paper while I do the dishes. When I finish, we'll talk for a while, as I stroke you. You'll be so tired that you'll fall asleep, with your arms around me. My darling, I love you for better or worse, in sickness and in health. All this I would have done yesterday, or any day, had I been there with you. I do hope you're well now.

I'm so happy to have these pictures of you—now I'm going to show them off to every one…. So, for a while I've just been staring at you. You're so very handsome! Wow! I sat in the library today, and tried to read "*Souls of the Black Folk*" by W. E. B. Dubois, and somehow, the words of the two letters that came yesterday kept interrupting the Civil War and Booker T. Washington. And I really wanted them to go right on interfering, frankly. I had a terrible sinus headache— it's the damn (whoops) weather changing from one day to the next—and believe it or not, of the medicine I took didn't help…**but as I sat and thought of you, the pain went away and didn't come back. Wow! I was impressed!**

Anyway, I was thinking of your description of our wedding night and brother, I really got lost, and it was marvelous. The description was beautiful, Patric, and it was just perfect.

Sometime the thoughts I have may formulate into words, then I'll be able to "fill in my side" as you said…. My friend Lyle came in… He sat down with me, but we didn't say anything because we both had to read. Suddenly, I was once again lost—I was in bed with you again on Saturday night [January 11th] I was feeling your tender arms holding me, and we were kissing each other's lips so warmly. And events of that weekend passed before my mind's eye, and I was really re-living them. I was walking into the bedroom and seeing you lying there waiting.

My heart leaped for joy, just as it did at the time. I was watching your face again as I rather self-consciously stood before you and I was seeing your eyes again as they swept over me, longingly perhaps, and gently. I wanted to be everything that you hoped I would be then—and I guess that I was aware of the fully lit corner of the room in which I stood. I'll never forget that moment. I'll never forget most, if any, of the moments that we shared, especially that weekend. I was once again looking at you, feeling somewhat awed by the tremendous masculine beauty of your body. I was touching you, kissing you, holding you, and loving you.

You. My God, Pat, I love you so much. You make everything so beautiful…so wonderful and warm and exciting. Each embrace, each kiss, each caress is an adventure, a loving and tender expression. At one time in particular, I was reading the words of your letter in my mind, and then I was lost, in the dream of our first night as man and wife. And it was just as you said. I was at one point, lying in bed with you, and we were whispering. And as we began kissing one another, exploring each other, I felt an anticipation of the joy of reality that can only come when you know that what you're dreaming will come true. And there I was, waiting for you, expecting you. I love you so…it was a strange feeling to wake up to reality then—there I was in the school Library. And there was Lyle sitting and looking at me. Lord knows how long he'd been staring at me, when I wasn't aware. He had a peculiar look on his face and I was a little flustered inside. I'm awfully glad he doesn't have ESP!! He said, "Boy, I'll bet I can guess what you're thinking about." I said, "well, I hope not," but he didn't hear me…. "Well, if you don't know" "Ha, ha." "thinking about Pat" "how'd you guess?"

Gayle is a wonderful person, and she has influenced me and my life tremendously. She has done more than any other person **to break down the wall that I've built around me since I was a very young child.** When I feel very deeply for someone it's extremely difficult for me to express it in words.

I'm listening to an old album of mine—I think I've had it since 9th grade. It's the first recording that Marianne Faithful ever made—She only made 3 or 4 albums. I used to really look up to her, and I imitated her style for a long time. At any rate, I haven't listened to this record in a very long time, and it's bringing back some memories. It's strange to remember like this…what kind of life I was living then; the people I knew… and while I'm remembering, I write to you, my present and my future. There are so many happy memories to remember. I'm remembering, I write to you, my present and my future. **There are many happy memories coming back, and there are many painful ones. Growing up is very difficult for emotional children, and the pain I feel now is not because I feel sorrow now, but because I am remembering some of the sorrow that I'd try to chase away by listening to this album.** And it's odd to sit back and view my personality now as compared to then. All of the changing! I've had a quiet life, and I know now that that it's been a very easy one, physically. **But my emotions put me through several hells. Thank God I am able to create, and express myself that way.** My creativity is limited, I realize, and it isn't anything great…but I don't care to be "famous" anyway. It's done me a world of good, and given me something to give to others…. I think during our married life I will need sometimes to be all alone to create. I do have to be alone, and my love for you will always give me a great desire to write music.

I don't know whether to say that you are the exception to this, or whether, in truth, I am unable to express the extent of my feelings for you…. Well anyway. Thank you for encouraging me to confide in you, my darling. I can assure you that if your letters were not so warm and personal and expressive, I would never have been willing to talk to you in such depth…rather, write. I am inhibited (do tell!) and I always have been, ever since I can remember. Well, I've just done enough talking about myself to last through the next 20 years! Blah. I'm rather bored with me now. Bet you are too!! Horrors!

I'm sitting up cross-legged on my bed now…I couldn't stay in the position I was in for another minute. I really am glamorous and sophisticated, let me tell you. My hair is set— by that I mean it's wrapped around my head in turban-fashion, with clips here and there to hold it. That's how I "set" it. And I have on a pair of blue and white checked-pajamas that I think I've had since I was in the 8th grade. The tops are too short and I look as if I weigh about 200 pounds! (Of course, that's not too unusual.) Well, if you keep telling him about the real you, he may wise up and find out that you really are as UGLY as you say you are! Oh my gosh. Don't let him do that! I'M

BEAUTIFUL, PATRIC. (Choke, choke, cough, sputter, gag, wheez, wheez.) Well, so I'm a lousy liar. Sigh….

This is getting ridiculous. I'm going to stop now, so I can wake up a bit and finish this letter half way decently. I've nearly put myself to sleep. Bet you're dozing now too. Ah, togetherness.

Patric, I've been looking at these pictures—especially at the only one I have of us together—the one by the Christmas Tree; I'm glad to have one of us—I also want those at Chamberlains'.

On weekends I have more time to relax in bed, and think. It's good for me, and it's also sad. This morning I thought about you forever so long, and I missed you so much that I began to think that I'd never be able to stand another week without you…. Your letters are invaluable now—they're what keep me going. Perhaps that's partly the reason that I write such lengthy letters to you, you know "Do unto others." And this torturous endurance test that we are both going through will always be remembered and talked about when we're married. And we'll remember the pain we felt, and we'll smile sympathetically and we'll look at one another. We'll hold each other then as we recall the loneliness, and we'll love each other all the more in appreciation of our happiness in being together forever as long as we live…. Absence does make the heart grow fonder.

God, Pat, I love you so much. I am yours, Patric, to have and to hold forever. "My cup runneth over with love" I do love you. You are my Prince my joy, my friend. I like you, I love you I adore you. I respect you, I value your opinions, and I thank you for letting me be myself. I cherish you. I long for you, for your loving kisses, your tender touch; your gentle embrace and your powerful, crushing squeeze. I love you.

You have made me the happiest, luckiest girl in the world. The awesome power of your masculinity makes me so happy to be feminine, to be the recipient of your love. I give myself to you, with my love. I need you, I love you, and I want you, my darling. Lovingly yours forever, xxx Shelley xxx.

I really don't know why I'm adding on this extra page… perhaps it is just because there's no moon for me to see at the moment, **and it's rather lonely looking** out my window. Perhaps it's because I keep looking at your pictures and wanting to reach out and have them come to life. Perhaps because I want to tell you not to feel sad because I want you to be happy, and well.

I love your letters, and the way you talk to me in them. And I love the way you express your feelings for me, your descriptions of every aspect of our love—spiritual and sensual. You are such a romanticist and that's becoming very rare these days.

Your doting considerations, your devotion, your gentleness, your tenderness, your sweetness and kindness all combine with the countless other qualities of your personality to make you what you are—a total man. You make me feel secure, and you make me feel feminine. You are my husband, and I am your wife. We are two, and we are one: you, I and We. I look forward to the days when I can show you by giving you love in every feasible way how much I love you, and to the days when we won't have to communicate indirectly. My darling Patric. To live is a miracle, a wonderful gift. And to live with your love is what purpose is all about; what happiness in life really means. Take my love and please give me yours, Patric, and together we can share the miracles of life and love. Take care. I love you. I miss you. I love you.

[A letter from the person of Shelley's Affections: Patric Spencer From the Garden Spot of the World: Los Angeles?]

January 31, 1970, a Saturday

Greetings to my very beloved Shelley,

This letter is to confirm the phone call I made yesterday. Where I confirmed it verbally, beyond a shadow of a doubt, that I am indeed, very much in love with you. You said to be sure and write even when I was tired and low. Well, here I am. Down with a cold, discombobulated, and tired from working hard all day, unpacking the car and finding places for all of my stuff and junk and such. Not to mention the misery I feel by missing you so very much. I think one thing that I probably would have said in that letter "to be CONTINUED," is that I was used to pulling in my emotions, ignoring the pain of parting, you know, chin up, stiff upper lip, and all that tommyrot. It is easier parting that way, or being away. But you mean far too much to me, to ever pull back from you. So I am resolved to just stick it out and endure the strain and pain of being separated from you. How I wish you were here to kiss and caress my poor tired head.

By the way, I made it here to Los Angeles Safe and Sound. My mind, heart, and soul, however, are still spread out around the country. Most of those "Wraithlike Spirits" seemed content to hang around your house, so feed them well, won't you??

Today, the mailman arrived bringing with him your little card of good wishes. That card meant all the world to me today. I have been feeling very poorly with this cold, and I am going through the customary let down, after such a long and exciting month of adventure. I was just feeling on the verge of rotten. Then I got your card, and all the love sprang to me, and lo and behold, I immediately felt much, much better. Shelley, I deeply appreciated your card and many wonderful letters. They have helped immeasurably to make my trip cheerful and pleasant, but more importantly, they have eased the pain of being away from you. Just like we discussed several times together, when contemplating our relationship, it just gets to seeming wonderful, as to not really be possible. Can anyone really love me like you do?? Your letters come and shout "yes, yes, and yes!!!" Shelley, I thank you for writing them to me. I love you. I love you. A hundred times I love you, and each new day brings another reason for blessing you.

I was so excited to tell Dad everything about you when I arrived. We got so excited that we stayed up until 4:30 A.M.!!! He was very happy for us. In preliminary negotiations for next summer, he thought it was an excellent idea for you to come and spend as much time as possible. He reasons, as many others did, that you and I have not enjoyed each other under ordinary day-to-day conditions. Ours was a holiday affair. He feels that it is very wise to see as much of the other person under varied circumstances as possible. It is better to find out before the marriage, than afterwards, plus a few children.

Naturally he brought up the sex issue and wanted to know what his responsibilities would be, and what would be the sleeping arrangements. So I took a half hour to explain to him that you were a virgin, and that it was deeply important to us both that you remain so. That a definite commitment had been made between us.

Well, I am tired, and discombobulated. After the sex discussion, Dad said, "Well, if you two can manage to control yourselves, I think it would be a very fine thing. He started talking about your being able to work in the music field out here. He said there were many musicians and writers living in the area who may need assistants.

At any rate, I think that even at this early date, you can count on my father to support us in the idea of you staying all summer. Of course, I don't fully know how you feel about it, or are able to do about it, much less how your mother will view it. It would be a good idea to let me know what letters of invitation are needed, from me or my father. I would prefer if nothing were specifically stated about sleeping arrangements. I naturally would like to have my arms around you every evening. And apparently your mother is satisfied we won't have relations (Intercourse). And my father isn't upset by it, just so long as, again, we don't have relations (or rather, something unpleasant doesn't happen, meaning pregnancy). Well, I do hope that a good opportunity will arise for you to present the particulars to your mother. And naturally, I hope there are no snags.

What a dream!!! Three months of living with my love, Shelley. That's that truly feminine girl who has the lovely long brown hair, the enchanting blue-yellow eyes, the silky soft skin, the tender responsive lips, the warm matching hands, and the very warm and soft torso. She's the girl that grasps my arm with both her hands, so securely, and looks deeply into my eyes.

Would you imagine that I could fall for a girl like that?? Well…you better believe it, and how!!!

The last few days of my trip were very quiet. The evening I arrived at Ruth's house in Reno, I felt drained of energy, and was aware of a throat about to become sore. The next day I felt lousy, as I wrote to you at that time. I stayed home, cooked, with no good result, and wrote to you. In the evening we went to the next-door neighbors to celebrate the birthday of their nine-year-old daughter.

On Thursday I felt much the same, so again I stayed home. In the evening, Ruth took me to see a Community's Players' production of *"The Philadelphia Story."*

I slept late on Friday, rising at 9:30 A.M. I left Reno at 10:30 A.M. It was 500 miles to Los Angeles. I had never before had the opportunity of driving down U.S. 395 from Reno to Los Angeles, along the back side of the Sierra-Nevada Mountains. [This is the same route Shelley and I drove six months later as we were on our Honeymoon.] It was simply gorgeous and spectacular. And I kept thinking what will it be like to drive around and show Shelley this wonderful country. You truly have been with me on the trip; every restaurant I sit in, I look across the table and see you looking back at me, or, enjoying the view out the window.

I did really enjoy that drive, despite the cold. I made good time, and arrived at my father's house at 7:15 P.M. We just sat around, chatting, drinking beer, and talking about that magnificent new woman in my life. Then he fixed a marvelous steak dinner, complete with baked potato, lima beans, and salad. I also met "DOC" who now lives with us. He is a fellow who has worked very hard all of his life, had a wife and nine children, then when the wife went through menopause, she went wacky and divorced him. Now he has no home and no wife. But still has to work hard to support the children. So now this is his home, too. He will probably be with us next summer when you come. Then if my daughter comes up from Solana Beach, or Dad's children come down from Modesto (my half-brother and sisters) for a visit, we will certainly have a house full.

Well, as I said, Dad and I stayed up until 4:30 A.M. Then at 9:30 this morning, I woke up and couldn't get back to sleep. So I got up and commenced unpacking, and some house work. There is a lot for me to do around here, so it should take my mind off of you once in a while, or at least help to work out some of the tensions I feel, when I miss you so. You are very right, Shelley, no little typed words on this sheet of paper begin to make up for you. I love you, Shelley!

February 1, 1970, 2:15 P.M. (Sunday)

My Darling Patric,

This morning in church, I kept thinking about three weeks ago this day, and also about 1 month ago today. Both are very precious memories to me now. And at about 2:00 A.M. tomorrow morning, one month ago, you asked me to marry you. Well, these are the many memories running through my mind, and I'm sad and happy.

When you walked into church with Sally and my mother, it was the first time I'd seen you in quite a number of years. **"My gosh" I gulped to myself, "He's cute!"** I couldn't help wondering whether you and Sally planned to meet there and I sort of assumed that you'd come over for dinner that afternoon. To me, you previously had been just a name and Sally and I would talk about you and I really had no idea what the true extent of your relationship to one another was. I teased Sally a lot and she loved it, I'm sure (knowing Sally).

Anyway, I was impressed when I met you and you shook my hand very warmly and firmly. I liked your hand then— but it was just a fleeting thought. When I got home, I changed my clothes and put on that "sun suit" or whatever it is. I wanted to look pretty and I really didn't know or care why. I rushed around the house trying to pick up some of Sally's junk. Then you came home finally (!), and mother told me not to help her with dinner, that I should go in and keep you company. I was a bit—well, self-conscious perhaps, because I didn't know you and I felt shy. And I was feeling a bit peculiar because I was wondering what the afternoon would be like with both you and Clifford there. So I went in to sit with you, and I really enjoyed your company. I suppose I figured that I was "safe" because I didn't have to impress you, because I figured that your concern was in Sally and I really didn't fit in to the picture at all. Well…then later Bryan had to go and put me in a most embarrassing position by bringing up the party he was having the next evening.

This I have mentioned in my diary. Well, just before dinner (Pat stayed and Theresa and Bryan also came) Bryan and Sally got into a discussion about tonight's affair (I wrote this Monday night September 8th) and it turned into a big mess. With Pat standing there, Bryan expressed the feeling that I shouldn't come with Pat; rather, Bryan had a young divorcee whom he thought should meet Pat. In the meantime, I was wondering how on earth I got dragged into any of it— They talked me into going—Bryan (After apologizing to me) Sally, Mother, Aunt Florence and Pat. I really didn't want to go and up until the last minute I was going to chicken out. I felt funny. Then Pat came over and we all went together… "I wouldn't have known what to do if we hadn't." So much for the quote. I remember that Sunday so well. I wanted to sing for you to see your reaction. For some reason, I wanted you to know that there was something beneath that kid-sister surface. I kept feeling a great deal of warmth flowing from you. I was aware of some of the events of your past and I was surprised that I didn't feel sorry for you, but that rather, I felt very sympathetic. But I respected you too much from the moment I first saw you to feel any pity. I don't know if I'm telling you what you wanted to know or not. Well.

All day the next day I was tormented—should I go to the party or not? I wanted to go—I wanted to be your date, but I didn't think that that was the arrangement. Still, I had a special feeling that day and knew that I had to go, because I was curious about you and Sally, and I felt that the experience, whatever it may be, would be good for me. Everyone kept saying, "Pat would love to have you go." By everybody I mean Sally; I guess, "he'd love for you to sing more—yeah free entertainment." I replied. I was a bitch to everybody that day because I was frustrated. "He specifically asked if you would be going," said Sally. I responded: "If he wants me to go so damn bad, he can call me up and ask me!" Well. So I went and I was nervous!! Let's see what my diary says. Remember, this was written with no knowledge of the future, and the confusion expressed was very very real. (I am quoting verbatim) This was when we were at the party. Diary entries: "After a while, I noticed no Sally or Pat—I discovered them on the front porch. I was furious and upset—there was Clifford in the other room, ignorant. I got Bryan to go out there…I was so angry. Bryan and Theresa got Clifford out of the house to get ice. Sally and Pat disappeared, but I could hear them talking. I sat and played with a puzzle and when Sally approached me, I had all I could do to keep from crying—which I did when Pat came in, so I went into the bathroom.

Pat later talked to me more or less in code [Patric: I have no idea what that meant] and I replied coldly—and Clifford sat there....I felt so badly for him. And I felt like an ass, because Sally had led me to believe Pat had really wanted me there and I'd gone—providing them with a perfect set up. The thing is, Pat is so sweet and has had it rough—and he couldn't possibly be thinking of getting serious with anyone now.

I refuse to judge and I can't become involved.... After dinner, Pat asked me to listen to a particular recording [Miles Davis doing "Sketches of Spain"—one of the most famous jazz albums]...so we sat for almost an hour in the living room with only eerie candle light—and we never said a word—just listened to music. **After that, he acted very affectionate to me. And damned if I wasn't really attracted to him.** I could have shot myself for thinking that way. I don't know Pat very well—my common sense tells me that he was only being nice out of duty—that it's Sally he's thinking of. But I guess I'm such a naïve prude that I can't believe he'd be that way. I could very easily be interested in him. He's supposedly coming Thanksgiving and Christmas—and Sally won't be here maybe for either. So what's going on? I don't think it's very fair for Sally not to let me have the slightest idea what's going on."

That entry was dated September 8. The next entry is dated the 12th and I'll give you parts of it...

"I really don't know what to think...I guess there's nothing really that involves me now. I am rather hoping that perhaps Pat will write a line or two to me—about what, I don't know...maybe I could tell something from a letter from him: is he interested in a potential relationship? Or am I just Sally's little sister? Or, am I second fiddle—since he can't have her, he'll take the next best thing. Am I the next best thing? I really can't tell anything from the other night.... What bothers me—really bothers me—is that I can't help but hope that he does come home Thanksgiving and that he wants to see me. Well, things are going to start jumping soon with the beginning of school. I'll probably forget about Pat S. and Pat will forget about me. I am also bothered about how "attracted" to him I felt—and how aggravated I was that Sally and Clifford were there at the end—I actually wanted to see if he'd kiss me. Maybe it's better not to know. What a bunch of "Peyton-Place-ish" sounding bunk. I am very young and fickle and I don't know what…lonely, I guess."

The next entry is dated the 14th and it's a longy, so I'll just take a couple of parts of it—most of the length is due to my…due to my recounting a dream I had, which I'll let you read sometime because it was about you and very strange. Well anyway, you realize that the "…" business is where I'm skipping ahead. This was a Sunday.

"I borrowed the *"Sketches of Spain" [by Miles Davis and Gil Evans orchestra]* record from Bryan. It's too bad that the record appeals to me—every time I play it, I think about Pat. I mean enough is enough already, this is the strangest thing. I do manage to get into funny situations. This is a funny feeling. The way mother and Bryan and even Sally talk—it sounds as if they think Pat's interested. Well, if he is, I guess he'll show it. I really don't expect it. I've got three more years of school…while Sally and Clifford are here to remind me of him, I'll keep thinking about him—& yes, even hoping that he'll come home Thanksgiving as he said he would if he could. By now, he's probably forgotten all about me— and I should do the same about him. I will, soon enough. But Thanksgiving will be a reminder. Gee, I wish it'd be a warm romantic Thanksgiving—like Pat and me sitting in the living room with the fireplace going & the music playing—all wrapped up in each other. Well, "better luck next time!"

Drawing of Shelley and Patric snug on the Bench

And that, my love, is the last time you are mentioned in my diary until Thanksgiving night. And I might as well let you read all that, because from there on out there is an awful lot of you in my thinking. As you can tell, I really didn't know what to think in September. I was afraid to even go deeply in my thinking of you to myself. I didn't want to hurt myself. But I kept thinking—and never admitting it—that somehow, this time it was different. I only shrugged the thought off with "yeah, that's what you say <u>every time</u>." So. This is strange. I've been involved with remembering in these pages, that it's a little hard to bring myself to the <u>now</u>.

It's as if my empathy to my own feelings is so strong that at the moment I'm feeling now what I did then. So much has happened, Pat. I went through a lot of anguish and wistful thinking and fear and hoping, and yes, pain too. It only lasted for about a week and that seemed like a century. If I told you <u>now</u> that I was in love with you <u>then,</u> it'd be a lie. But I can tell you that I wanted to know you better—I wanted to share experiences with you, even if we never became serious. And I knew that I could fall in love with you, at the drop of a hat if I'd let myself—but I fought hard. And I won—by losing. God.

What can I say? I really don't know what it was about you. The qualities I looked for in a man—whether or not you possessed them I didn't know in September. I didn't know you. *I was very lonely at the time; and so perhaps that's one reason I wanted to see you more* often. There must have been something—I am seldom ***"turned on"*** by a man before I at least get to know him a bit. But you really are an exception there. You're very SEXY, you know, and I think you're very handsome (or have I told you…).

That's a really dumb, perhaps materialistic statement. But you see, my love, when I was a kid, for as long as I can recall, I always was the tallest of my playmates. ***AND FAT!! I WAS SO FAT! And I have the world's biggest inferiority complex still. When I was 11-years-old I weighed 136 pounds—& I was only about 5' 3" then. That's fat. And for an 11-year-old, that's pretty tall I think.*** So, with your height & and your strength, *you make me feel **SECURE**. It's hard to shed **complexes that plague you for years.*** The height is OK now because, I didn't grow all that much more. But the weight still bothers me, and maybe it always will. So don't worry, darling, I'd never try to look like Twiggy [a famous British model and actress who was famous for being so thin.] I'd never make it if I wanted to. But I'm on a constant diet, which is kind of dull, I guess. If I am not careful, I'll go right back up there. ***When I finally went on a huge diet, the starting weight was 163 pounds! And I'm never going to get anywhere near that again. It's just awful.*** I don't know how I got on that.

[Bryan's dog, Fritz, wandered away from Shelley's house while dog-sitting.] I spent an hour before church & a half hour afterwards driving and looking but to no avail. Fritz finally came home at 1:30 & and Bryan came and got him at 4:00 P.M.

…. So mother is still in an ugly mood. When she gets depressed, I'd like to sit around and cheer her up, and she wants me to, but she has the damnedest way of showing it. Last night she started out on a vicious verbal attack toward me. And I knew if I sat there, I'd lose my temper, so I came up here and wrote to you for 2 hours. So then she started in how I don't care about the dog, etc. etc. Tonight I really don't know what her problem is—she's depressed, and so I say OK, you have your days now and then. But I'll be damned if I'm going to sit around and *BE A TARGET FOR THE MEAN REMARKS SHE COMES UP WITH. My mother is a fine, good person.* But *SHE HAS HURT ME SO DEEPLY AT TIMES THAT I JUST WANT TO GET OUT OF HERE AND NEVER COME BACK. I CAN'T TAKE HER SOMETIMES—AND TONIGHT IS ONE OF THOSE TIMES.* It's funny—three weeks ago tonight was another of those times and I stood around and bitched to you then too. Forgive me, Pat, I don't want to spoil this letter. But if I should sound low for the rest of it, you are entitled to know why. *I DON'T INTEND TO LET HER GET ME DOWN. I AM AMAZED AT MY MOTHER'S CAPACITY FOR LOVE AND HATRED, NARROW-MINDEDNESS AND LIBERALISM, KINDNESS AND CRUELTY ALL AT ONCE. LAST NIGHT AND TONIGHT SHE WAS CRUEL TO ME.*

And when she gets that way, I won't fight her. I creep up here like a hurt puppy with its tail between its legs. But enough. I feel better now—and I'm in too good a mood to let my mother ruin it.

I am so thrilled that you called tonight—I'm afraid we went over 10 minutes though. Please, you mustn't spend your money anymore, as much as I love and want to talk to you. Bless you, Pat, you're so wonderful. Please be cautious.

I didn't think you meant that you'd still call me tonight when you asked me when I'd be home. I thought that you were thinking that today was the BACH DAY. Anyway, I decided to stay home from the recital right after I stopped writing in here around 4:00 P.M. Then Bryan came over and he and mother got into deep and serious discussion—and proceeded to devour a good bit of wine between them (one of the reasons for her mood tonight).

So, not wishing to participate in the discussion, I excused myself and tried to read my "Souls of the Black Folk" again. But Bryan and mother were talking about children and teenagers, etc. I started thinking about our children, and wondering what kind of standard you'll set (and me of course) in raising them...I can't imagine looking at our child for the first time. And I'm a little worried about you being in the delivery room when I have our first baby. You know why? Because my dad was in the room when my mother had Bryan, my Dad became so upset at seeing the agony she went through that he completely went to pieces—and vowed they'd never have another child...don't get me wrong—I don't object to your wanting to be there at all. But I'm not too sure whether you'll come out of it weeping for joy or not weeping maybe...No, my love, I'm not teasing or making fun. I'm perfectly serious. If you are there, I want it to be a rewarding experience for you—not a dreadful one, as it was for my father. I love you so much, and I love the thought of carrying your child. I love you, and to have you, and to have you by my side during birth would be tremendous for me—but only if it would be for you.

I feel better now. I've been wanting to say that for a while. I love you my darling. Right now, I am thoroughly immersed in a stupor of love and it's wonderful. But it would be greater if I were with you. These months will seem endless, perhaps. But we'll trudge through each day and live in a world of loneliness, dreams, letters and love…

Bryan was talking tonight about Theresa's brother and sister-in-law and how they are separating. I am shocked—they seemed so close. And as I listened, a little shadow of terror crept into my mind. Pat, I have committed myself to you. I love you deeply, and devotedly. *I COULDN'T TAKE IT IF OUR MARRIAGE DIDN'T WORK. I DON'T BELIEVE IN DIVORCE AS AN ESCAPE—AS A WAY OF RUNNING AWAY FROM PROBLEMS.*

I know that I will never fall out of love with you. I know that…. I have no doubts about our marriage. I have never known such happiness, and I never believed I would. I love you, Mr. Spencer, my darling, my fiancé, my husband, my love.

Pat, I can't believe this letter. Here I wanted to make it such a romantic letter…I felt romantic when I started…. God, I miss you. You're so sweet my love. Goodnight, darling… soon, I'll whisper that in your ear. *You may laugh—and I guess I may too, when I say it, but honestly, I do look forward to sleeping in the nude with you this summer if we can. I am shy about expressing myself that way—but in case you hadn't noticed, I do enjoy SEX.*

That's a cue to laugh. I can't end a letter like this—right before I turn out the light: I'll never get to sleep. I'm beginning to wonder if I am not some sort of fiend or something! Well, anyway. Goodnight, my precious. Think of me—and I think of you. I love you. Shelley.

Monday Night, February 2nd, 9:15 P.M.

Your manuscript came in the mail today. Really, I've never received a typed letter that I so much enjoyed until today. Somehow, your warmth and love melts the coldness of a typewritten page. And the drawings—well, I love them.... Thank you for writing such beautiful letters, my love. They mean ever so much to me...You are simply wonderful to take so much time for me...your letters never cease to amaze me with their warmth and eloquent simplicity.

[Please note, that my love for Shelley motivated me to pour forth my poetic writing...unfortunately I didn't keep copies of all my letters, but obviously I was bitten just as hard with the love-bug.]

About the wedding—I will talk to you about it more, perhaps in the next letter...

I'm glad you told me about some of your feelings from your experience at graduate school. It was a hell for you that I thank God you are out of now. Always feel comfortable telling me anything you want....

My mind went back to that Tuesday night, December 23, and our walk in the snow. It carried me all the way through that evening, and then proceeded on to the 25th when we sat in the living room alone, after everyone had gone to bed. Then it continued on through the party the next night, and on to the following Sunday...and then of course, the last weekend. [Before Patric left for California to live with his father.]

As I thought about it, I realized that to be physically separated is very difficult, and that the memories of our moments of sensual pleasure are bound to stir within our minds now, with the loneliness. Oh Pat, we had many beautiful moments together. You gave me so much, and I know myself well enough to realize that I would have received no pleasure if you had only been seeking physical gratification. Well, that's putting it mildly—I'm too much of a prude in my ways about SEX, and I never would have let us go so far if I wasn't sure of myself, and of you. But I knew it was right. I thought and pondered and the answers came to me. I gave just so much and waited for you I guess. I waited for you to fall in love with me before I could let myself admit to myself how much I love you.

In our experiences with one another, I let you lead the way for many reasons, all of which I'm sure you're aware.

Before you came along, I was very backward in even any desire for sex—part of this inhibition bit. **Anyway, I can't stand the thought of sex just in itself.** That's why I was so amazed at my attraction toward you (or is that vice versa?)—you really ***"turned me on."*** But I loved you. And I do love you. When I kissed you, all of my kisses were out of love. Every caress, every hug, everything—all were expressions of love, and will always be. *You stimulate every nerve in my body, just having you near me made me tingle. And to lay on you, or with you, or under you, that was so wonderful.* Oh my darling Patric. Sex can be so warm and kind and exciting when it's <u>right</u> and we were right. Don't worry—I don't have any hang-ups with you. I desire you, with all my heart, but only because I love you. No, sex is not the main event in marriage, but it's a very important one. And to be without you makes these memories come back time and time again as I miss you. And I don't merely have sex on my mind—I'm sure you know what I am feeling.

I'm rather surprised at myself—in each letter I find myself revealing more and more to you...discussing sex has never been easy for me when referring to myself,

until now. I enjoy the way you express the thoughts and feelings that you have about our relationship—spiritual, mental, and physical. Don't ever let yourself think that you can't write, Patric. Your words flow artistically, intelligently and with great warmth and sensitivity. If I ever described one of your letters to anyone, that person would swoon. I can't tell you how much your frankness, honesty, and very loving romanticism means to me, and how deeply it touches me. I hope you understand some of what I've tried to express to you. Last night I was up thinking until after midnight—and so I'm tired now. It's past 10:00 P.M. I love for you to express yourself in your letters, because you seem to like to let me know. There are so many things I'd like to tell you, my darling, but I don't know how. Again, physical contact can help there too. Send me your caress, be it gentle or full of fiery passion. Send me your kisses, all of them. And as you send these to me, close your eyes and perhaps you will receive those that I am sending to you.

Now I am delicately touching you, exploring your warmth, feeling your heart beat a bit faster as I gently kiss your breasts. And now I am giving you the ever-expanding passion which sends us quivering into the depths of sensuality, sexuality. And as you sigh from exhaustion, your arms still around me, I am kissing your lips, your face, your neck, and feeling your breath upon my face as I do so.

I am feeling your hands upon my breasts, and I am saying to you that I love you in your nakedness. We have so much to give one another. Patric and I love you very much. I need your love. And I offer you mine, in every way that I am capable of giving to you.

I must get some sleep now. I miss you all the more now. I lie in bed at night and think of the mornings when I'll wake up to find you holding me, and kissing my forehead. I think of the days when I will gently kiss your lips until you realize that you are about to wake up, and when you realize that you are about to wake up, and when you open your eyes, then I'll kiss you again, just to let you know that you're not dreaming. I look forward to waking before you, and watching you sleep, as I did for about five minutes on that Sunday. I look forward to lying in bed with you, and being clothed only by the finely woven, soft and sensual threads of your love. God, Pat, I miss you so much. I'm going absolutely crazy!! But knowing that you love me will carry me through. And perhaps you may feel my presence. I am always with you, my darling. Sleep with me, dream with me. Tomorrow will soon be yesterday, our loneliness will soon be gone. I love you now and forever, Shelley.

Wednesday Evening, February 4, 1970, 5:45 P.M.

My Dearly Beloved Patric,

Would you appreciate my telling you that I'm lying here in the nude as I write to you? When I came home today your letter was waiting for me, so I brought it up here & let it rest on the bed, unopened, and I ran downstairs & took a shower. THEN I came back up here, feeling refreshed and warm, and I opened the letter—and tremendously enjoyed the fragrance that greeted me as I read. Thank you—that was (is) lovely, and it brings just a bit more of you to me. Your letters are so warm and loving that they give me chills—you remember the goose bumps? God, Pat, I wish that this very minute you would walk through the entrance here, and take away this robe that covers my legs & feet, and take me into your arms, pressing me against your warm skin. I wish that we could just stand before one another and gaze upon each other's humble nakedness. And I wish that, when we could no longer tolerate this separation of even a few inches, that we could stand embracing one another, and share our bodies that lovingly kiss as our lips meet. I miss you so.

My heart cries longingly to once again feel your hand upon it...my breasts meekly await your tender caresses... and everything that is feminine and womanly within me desires you and only you, Patric, the manly...the missing half, the beloved. I love you so.

Well, what a way to start a letter. I am acutely aware of my nakedness as I write, because I know that you can see me, just as I can see you. In case you're wondering, not to spoil the picture or anything, I have to dress shortly.... But for now, here I am.

Perhaps soon, I won't be writing to you as I lie in bed, but merely waiting for you to come into me. And so, I figured if I were going to write to you like this, that you might as well enjoy the fact. I miss you so, Pat. Don't worry—I'm not generally a sex fiend or anything. Only specifically!!!! Specifically, meaning YOU. You've got to be the SEXIEST man alive! But don't tell anybody—I want you all to myself. Selfish? YOU BET YOUR SWEET Bippy!!!! [From the TV show *LAUGH-IN*].

I guess that writing to you is a release of tension for me... in case you hadn't noticed. This past weekend—and this week too, I've been pacing the floors, nearly out of my mind over you. I didn't—and don't know what to do with myself. Sometimes I'd just picture you sitting in the rocking chair— while I was downstairs washing and hanging laundry. I can't tell you what your letters mean to me. I felt rather hesitant about mentioning it too much, because I don't know if writing to me as you do is too much of a chore. I don't want you to pressure yourself into writing because you feel obligated. I would like your letters to be completely willing, perhaps even eager—even if it means that you have to write less often.

To be honest, I need you, and I need your letters, and I look forward to hearing from you perhaps more than I should. But you must decide, my love. I enjoy writing to you, because you enjoy receiving my letters. I enjoy trying to explore the language, in an attempt to express myself. And if I can tell you about what kind of mental and physical state I'm in, it makes me feel better. I keep telling you that I'm shy, but the more I write to you, the more my letters seem to laugh at the concept of my being shy. *I must be writing faster—I can't read this....* **SEX has never been discussed around here, believe it or not.** *Since they know that I am aware of the "facts of life" they are more open (especially Bryan). But finding out was a real chore. I was so stupid—well naïve— that I thought women could get pregnant with their clothes on until I was "____" years old. (That I won't tell!) When I had my first period 9 years ago, I thought I was dying of cancer or something because I couldn't think of any other reason for the "hemorrhage."*

So my parents gave me a book. Well, now that you know the life history of the naïve Shelley, stop laughing long enough for me to try to figure out what I'm leading up to. If I could stop laughing it'd be a whole lot easier! My friend, Charla Anne, and I used to take turns teaching each other the facts.

Well, I guess what I'm saying is that until you came along, no one had really spoken frankly to me about SEX— man to woman. I appreciate your honesty and I found it really unbelievably easy and inviting to reach out to you and respond to you.

My parents have been very Victorian about educating me, and although I learned, I am somewhat…well…I don't know what the word is—shy again? About even thinking sometimes. So you see, my mind has been in quite an uproar, not because I disapprove of my thoughts and memories, or losing myself in my love and desire for you. But because I'm not used to thinking this way. Your letters have been very reassuring, perhaps without you even realizing. Thank you. You see, I am naïve in many ways—but I try! Ahem. I love you so and I have never expressed myself so frankly and honestly to anyone as I do to you. Because I've never loved anyone as I do you.

I've never let myself TRUST anyone as completely as I trust you. Believe me, I've never written letters before the way I write to you. You. You are my love. And I am yours.

I wish I were with you. Just because it's warmer there, you understand. I really don't want to see you—I just need a foot warmer. If you believe that, I just may have to fly, right out there and set you straight. I think I am going to cry.

One of these days we're going to be sued for $1,000,000 because the mailman is going to break his neck—if he doesn't watch where he is walking as he comes down the street because he's so busy reading your <u>ENVELOPES</u>!! My funny, sweet, lovable Patric.

Well, I was going to answer your letter, but now I haven't time. Anyway, I have to do some more thinking about California yet.

I hope you're feeling fit and fine—by the time you get this (Friday?) Did you get the little book with the flowers on the front? Gee, Pat I love you so. I was thinking that I wouldn't be able to write you this week, but I haven't done so badly….
Give my regards to your father, please. Tell him to take good

care of you. You realize, of course, that I'm jealous—he's there with you and I'm stuck out here. Now I'll CRY!!

Pat, I love you so. I wish I could end this letter with some deep statement or something. But I can't think now. I can only think that I miss you terribly. I can only feel my heart pounding with love and loneliness. And I can only wish that you were with me now, as I sit here exposing myself to you alone. I love you deeply, sensually, spiritually. And I want to devote myself to you, expanding my life & mind, and sharing the life with you. Bless you, my darling, and do take care. I love you so. My love is yours for free, forever. I miss you, my Prince. Faithfully, devotedly, and always lovingly yours, Shelley

P.S. ...Only one element (of the recital) was bearable—and that was you. I gazed at your picture in my wallet when the house lights were on, and at times, I became so engrossed with my thoughts of you that I forgot to clap for the performers. And I missed you so right now. I daydreamed coming home and finding you in a rocker reading and waiting for my return. I came in exhausted as I am now. I sat in your lap for a few minutes telling you about the concert. I was very tired, so we went to the bedroom and slowly undressed each other. We held each other for a while, absorbing each other's warmth under the covers. And then I could feel myself falling asleep, securely resting in your arms. How I do miss you. **I don't need intercourse right now—I need you.** As much as this letter may seem obsessed with SEX, which really is not the object upon which my attention is focused. Either one of us could go to the other sources to satisfy purely carnal needs or desires, but that is the farthest thing from my mind. I'm missing you, Patric, every bit of you. And perhaps the fact that I miss you so much can give you some comfort. I hope so. Bless you, Patric.

Your letters are sunshine to me. I read them ever so slowly and then I read them again, trying to absorb and soak up all the love that comes to me through each of your words. Thank you for being so good to me. This letter is very strange...I've felt as if I'm not present as I write it—I am with you, not here. Are you writing to me now? Is that why I feel this strong closeness to you? Are you thinking of me? God, I am so in love with you, Winston Patric.

...Thank you, thank you darling, for all of these precious letters. I treasure everyone. I treasure you. I will write when I can and will be looking forward to your letters. I love you, Pat. I deeply love you.

Yours alone, Shelley.

Thursday, February 5, 1970, 12:10 P.M.

To my dearest and most beloved Shelley,

I have just received your latest and greatest eighteen (18)-page epistle, and I wish to comment upon it immediately, as my reactions are most fresh in my mind. I AM QUITE MOVED BY YOUR MANY WORDS.

If you really do not mind, I will type many of my letters. Actually, had I not already made that long tape to you, I would be putting this on tape. By the way, I hope you had no trouble in playing that tape on your machine. If you did have problems, let me know. My desire, when communicating with you, is to have the greatest possible freedom to say what and how I wish. The ultimate in one direction, is to be able to see you in person. But there is something about face-to-face which affects how we communicate. We are sometimes much more aware of our surroundings and circumstances, then, and have greater difficulty in contemplating our thoughts. So that in another direction, taping gives me the greatest freedom. Next to taping, I find that typewriting gives me the desired freedom. I know that handwritten letters are warmer, and perhaps more desirable, but for me, I save that style for a time when I am completely relaxed, and have lots of time available, such as in the Shenandoah Cave cabin. Today, I feel I have quite a bit to say, in response to your very provocative letter.

As soon as I received the letter, I took it outside to the outdoor living room, where I could be surrounded by flowers and trees, and could feel the warm sun beating down upon me, and could smell the fresh air. Somehow, that seems most appropriate for the reading of your sacred words. I say sacred, because I believe that through our communication we are putting together a most holy, and sacred relationship; one that is available to the man animal, but one which so few persons ever bother to look for and go after.

It took me well over an hour to read all of the words. I read very slowly, very carefully, very deliberately. And I stopped often to reflect upon your ideas.

I was struck by a thought of my own: maybe this period of long-distance physical separation is a kind of blessing, in that, here we are, having to relate to each other by letter mostly. And there is great drive on both of our parts to reach for the other, and to let the other know as much about ourselves as we can at the time. Your letter is so filled with gigantic thoughts and feelings.

It goes to great depths. Would we communicate so, if we were seeing each other every weekend?? I don't know. We certainly would communicate, but I wonder if we are not exploring some very important dimensions this way.

There are times too, when I am pleased that there are two and a half years before our wedding. Notice I did not say marriage. Marriage is a spiritual thing, which can take place before the wedding, or, during the wedding, after the wedding, long after the wedding, or, perhaps, never. You and I are already married. My soul and spirit have found a home with you, that was never thought to exist in, is such fine proportions. I am pleased that the two and a half years are there because I see us using that time to explore each other, and relate to each other in a fashion that is not called forth, when two people are all the time with each other, as in marriage. Or, maybe you and I will go on it after the wedding. It is so hard to make accurate statements about what will happen then, because I see us putting something together that is rare, unique, and ever expanding.

Anyway, I think that what communication or communion that passes between us this winter and spring, will be a strong prelude for next summer, which will build upon it and contribute other greater dimensions. And so on, as next winter comes and I come to spend a month with you in OUR TOWN. If I have not said so already, I do and will accept the invitation to stay with you and your folks most, if not all, the time of my visit next winter. I may stay a few nights with my mother, and/or some of the family may go to the Shenandoah cabin again. We, my mother and I, are thinking of bringing Heather, my daughter, to the Our Town next year.

Pardon my digression. I was building on the thought, that given the rate you and I are now growing toward and with each other, we will have a very strong, solid, stable, and intricate platform of relationship already in existence by the time we walk down the aisle. We will take our time, and think, and plan, and research our goals, values, and needs carefully. We will build the Ark that sails for us.

And now I turn to responding to your letter. Since you have very carefully described your feelings toward me in September, [1969] let me reciprocate, although I have no written material to guide me. Sally and I had written to each other previously; we knew we would both be in town in September. We were hoping to have a chance to meet at the church and sit with the family, as it did happen.

I was able to spot you in the choir immediately. I had enough dim memories of you to remember your general features. I was pleased by the developing young lady I saw. After church, I was pleased when you and your friend Gayle came up to meet me. You were very attractive, and I couldn't help noticing you. Later, I came out to the house for lunch. I had been quite content to sit quietly in the living room, while everybody else fixed the food. I was rather flattered that you came in, sat down, and began a good conversation with me. And I suppose I was a little embarrassed for a few minutes. After lunch, you sang for us, and I, being informed that you had written all of your own songs, was deeply impressed by your singing. And I felt a great depth of person, and feelings, underlying your music. I did want you to know how I felt about your music.

Later, outside the house, Sally and Bryan told me about the party and wanted me to come. I thought I could make it, and I did specifically request that you be encouraged to come, and perhaps sing some more.

Now, it is necessary to try and express what was my orientation toward you, as best I can recall. Well, to be frank, in spite of my warm responses to you and your singing, I basically saw you as the very young kid-sister of Sally. You were 19 years old. I had a funny little game of saying I would not even consider dating someone under 23! Because of the gap in the experience and understanding.

I wanted to do nothing to upset you. I had not the slightest concept of looking for someone with whom to become serious. I had several years of school ahead of me, and did not want to be encumbered. And I was Sally's very close friend, and so was wary to show attentions to her sister. In short, I held no concept of "dating" you.

Even to the party, I saw myself more as an escort, than a date. At the party, Sally and I did look for an opportunity to be together and talk. That was prearranged. And I, not feeling like a "date" for you, didn't feel I would upset you if I talked to Sally. And when your tears in the bathroom came, I was most perplexed and shook up. Obviously, you and I were viewing the situation from much different perspectives.

Let me say, though, that I did not view my escorting you to the party, as a "set up" for Sally and me. I saw you basically, as Sally's wonderful kid-sister, who would be a nice addition to the party, who might sing some more for me, and with whom I might converse, _because your personality was intriguing. But still, because of my_ mind-game with your age, I didn't view you as a regular date.

Later, after I returned to Chicago, I wrote to Sally and asked her to explain to me, what happened at the party with respect to you. She wrote back, explaining as best she could what happened, and indicated that you were quite taken by me.

I was surprised by her words, and mused over them, thinking about relating to a 19-year-old. Finally, I wrote back to Sally, and said that I was very impressed with you, and did want to see you again, and get to know you much better…like I did envision asking you to go to the museum with me. But still, I saw myself in the role of a warm, gentle friend to you.

Sally, in her letter, indicated that with regards to her feelings, you and I were free to date each other, and she even sent me three pictures, two of you, which she had taken in September. It is kind of telling that I kept those pictures out by nightstand where I could view them often. Well, I became embroiled in the personal trauma at my graduate school, and I didn't have the time and energy to think that much about you.

Then came Thanksgiving. Thursday was a day of surprises. I called your house and was surprised by how warmly you greeted me. When I came to the house, I was surprised by your getting and playing the _SKETCHES OF SPAIN JAZZ ALBUM by Miles Davis_ (which I had introduced you to in September). I was even more surprised by your Mother suggesting I escort you to the Xmas Concert. At that time, I was quite unaware of your strong feelings for me, and if anything, I thought your mother would be quite concerned if a 29-year-old man wanted to date her 19-year-old daughter. But, it sounded like a nice idea. I was embarrassed for a while, as well as pleased.

Well, then it seemed alright to ask you to go to the Pink Floyd Laser Light Beam Art show. I was going to ask you anyway, but the Xmas Concert invitation made it much easier. Then on Friday, as we went to the Art show, and I held your hand, I was very apprehensive. I wanted to hold your hand; it felt so nice, and was such a pleasant experience; but I did not want you to be lead-on by it, or think I was being overly forward. I enjoyed the trip to the museum very much.

Then came Sunday and I sat with you in church. You were lovely as the yellow light from the stained-glass window fell upon you. But I was again surprised by your willingness to walk me to my car. And, I believe I shook your hand good-bye.

And so I returned to Chicago quite pleased to be your escort. The next two and a half weeks I was very busy with wrapping up my affairs at school. They were very emotional and dramatic weeks, as I prepared to withdraw, and many students, 25 out of the 31, gave me an overwhelming response of warmth and appreciation for my teaching, and expressed great sorrow and disappointment at my leaving.

Came Xmas vacation. I called you on the phone, and for some reason, was again surprised at your very warm greeting. Came the night of the concert. I was slightly embarrassed when Bryan had us sit in the back seat of the car. And then, you held my hand again! I thought to myself, "Keep it real, Patric. Don't lead this girl on, just be her friend and let her know you genuinely enjoy her company."

Came Saturday, no, Saturday evening at the Chamberlains, and from there on, I think you knew how I felt. You know the struggles I went through, readjusting my thinking all over the place; changing conceptions like mad; finding a new way to perceive you.

I can recall your saying to me, "Please don't fight me!" and I had to ask what you meant.

It was Xmas Eve, when I went to the Candle Light Service with Mary Chamberlain, and where I had a good hour to think quietly to myself, surrounded by exciting music [Hand Bell Choir] and imposing church structure, when I finally came to the realization of what was before me: you and your greatness, and were asking in stentorian tones, to become part of my life. I decided, by God, I cannot turn a deaf ear to all this, it is too beautiful. I have never experienced anything like it. And so…here, we are.

You mention your height and weight. Yes, you were big for an eleven-year-old. I was only 5'4" when I was fourteen years old. But what I want to say is that how well I understand how we all do get complexes. Much of our society has such rigid standards of what or how we, as human beings, ought to look, behave, act, think, smile, dress, ad infinitum. And very few of us actually do measure up, or ever could. How many men can be "Tall, dark, and handsome?" How many young people can match the guys and gals on the Pepsi Generation Ads?

I love you, Shelley, because you are genuinely you. I love you just as you are, and as you develop along with the maturing process. Let me just express some honest feelings. I would not like to see you gain back all those pounds (Shelley was very overweight in her mid-teens) because it would be harmful to your health. As a matter of fact, I look forward to our meals being planned with weight watching in mind, and cholesterol content minimized. I would personally like to lose a few pounds, or at least maintain my present weight of 195. My father, due to his own weight problems, has a wealth of information of good eating habits; you might talk to him while you are here.

Saying all that about weight, I don't want you to feel badly. I love you just as you are, and if you gain a few more pounds from time to time, well, it will be just all right. Certainly when you become pregnant, you will shoot up another 25 or 30 pounds. May I say too, that often (but not always) fatness is due to mental and emotional unhappiness. And I would hope that the happiness we generate will help you.

A thought occurs to me. Maybe your weight isn't the only contributor to your feelings of inferiority. If that is so, and you would like to discuss it further, I hope you will feel free. The best way to free ourselves of nagging little anxieties and tensions is to talk about them.

We all of us have some feelings of inferiority for this or that reason. I certainly have mine. Like, for instance, in relationship to my mother, nothing I ever do, or how I feel, is quite how she would see it and lets me know about it. So frequently I have to contend with great feelings of inadequacy. And also, instead of objectively viewing my successes and failures together, I tend to remember the times I did not do so well, and forgot how really well I did something else. Your love and acceptance does a lot for my soul. May my love, acceptance, and devotion to you serve as a freeing agent for you.

The subject of raising children is a big one. Let me just say a few things now, and maybe we can wait until this summer for a longer discussion and exchange of views.

It is my philosophy that what is of vital importance in this area, is that there is a strong sense of family unity, composed of <u>love</u>, devotion, and consideration for every member of the family as a full-fledged human being, with all the rights as such. I think that when a child grows up being allowed to believe in himself/herself, and accepting himself/herself as he/she really is including her/his limitations, and knowing by word and deed, that he or she has high esteem within the family, that she or he develops an attitude toward the self that encourages the child to do those things, and act in such a way, as to contribute positively, to self-growth and development. Many persons in our society have very negative concepts of self, and are bent, either consciously or unconsciously on self-destruction. And frequently they try to destroy other people as well.

I think that when parents relate to their children in a manner that is loving, humane, and just or fair, that there will not occur the kinds of problems that develop when there is great tension or animosity between parent and child.

A child's view of a situation may be quite different from the parents', but it often is equally valid, and must be recognized. A child's feelings should always be considered. Just as a child should be taught to be aware of other persons' feelings, and to consider them.

Nothing destroys a relationship faster, or the people in it, than for one party, particularly the party in power, to act as God and to decree just exactly how the world is to be run, or, which view has reality, and which does not.

Certainly there will be times when discipline is necessary. Between any two people there occur differences of opinion and interest. There will be conflicts, and there will be times when I or you feel that our plan is the wisest and safest. And we will prevail amid cries, cries, and screams.

Hopefully, our children will be raised in such a manner as they learn to use their own minds, and depend upon their own values as guides to their behavior. I, for instance, have been quite free and independent all of my life, really answering to no one, (except for three years in military school). And I developed my own standards and obeyed them. And I think participating in a Church youth group was a good experience, in that we had all the responsibility of making our events, our conferences happen. In my experience, no adult would try and take over, even if we were shirking our duties. It was a good learning experience and growth-producing.

As a final comment, I think that in parent-child relationships, I think all decisions should be open to question, explanation, and negotiation. No two persons view the world exactly alike nor do they feel about it, exactly alike. You have to be careful not to stifle your child's life, by making him or her adhere to your views alone.

On the subject of childbirth, I have thought about it quite a bit. I was very sad and disappointed when I couldn't be present the last time. I will think more about it, and we can discuss it further when you come out, and when the time comes. But my feelings now, are, that it would mean a great deal to me to be there.

Besides, childbirth has often been painful due to lack of understanding and knowledge of the process; plus the psychological set one gets from just hearing how bad it is. Now-a-days, with natural childbirth, means are devised for giving birth with only a minimum of pain. Childbirth is a part of the miracle of life. I would not want to be denied the privilege of experiencing it with you. A couple of quickie items. With regards to divorce, I share your orientation. If it means anything to you, when my last wife and I were having our problems, it was I who kept trying to go to counselors, and to work things out, and it was she who refused. But I hasten to add, it was not a good situation and I didn't really have the emotional maturity to love her anywhere near the way I love you…it was I who was too bottled up inside to know just how I really felt about anything. When I went back to college in the fall, I enrolled in counseling therapy and was able to get in touch with my deeper feelings, and accept the responsibility of becoming emotionally authentic. [This may also help to explain the "vibrations" that I was transmitting to Shelley, as well as to be able to receive and respond to Shelley's "vibrations" toward me.] We can discuss that further if you like.

I do not mind a bit that the letter is not "romantic" through and through. What you put down on paper is very important. We need to spend our time discussing the serious things as well as the light ones. Do not ever feel, on my account, that your letters should be a certain way. Let's talk about whatever deeply concerns us. If something is worrying you, talk about it, like your grief for the university co-ed who was shot and later died. Which, incidentally, I was sorry to hear about, and felt a sense of anguish at the senselessness of it. Not that it was senseless from the attacker's viewpoint, but that an innocent person was deprived of life and health, by another's maladjustment to life. I say again: one of the most important things you and I can do or accomplish in this life is to create a family where there is life, love, and the love of life: our own, and others'.

I am not laughing a bit when you say you honestly look forward to sleeping in the nude with me this summer; I am pleased, very pleased, that you feel that way. I look forward to that myself. But, more importantly, I recognize that sex is something with which you have just begun to think about, and feel about; in very real terms, and in immediate relation to yourself. Certainly, you walk and talk cautiously about it, not knowing always, if what you do is acceptable.

I accept whatever view or way you wish to express a view concerning sexual matters. It is all right by me for you to have whatever questions, doubts, thoughts, fantasies that seem to come to you. And you are always welcome to express and discuss the concern with me. I think I can empathize with you for the most part, because in spite of my great independence as a youth, I was very cautious when it came to sex. I was very concerned to be the gentleman, and to be proper toward women [I was 21 before I had my first taste of intercourse].

As for your fantasies about sex, and how you might like to experience it, you are not, by any means a fiend…but rather, a very much "in touch" with your feelings and desires—you are a human being who allows herself to experience such thoughts. You just go right on dreaming and desiring. It's good for the mental and emotional health. Many thousands of persons cripple themselves by suppressing such thinking. And, when you come out next summer, we will put as many of your dreams into reality as possible save intercourse. I have dreams, too, you know; or could you guess that? I don't believe I have finished kissing every square inch of your body. I guess I keep getting sidetracked by certain parts. Like your feet, for instance. I get a thrill by putting your toes into my mouth, and caressing them with my tongue. I enjoy your fingers in my mouth for the same reason. I like putting my fingers in your mouth, and feeling the warmth and softness of it. I like covering my face with your hair, and experiencing the smell and warmth of it. I like you to run your fingers slowly across my forehead and into my hair. I like you to reach around, grabbing my head, and bringing it toward you to kiss me. I like fondling your breasts; playing with them lightly and gently, and then burying my face in them, smothering myself with that warm soft, sweet smelling flesh. I like to take your nipples in my mouth and to caress them with my tongue. I like to have you hover over me, so that just the nipples graze my lips. I like you to draw me close to you, and put my lips on your breast.

I like to move along, and kiss up under your arms, and down the side; across the stomach, stopping at the oasis of the navel. My, you have a deep one!

I like to move on down to the pelvic region, and then stop. And begin kissing your foot, and then slowly work my way back up the leg to your vagina. There, I like to smell the faint, pleasant feminine odor of a woman; and to feel the soft, moist tissue of the vulva with my face. I like to excite your nerve endings with my tongue, and give you as much pleasure as you can stand.

As I caress you with my mouth, I like to reach up and pull your body toward me, to caress your hips, massage your stomach, and fondle your breasts. I like for your legs to rest on my back, and move gently back and forth. I like your hands to stroke my head and ears, in response to your pleasure. I like to hear the sound of your heavy fast breathing, as your whole body moves in excited motion. Sometime, perhaps, this summer, if you would desire, I will climax you by kissing your vagina.

And I like all the things you do for me. Just reading your words caused me to shiver and shake as I did when you climaxed me. Thank you ever so much. You are so gentle, yet firm. You show well your loving tenderness. And my body responds. And then, to lie quietly afterwards, with you on top of me. Just resting, happily, listening to the warm; my arms around you, and yours around me. Yes, and there are many exercises described in the book ***Explorations in Sensory Awareness*** which we might like to try. That is the book that Theresa and Bryan got for Christmas. One of them, for instance, is where one person "taps" on the body of another, with the tips of the fingers, until the other person feels that it is enough. It seems to be a form of massage, blood, nerve, and muscle stimulation, which leaves one feeling relaxed and excited.

Yes, my love, you just fill your mind with whatever dreams your sensual imagination can create for you. This is part of what it is to experience human life. Let us not ever need to turn to artificial means, such as drugs, cigarettes, and the overuse of alcohol. But let us always make the best use of our own natural body sensations.

And you are right. It is not done for the sake of physical gratification alone. There must be feeling, and be love. I know how when I was in the Orient for six months on two occasions, I often longed for sexual gratification, but there was no one there whom I loved, and cared deeply about. And may I say that bars are filled with prostitutes [which were legal in many Far Eastern countries] and you frequently have to fight them off. I thought about it, having intercourse with them, but it somehow seemed so empty, so physical. I could not see any point in it. So I didn't.

But you and I have some things else going for us. Something marvelous. I have never felt the love before, that I hold for you. My soul and spirit have never found such a beautiful and more welcoming home than with you and yours. I have never had someone with whom to explore the far reaches of the universe. I have never before, been able to meld my physical and spiritual love together, as they have with you. So, I am exploring new horizons, as I take you into my arms. I love you, Shelley. Everything you are, everything you have been, everything you will be. My love for you knows no limits because you put none upon it; and none upon your own.

May you look back upon your own past, and now giving blessing for it, because it has contributed to your becoming the tremendous human being you are, so capable of feeling and understanding and living in area that others have long ago closed themselves away from.

It is February now. And I am here in California, miles and miles from the person I most love. And in my quiet moments, my mind is like a fountain, pouring forth many thoughts, dreams, hopes and many other connections with Shelley:

"SHELLEY.
DARK, RAINY NIGHT. GIRL SITTING CROSS
LEGGED ON BED: WRITING.
WARM. WAITING. WISHING.
SO BEAUTIFUL, WHAT WE DO, THESE DAYS.
THESE DAYS SO BRIGHT, SO HAPPY.
LOVE.
SHELLEY. A GIRL. MANY HARD DAYS AND
THOUGHTS HAVE VISITED HER—WITH THEIR
PAINFUL TOOLS, THEY CARVED A SENSITIVE
HUMAN BEING OUT OF HER.
SHE KNOWS.
SHE KNOWS WHERE IT'S AT.
SHE KNOWS HOW TO GET THERE.
VERY FEW OTHER PEOPLE KNOW THOSE
THINGS. SHELLEY CRIES, STANDING BEFORE
THE MIRROR;
HOW IT HURTS TO DENY THE SELF: 'SEE MY
UGLY BODY' COMPLEX.
HOW MANY OF US MAKE IT THROUGH CHILD-
HOOD WITHOUT COMPLEXES.
I KNOW NO ONE.
COURAGE. STENGTH.
SHELLEY DISPLAYS THESE AS SHE STANDS NUDE
IN THE LIGHT: BEFORE THE PERSON SHE WANTS
MOST TO LOVE HER.
RISK. FEAR. FRIGHT. SELF-CONSCIOUS. YES.
BUT STILL: SHELLEY STANDS NUDE BEFORE
THE LIGHT.
PAT DOES NOT SHARE SHELLEY'S COMPLEXES.
HE HAS PLENTY OF HIS OWN.
PAT BELIEVES SHELLEY'S BODY IS BEAUTIFUL.

HER BODY IS FULLY DEVELOPED, WARM, SOFT, CUDDLY, AND NICE.
ALTHOUGH SHELLEY'S BODY IS SO YOUNG, FRESH, AND INVITING,
PAT IS NOT MARRYING SHELLEY 'FOR HER BODY.'
TOO SOON WE ARE ALL VISITED BY NATURE'S AGING PROCESSES.
SHELLEY. TO BE A WIFE.
WHY?
I HAVE A VISION.
I SEE A PATH.
LOVE AND BEAUTY, AND ACCEPTANCE WALK ALONG THAT PATH.
IT IS NOT A MATERIAL PATH.
IT IS A SPIRITUAL PATH.
SPIRIT IS THE ONLY REAL REALITY IN THIS, OUR HUMAN WORLD.
ALL ELSE IS TRIMMING AND TINSEL.
DROWNED AND LOST IS HE WHO JUMPS IN TO THE WATER, IN QUEST OF THE PRETTY REFLECTIONS.
SHELLEY OFFERS ME MORE THAN ANYONE ELSE COULD. AND SHE RECEIVES WELL THE GIFTS I HAVE TO OFFER.
VERY FEW UNDERSTAND.
VERY FEW OTHERS APPRECIATE.
I AM LEFT HOMELESS AND WANDERING.
I AM THE PROVERBIAL SHIP WANDERING THE SEAS, AND SHELLEY IS MY PORT.
SHELLEY...
FEEL THAT 'HOME IN MY HEART' GROWING, GROWING, GROWING INSIDE OF YOU.

WHEN YOUR SPRITS FEEL LOW AND TROUBLED,
PUT THEM INTO THAT HOME. THEY WILL BE
NOURISHED THERE.
THEY WILL RECEIVE SUSTINENCE.
THEY CAN REST, IF THEY ARE TIRED.
THEY CAN BREATHE REALITY, IF FEAR HAS
MADE THEM BLIND.
LOVE.
SUCH A SMALL SYMBOL. STANDS FOR SO MUCH.
MUCH OF WHICH WE ONLY BARELY
COMPREHEND AND HAVE GREAT DIFFICULTY
IN EXPRESSING.
BUT, I KNOW THIS:
WITHOUT LOVE, THERE IS NO LIFE. WITH LOVE,
GROWTH IS BOUNDLESS.
TIME IS ETERNAL, AND I AND YOU BECOME AT
ONE WITH THE UNIVERSE."

You are the greatest Shelley, and deeply beloved by me. Good night. Patric

CARD:
I DON'T KNOW WHAT'S UP WITH YOU!

My Darling Patric,
When I went to buy a book just a few minutes ago, this card said, "Hey, send me to Pat." So I am. It's 2:00 P.M. Thursday, and I am in the Library—with all my books staring at me. But I miss you very much right now, so I wanted to talk to you. I hope that you're feeling much better now. I've been thinking about you all day, and last night I dreamed about you. Heather (Patric's 6-year-old daughter) was in my dream. The three of us were at your father's house. And when I woke

up, you were on my mind. I love you, Pat, and today is a very lonely one. But I have your picture with me, and your love for me keeps me going. Bless you, Pat.

Page two of card: **I LOVE YOU**

[I don't know what's up with you!] BUT I WISH IT WAS ME! XXX

This is probably confusing for you to read.

There are so many things going through my mind now. What are you doing, as I write this? We have a beautiful love, Patric, and nothing could ever change my feelings for you— unless of course the "change" was loving you more each day. And I do. Think happy, my darling, for you have my heart and my love with you always. Lovingly, Shelley.

END OF CARD

Thursday, February 5, 1970, 5:15 P.M.

My Dearest Patric,

Somehow, I have been unable to resist writing to you in every free moment I've had this week. Perhaps it's because I don't think I'll get any letters off to you next week and so I'm trying to make up for it now. Next week I have many long rehearsals for both the Music Academy Production and also the Church's musical service. Also, for theory, I have to compose a minuet and trio in classical style and form besides all of the other routine stuff for other classes. Right now, I'm sort of in shock, as I foresee all kinds of strenuous and trying moments coming. I'll be so relieved after next Sunday that I'll hardly know what to do with myself. Well, it will pass. I apologize for complaining so much about it—I feel rather like a fish swimming in mud.

I like the Music Academy, but the constant pressure really drives me out of my mind. So, please excuse me. Every quarter I swear I can't take another, but I do plod on through, and somehow things manage to work out. But I can't tell you what a comfort it is to sit down and write to you, sharing my better times, as well as the not so enjoyable ones. It's such a source of warmth and light in any of the cold dark periods. To know that you're there, patiently listening, lovingly thinking thoughts of courage and strength to me; and to know that you love me is the most wonderful feeling in the world. My letter last night and tonight's too, aren't up to par, I don't think. I didn't read that one over last night, and may not have time to re-read this. If I sound low or disturbed, I guess it's because I am and yet I want to be cheerful for you. But I'm so tired now and I guess just a bit frustrated, and so I write and write.

If my letter sounds slightly insane, it's just because that's how I feel!!

And so if there's a rushed tone in this, I must be honest—I am too short of time to think very much as I write. Do you understand? I like to write to you very slowly and think about what I'm saying… because I think that you deserve the very best that I can offer. But you also need to know me in my more scatter-brained, dimwit, everyday moods. Patric, I have once again lost me train of thought. This letter so far has been pure madness.

Now I'm debating whether or not to torture you with the garbage that has thus far seemed to litter this letter. Now I'm finding myself worrying about what I'm writing again. Well, I figure that I want to hear from you, no matter what mood you're in, if you feel compelled to write me. And my urge to write now would drive me even nuttier if I didn't take heed. Please understand. Do you know what I keep regretting? I wish during your stay at graduate school, that we had been close enough for you to write to me and get some of your tension out of your system, just as I am doing now. What a horror for you to have gone through. Perhaps I wouldn't have been any help to you at all, except as something secure and solid backing you up and encouraging you in your black days. I wish you could have had a happier experience there, and I worry so about you now. I hope that soon you will be mentally and physically relieved of the burdens and stress which you were cursed with at Graduate School. My love.

Always remember that you can turn to me at any time, no matter how busy I am, or what stress I'm under, or how tired I may be. Always know that when you're happy, you can bubble over with cheer and I'll feel that gladness with you; and when you're sad or upset, you can yell and storm or shout or weep, and I will listen and try to be a comfort to you. I want to share with you; I want to be a part of you, as you are a part of me. If you need to talk, I will listen; if you need to converse, then I will try to do that too. If you need someone to yell at and scream at, just to relieve yourself, I will be there if you let me know what is wrong. Talk to me verbally, physically, or even silently. All this is so very important to keep a marriage going—to relate, to communicate. And sometimes you'll want to be quiet and you won't want me to interfere with your thoughts if you let me know, I will understand. All of this will probably go for me too, I guess. Just having you around will be a wonderful happiness for me. I love you so much, Patric. Remember that above all.

And now it is nearing 6:00 P.M. I may even mail this tonight on my way to choir to keep myself from staying up and writing more after I come home tonight. I feel better now—I have released some tension. I do hope to hear from you soon. We need each other now very much, to keep each other from losing our minds.

6:50 P.M. I was downstairs for a while. Today and last night, I was daydreaming about you. Last night I was thinking about December 17, when you and I were sitting in the living room together. I was once again standing next to you as you sat in the rocker, and you held my hand, and put your head against me. My other hand rested upon your left shoulder, do you remember? I thought then about the drama of the situation, as I stood there fighting off mysterious tears. I wanted to stroke your hair then, and massage your shoulder. I wanted to feel you hold me. But I was so afraid that my hand froze as it lay on your shoulder. Every once in a while you would shake your head as if in disbelief in the hopelessness.

I wanted then to ask you what you were thinking, but I was afraid again. And one expression of such sadness came over your face that I wanted to run from you and never see you again, because I didn't want to ever be one to cause you as much pain or distress as I beheld on your countenance then. Before you left, I thought I saw tears in our eyes, but perhaps that was a reflection of my tears that seemed to want to fall. I was so confused. And I was so lost in your arms when you held me by the front door. I knew then that I probably was in love with you, but I resolved that I would never reveal that to you unless I knew that it would neither drive you from me nor hurt you. And then I resolved further that I would try not to think about it and not admit it to anyone or myself again. Well, my, I just got lost again, didn't I? Those were some of the thoughts and feelings that I was re-living last night. It was wonderful to re-live them because I was with you again. Today, in theory lecture I found myself wondering about the future, and about California, and about our marriage. Sometimes I become afraid, Pat. Not because I doubt you or our love, or myself. But just because you're so far away and out of reach and sometimes, I just need reassurance.

I try to envision our getting married, but somehow it never really develops into a picture that my mind's eye can focus upon. I don't understand this; I guess. When I was younger, however, and wanted something to happen very badly, if I couldn't quite picture it happening, it always came true. And if I did picture it and was able to see it, most often, it didn't come true. So, perhaps that's what this is. It's so far away—2 ½ years. *I never felt so sure of myself before, and I've never known the happiness of completely trusting another person and having faith in someone else. At times,*

I've been very cynical and pessimistic about life. But it was only a defense mechanism.

I have to finish this now. I love you, Pat, with every bit of emotion and thoughtfulness in me. **I need you**. I've never said that to anyone before you. But I do need you. And I want you so, in every way. I'm thinking of you always, and loving you. Thank you, my darling, for being the man you are... Patric, you're so very precious to me. Think of me, my love, and know that I give you my heart. Bless you. I love you.

Ever devotedly, your loving Shelley.

P.S. It is now 11:00 P.M. and I want to add something. First, when I have time, I intend to sit and write out all my feelings and thoughts about California. My parents are being very understanding, but there are still some snags, as can be expected.

The real reason for adding on is that suddenly I realized that I haven't even asked you about what you're doing about a job now.

I've been wondering and wondering about your finding yourself a position and so your brainchild forgets to ask you. Sometimes I think I'm getting senile. Please tell me all about what is happening—I do want to know. Best of luck, my love, in finding a good job. I'm thinking about you, and hoping that you're well now too. Forgive me for not asking about your job, etc.—I have been thinking about it, but I get so involved at times that it slips my mind. I'm sorry. And I'm very interested to hear.

Please give my regards to your father. He must be a wonderful man, and I respect him tremendously—and I don't even know him. Your feelings rub off onto me. Tell him hello for me, ok?

I must get up at 5:50 A.M. tomorrow and tomorrow night I go to two recitals with Charla Anne. Nausea. Well...I love you so much, Patric. Take care of yourself and get plenty of rest. I am with you. Soon we'll be together again. Did you Receive the little Flowered Notebook with a poem inside that I sent you?

My sweet love, you're so wonderful to me. I love you, Patric. Your Shelley xxx.

SMALL FLOWERED NOTEBOOK POEM
2-2-19
MY LOVE

To my dearest
    Patric…
        …my Love.
Now you're gone
    for a while,
       and I miss you,
          my love…
   …as each hour
    Brings back
       memories of You.
    When the
      sun shines,
        I think of
          my Love…
   …For the warm glow…
     reminds me of You.

When the
    rain falls,
      the sky weeps,
        my Love…

…Sharing tears
that I shed
without You.

When the
wind blows,
the leaves sigh,
my Love…

And they
Softly say
"I need You."

When the birds
gently sing
their love songs,
my Love…

…Every note,
every tone,
is for You.

And,
when the flowers bloom,
I'll smile,
my Love…
…For their births
bring me closer
to You.

And,
when summer comes,
I'll be with you,
my Love

...To kiss you,
and hold you,
again.
We'll share
many moments
together,
my Love
...And, make some
new memories
then.

And,
when I leave,
I will miss you,
my Love...

...Just as deeply as
I miss You
now.

But,
I know that
You're missing me
too,
my Love...

...So,
I'm sending to you
a vow...

...My
Darling
my Love...

...my Dearest Patric...
I'll love you
beyond the sheer
depths of my soul...
...forever...
...eternally.

With all my devoted Love. Your Shelley.

Friday, February 6, 1970, 5:20 P.M. Pacific Time

To My Precious Shelley,

I received both your "Small Flowered Notebook Poem" and "nude" letter today. And I thank you for both. I have read the letter three times already. In a way, I feel a little exhausted by all of our communication. Yesterday, for instance, I received the eighteen-page letter at 10:30 A.M. It took me until 11:45 A.M. to finish reading it! Then I immediately sat down at the typewriter to answer it. And did not finish until

4:00 P.M.!!! Would you believe six hours of communication?? Not to mention the tape.

But, somehow, your letters have a way of making me want to respond to them immediately. And I think it is better that I do it that way, when my mind is still filled with fresh responses. Particularly in these days, when I do not relate very well from one day to the next. Each day seems to exist by itself, rather than being a part of a continuum of days. I am very fortunate that I have not started working; otherwise I might not have all this free time to write. Speaking of work, only today do I feel like I am almost over the cold. I called the Personnel Office of the Bank of America today, and they would like to see what they can find for me. Most of the men they hire go into management Training. But that is not what I want. If they do not have anything, I will try a few more banks, before I look into factory work.

And, I am feeling better. I am happy to be here in Sierra Hills. It is very restful, and our place is comforting. It serves as a kind of touchstone for me. Like with all of my adventures and travels, I can still return to something that is very familiar. Dad has lived here since 1961…the longest he has lived anywhere. Today, it was a beautiful, warm, sunny day, so I went out to our outdoor living room, and did some yard work for three hours. I kept thinking about you, and how you would love it so; we could sit out there in the evenings and discuss whatever seemed worthwhile to us. Matter of fact, every time I do any work around the house, I keep thinking of you, and how it will be when you are here to share it. (The house, I mean, not necessarily the housework.)

Getting back to my original reason for beginning this particular letter, I wanted to tell you straight out, that it is not a chore for me to write to you as often as I do. I enjoy it, and it makes me feel good and closer too. Plus, I see it as an important channel for you and me to grow, either singly or together. I sense very quickly how much you are expanding by talking to me in your letters.

I probably did mention something about not writing too often. Because, normally, writing letters is a chore for me, and highly time consuming. I usually need a very relaxed period in which to feel comfortable writing to others. But, with you, it is different. For instance, I am not writing to anyone else, now, any more than I ever did. You are something very special to me. And I am anxious to build a strong union with you. And, more recently, I see how much this correspondence means to you. Like, through it you are exploring many important areas of your own life and thinking, as you did with the letter today. And I think it is great. We all need such opportunities to talk to ourselves that way, as we talk to others. Do you not feel that you are saying a lot to yourself, as you make the conscious effort to write your thoughts down on paper to me?

It works as a kind of purposeful focus. It encourages you to think and begin to crystalize, or give form to your thoughts. It lets you examine directly your own feelings and values. An immediate example of this is your feelings of "SHYNESS." In relationship to me, you are not very shy at all anymore, are you? What is "shyness" anyway?? Is it a hesitancy to exert ourselves socially, because we fear that we may not be acceptable for some reason or other? And with my acceptance of you, does that fear not diminish? No, I do not think the fear has disappeared entirely yet.

I think that in spite of your great love for me, and mine for you, your having lived so long with an inferiority complex, now that still plagues you, especially in your more down moments. Well, that is all very natural. It may take you several years before you feel completely free of those inferior feelings. Of course, all of us do some things better than anyone else, or most anyone else, and all of us are inadequate in performing other tasks and dealing with certain problems. So that objectively, we all can focus upon areas within ourselves which are inferior, and most likely always will be. But, perhaps your feelings are more centered around being accepted as a person. I really would like you to sit down sometime and just "rap" about your feelings of inferiority. They do not have to be logically organized on paper. Just set them down in any fashion...of course, this will all depend upon how you are feeling, and whether you feel like telling them to me. But maybe, it will feel good to you to express them me, just as now you feel better in all that you have expressed so far. I am immensely pleased that you trust in me.

My life was no picnic either. And I have worked for years to unravel a lot of feelings, and try to understand why I did not feel inside, more acceptable. A lot of my problems can now be traced back to the very achievement-oriented, authoritarian, and critical society, that does characterize much of our present society. There are always those standards, that others are so willing to wave in front of your face; the age-old pressure to conform to how someone else thinks you ought to live. And, through religion and other similar institutions, you better start feeling guilty about it, if you do not conform, or at least pretend. It is a problem, and the Flower Children Movement [that took place in San Francisco and a few other cities between 1965 and 1970; I was there and witnessed much of it] began as a healthy answer to it. I praise the day I began living in California, because here, there is far greater human freedom than would ever be present in some of the Mid-Western cities. My ear is always to your lips, Shelley, as you struggle with your own negative feelings. Nothing you can tell me can alter the beautiful person I know to be you who fits well into my life. Love Patric.

Friday, February 6, 1970, 10:15 P.M.

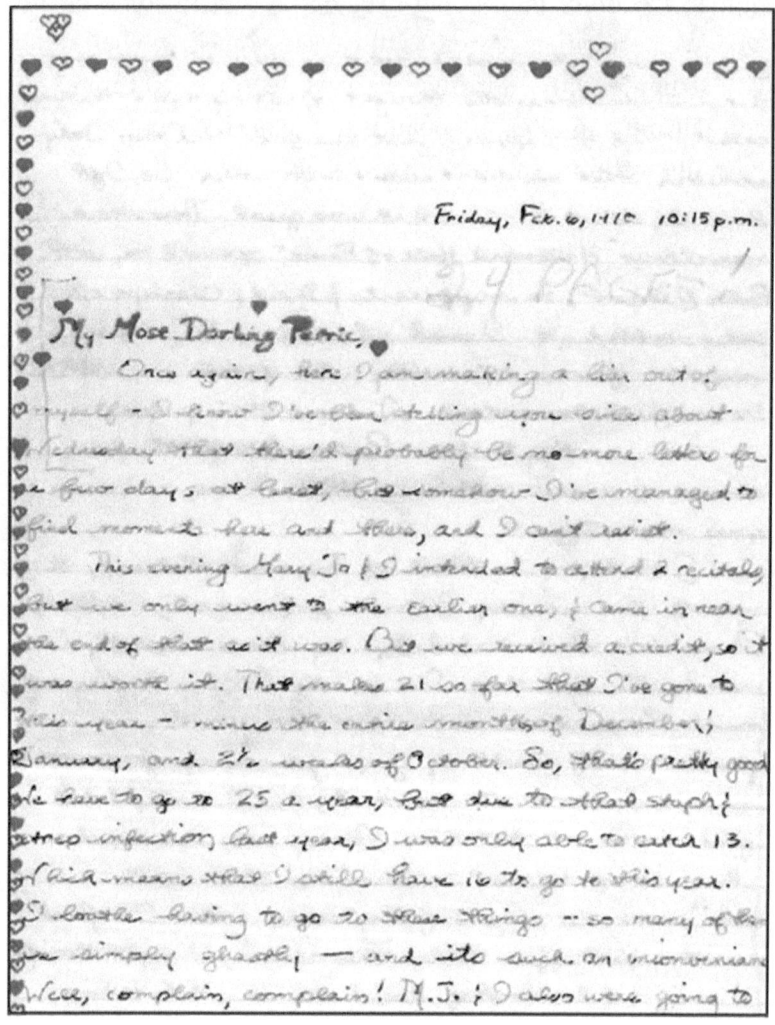

My Most Darling Patric
[Hand-drawn red hearts all around the border.]

Once again, here I am making a liar out of myself—I know I've been telling you since about Wednesday that there'd probably be no more letters for a few days at least, but somehow, I've managed to find moments here and there, and I can't resist.

Please don't be disturbed by my letters recently—namely the last two. I'm in the strangest frame of mind at one time in the not too remote past, I found myself suddenly groping aimlessly for something secure and warm to relate to, and I really didn't find it then at that time. At any rate, I developed a keen set of defense mechanisms that still are prone to begin firing away when I'm faced with hardships. When this occurs, I fight them if I can, but it's kind of weird. This is what's taking place now, perhaps.... I hope I'm not boring you. This week I've been very tense & mostly I don't realize it until my back starts screaming at me. But it's gotten to the point where suddenly I'm rather detached from myself to the extent that I really don't feel the pain anymore—which is great, and I really don't realize how tired I am—**that is** not so great for health. But so far, I'm in very good health & my system will survive the next week.

The pressures at the Music Academy are sometimes too light to be true, and at other times, too heavy to be believed. What I wanted to say is not to worry. I'm fine physically and soon much of this tension will lift and I'll improve mentally too. Forgive me for complaining so to you, Patric. And thank you for putting up with me. It's wonderful to be able to turn to you now in times of great need. Thank you, my love. Tonight, as I listened to the man singing in the recital, I wondered briefly if perhaps his wife was in the audience, and if she was very proud of him. Then I thought about you. I pictured us when we're married, and I saw you standing at a podium making a very impressive speech of some sort & I was feeling so proud. You were addressing faculty people etc. I watched you and admired you. And my mind went through the speech part to the party afterwards & everyone was commending you & very interested in your topic. I don't even know if you'll ever make any speeches, etc. and I don't really care.

But I know that there will be many moments when I'll be so proud of the admiration that others feel for you. My mind pictured us getting ready for the evening of my visualization. I was running around in my slip, trying to be very calm, but I was nervous about meeting other wives etc. You had picked out the dress you wanted me to wear—it seems to me that it was some sort of yellow wool or something. It was fun to get ready with you. I straightened your tie for you. And you zipped my dress for me, & we stood before the mirror a moment, with you behind me, resting your **hands** upon my shoulders. We both smiled & turned & kissed very lovingly....

Suddenly, I realized that people were clapping, and there I was, lost in my reverie. Pat, with all my heart and body and soul, I love you. I am awed by your intelligence and your inborn grace. I am delighted by your sense of humor. I am flattered by your attentions, and deeply moved by your devotion. And I am blessed with your love. I admire you. I love you.

Right now, it is 11:00 P.M. and my eyes refuse to stay open. It'd be so wonderful to hear from you tomorrow, but I know that you're very busy and I understand when you don't write. How is your health now? And your job-hunting? I'm thinking of you my love. "Goodnight sweetheart. Good night my life's sweet content." I love you, Pat... Sleep well tonight, and have peace in knowing that I love you.

Saturday February 7, 1970, 10:00 P.M. [same letter]

What a day! When I heard Sarabel barking outside this morning, I knew she was greeting the mailman. I knew there'd be a letter for me, **I CAN ALWAYS TELL!** Yes, there was your letter. But what's this? A tape—and a mysterious little package were also there...So the unopened Valentine's package sits on me dresser, teasing me. Your letter I read immediately. And Pat, it was just marvelous. The tape I had to wait to play until tonight because my little recorder can't take that size reel. So I borrowed Bryan's & picked it up on the way home from the extra choir rehearsal at church. It was a miserable day weather-wise—raining and cold. So when I got home at about 4:30, I immediately set up the tape, and then went and wadded my hair. After I took care of everything for the evening that I had to do, I came up here to listen—it was about 6:00 P.M. It was (is) so wonderful to hear your voice again, my darling. Thank you so much for your letter and the tape. You spent much time on both & and put a lot of physical and mental effort into both, and I want you to know that I deeply appreciate your thoughtfulness.

Thank you, Thank you. I can't make a tape of this size to you because Bryan's recording mechanism doesn't work at the moment. If he gets it fixed, or if I find another means to record such a tape, I'll buy a larger one and send it. Perhaps I can find some very thin Mylar tape that will enable me to put many many more feet of tape upon the small reel than regular tape. Well anyway. I'm very much torn between your letter and tape—I want to reply to both, but am so overwhelmed that I can think of no words to express my feelings about either. I am so very appreciative for both. Well, I'll just start writing and see what happens!

This morning I didn't get up until 10:00 A.M., so I had 11 hours of sleep. And boy, did I sleep soundly. I only do that when I get unbelievably tired. I had a dream within a dream—I was telling you one morning as we lay in bed that I dreamed that we weren't together at all—that it wasn't June & I wasn't really in California. You kissed my head & said, "Well, you're not dreaming, Shelley, you're really here and I'm with you, and I love you." And then I woke up & and reached over for you. It took me a few minutes to really place myself. For a moment, a feeling of desperation swept over me—almost as if I felt that if I shut my eyes & wished hard enough, the dream would come true right then. But then I turned my thoughts away from that direction & started thinking of when you were here four weeks ago. And I sort of went back to sleep.

There are so many things for me to tell you & I just don't have the time now. Today, I really relaxed—except for the rehearsal and took my mind completely off the Music Academy. You mentioned my education in the tape, so I'll tell you what I think. It would be a crime to throw it down the drain for nothing—here I am an honor student & I got a $350 scholarship this year...Anyway, it also would be a sin to throw away the money we've put in to it so far.

As your wife, I should have some degree...But I'm sure you'd feel easier if I could say that I have a degree. I have to know that I've got a green light from the Music Academy to go ahead safely on toward my (Senior) recital and degree.... Well, I sit and bitch & bitch to you, don't I? I guess I'm complaining so much because I'm scared—I'm really scared of my (voice) boards this May. And although Mr. Knissen doesn't act that way, I know he is (scared) too. And I've got a temper and a stubborn streak and I am bound and determined that if and when I leave the Music Academy…it will be on my terms, not theirs. I get frustrated when I write like this to you, and it's not because I want my letters to all be romantic, **nor because I want to keep these *ornery characteristics of mine a secret from you.*** It's just because I don't have time to get off on a tangent that I didn't really intend to start on in the first place.

Well, I kept my thoughts away from the Music Academy all day until now. And now I'm frustrated and angry and I feel like yelling, so I think I'll pick up your letter & just hold it for a minute, and smell your After Shave (lotion), and then I'll become serene once again.

I'm back now, & I don't know if "serene" is exactly the right term. I happened to turn at random to your description of what you would like to do to me…my God; you do know how to express yourself, don't you! So I sit here rather speechless or witless.

As I said before, I do have to talk to you about California & I think I'd prefer to do it on tape. Don't let that sound ominous— there are only two problems that I see now from this side, besides the financial angle. I'm very grateful to your father for his attitude about it. And I can't tell you how glad I am that you told him of our *vow to one another. I hoped you would, and I'm glad that you did.* I'm sure my parents will comply—there's been absolutely no fuss about it and if I logically try to work out any snags that they may feel are pending—it should be ok. Well, I'll tell you more later.

You asked the reason for my wanting to get a job during my senior year. It is because I'd like to pay for as much of the wedding as possible. It's such an expense & it seems to get more expensive sounding every time I turn around. So, that's why.

And no, I most certainly do not mind if you talk about Barbara [Your first wife.] I want to express something else, while I'm on the track. When you feel that the time is right, etc. I…well let's start that sentence again because I want to say it another way. I am looking forward to meeting your daughter, Heather. She is a very important part of your life and you are a better man for retaining and acknowledging the very warm love that you have for her. She is a beautiful little girl and just from her pictures I think she must be very lovable **[Heather would have been six years old at the time]**.

You told me to say whatever I think & feel so here goes. When you do arrange for Heather to meet me, it may seem a little strange for her, because she is so young. Well that's not the point. The point is that before & after you and I have our own children, I hope that you won't feel that you have to cut Heather out of the picture…I hope that her life will be very fruitful and happy and if there is some way in which I can contribute to her happiness, I very much would like to. I hope that you understand what I've tried to express….

Sunday afternoon, February 8, 1970, 2:30 P.M.

This letter is to go to that most beautiful, gorgeous, sexy, and desirable Miss Shelley Bennington,

My Dearest Shelley,

I had thought to start this letter out on a rather serious note, but I sat down in a chair to look at a cartoon book entitled "*Nude-Niks*" and I got to thinking about your great feminine pulchritude, and all the different poses I would like to see you in, and my mind slipped off of its serious track. How much I would like to come upon you reclining on the couch, clothed in a filmy negligee…yes? Or, how about if we were both nude and standing up, and you turned your back to my chest, and lay back against me, putting your head upon my shoulder, and I would take my large, warm hands, and starting with your hips, would slide my hands forward and upward, with a gentle but firm motion, until each hand was in firm possession of one of your delicately, warm and soft breasts. And then to caress them gently and tenderly. A good idea… yes? I must slow this train of thought down, for I am getting too excited.

In one of your recent letters, you ask about my happys and my sads, my ups and my downs. Well, I have them. This current period or phase of my life is one filled with a lot of emotional feelings. I have only begun to think about where I am now, and what has happened to me, career-wise. It is indeed a jolt, to be stopped suddenly, in my struggle to carve out a career for myself that is suited for me; one that feels comfortable for me, one that utilizes the talents and skills that I have. Especially is it hard, because I was making quite a bit of progress during my years in the Northern California State College. Now, everything will be delayed for a few years. But maybe the delay is good; maybe some important developments will take place. Of course, I have been thinking, that if I accomplished nothing else last fall than to meet you, it was all worth it.

Let me tell you a little of my background. This involves the more negative aspects. Starting at the age of five, I lived alone with my mother. She had three different jobs in order for us to live in a nice neighborhood and for me to go to a good school. Consequently, I spent a lot of time home alone. After the age of eight, baby-sitters were passé. I used to get money from mother and go downtown to the evening movies

(Usually a double feature plus a Newsreel, plus a cartoon). I became very independent, and was "doing my own thing," long before most other children.

But, I was very lonely. And I always had a feeling inside that I did not really belong anywhere. Everybody else seemed to have much more family life. They had mothers and fathers, and went places and did things together. I used to sponge off of others' families' lives. The neighbors would take me to the circus, swimming, or to the movies. But still, it was not the same as having one's own family.

I remember one day in particular. I was nine years old, in the summer of 1949. I had helped the neighbors pack their car for their annual trip to Florida for the summer. I waved goodbye to them as they drove off. I just stood there staring, and said to myself: "I never get to go anywhere, or do anything interesting!"

Somehow that image became deeply imbedded into my consciousness, and I have been making up for it ever since. For years, I have had the wanderlust and the curiosity about any and all places I have never seen before. It really is true, now, that I have been across the United States no less than 36 times! And my spirit of adventure has taken me to many strange places, and into several different situations. I have worked as a volunteer, in mental hospitals, and once in San Quentin Prison (One night a week for six weeks). I have picked beans in Oregon—like a migrant worker—to earn enough money to take me back to Our Town. Well, if I start telling you all the jobs I have had, this letter wouldn't be finished for a week.

Let's get back to my childhood. In addition to feeling lonely, I usually felt inadequate. I was a miserable student in public school, often sitting beside the teacher's desk, because

I always played with toys or bothered other students, rather than pay attention to the lesson. You might say I was the Dunce of the class. Except that I was not stupid, I just could not relate very well to what was happening. My needs were different from what the teachers were offering.

This aspect was corrected when I went away to a Military School. In Military School, life for me improved tremendously. Everything was orderly: you went to bed every night at the same time, you got up every morning at the same time. Meals were nourishing and always on time. There were roommates to play with, and a whole wood to play in. AND, there was a regular study period every evening after dinner. With all the regularity of study, I surprised the hell out of myself and became the No. 1. Student in my class. (Coupled with becoming the military leader of my class.) I remained number one for all of the three years that I attended. What a different image that gave me. Of course, too, the Commandant was on the scene and did quite a bit for me and many other boys, in building better self-images. Military School for me was a happy and progressive time. I owe a lot to it.

I keep trying to tell you something in this letter, but I seemed to get sidetracked. I was trying to trace some of my early beginnings and then show how some of them related to me now, but my fingers seem to want to say something else. Well, maybe this isn't the time. Maybe it would be better when you are in person.

Let me just say, that as a result of my background, one of my strongest drives has been to really make something of myself, with the specific target of a career. It was more than just wishing to be successful, or making money; it was as if my identity as a person depended upon it. And, as I could see myself making progress toward a career, I felt good about myself as a person; when I felt I wasn't making progress, I became depressed with many negative feelings and anxieties toward myself. It all seemed so hinged to just succeeding in a career. That is a pretty narrow base, from which to have self-esteem and respect and belief. But it is not all that uncommon in our type of society, which is so achievement-oriented. Just look at the symbols we hold to stand for success: money, big houses, cars, yachts, minks, jewels, etc. Very few people give others credit for being a successful person, in the sense of values and ethics.

It has only been very recently, that I have recognized how precarious my self-oriented thinking was. And now that I do realize it, it will be sometime before I can completely modify such thinking.

One of my lifelong goals has been to become the most mature person possible. Not that I had to compete with anyone else; but just that I wanted to grow inside, as much as possible, and be a very fine person, whose goals and values were wise and livable. And I must say I have had quite a bit of outward success there. I think, basically I have developed a character and a lifestyle that is effective and worthwhile. The problem is internally; I am not oriented to appreciate myself very much. My mother, and her mother, who had the biggest influence upon me as a child, are, for some very valid reasons of their own, very critical and demanding people. Nothing is ever quite good enough. One must always reach for the standard, but somehow, you are never quite able to. It is kind of like original sin: "everybody is a sinner; whether he actually sins or not." It is a very common bag; mother is more concerned with doing what looks proper, than with being yourself and accepting your own feelings and values. Indeed, Mother is sometimes insecure. And, her feelings have been passed on to me; such that I very **often am** concerned with **being** a person **who devalues** his own accomplishments, particularly as they do not correspond with common norms, or whatever standards. After a while, you do develop a generalized feeling that somehow, you are just inadequate no matter what. I don't know if any of your feelings are similar to this or not. Well, I have been working very hard during the past three years to become aware of how I think and feel about myself, and to modify the detrimental parts. Your overwhelming acceptance, incidentally, does me a world of good. Your letters mirror back to me many of the qualities I feel are important for me to have, and very rarely give myself credit for.

You say you need me, Shelley. That my love of you means the world to you, beyond expression in words. Well, as a fellow human being, I need yours too; very much. Your very warm and mature love makes me grow inside; reminds me of how great life is, and gives me personal satisfaction.

If what I have done with myself can make me into the kind of person that draws your love and respect, then I am well proud of myself.

I really mean that. I perceive you as a person of great and deep emotion, who, "does not fall in love easily." And if you love me, that is worth something. Oh, lots of other people love me too. But I want a special kind of person to love me; your kind of special person. One who means a great deal to me, one with whom I can build a lasting relationship. One whose values and needs, and desires parallel mine.

You may say to me, that you too, have difficulties with feelings of inadequacy and inferiority. And I accept them. But I see you as a case similar to mine; you are a person of far greater worth than you-yourself perceives. Of course, you have not travelled, lived, and experienced the ten extra years that I have. You have little to go on in comparing yourself with others. You are not yet fully aware of how rare and valuable is your deep love, and openness and honesty of emotions, to yourself, and to others. I know how much you are worth, especially to me, even if you cannot see it yet. Just as you see me differently than I see myself. So, as time passes, we will give to each other, and help each other. We will talk about our feelings, and try and eschew those that have little basis in fact or reality.

Well, getting back to the present, this period is a difficult one for me; I will have to do a lot of readjusting of my thinking, as I come to better understand myself, with my many deep and complex drives and needs as I come to formulate better systems of values and procedures. Your love and feelings for me are a form of radiant life source. And I thank you for them. They will make the road much easier.

You asked about my job situation. Well, up until Friday, I had a cold to contend with, so I did not do much more than rest. On Friday I called the Bank of America, and they are looking to see if there is somewhere in their organization for me. Mostly, they put young men into Management Training, but I don't want it. If B of A can't find anything, then I will try several other large banks. Basically, I would like a clean, regular 40-hour-a-week job in an office. But if that turns up nothing, then I will look into factory work, which pays more money. There is not a great deal of pressure financially at the moment. I have very few debts and I can live here with my father for nothing, until I start working. Besides, the rest is what I need.

I went to my father's chiropractor on Saturday, and he gave me a full treatment. He loosened up my whole body—a body that was full of six months' worth of tension. He found a knot (lump of muscular tightness) on my back that I did not know was there. It sure hurt when he pressed it, though. When the body is loose, the blood flows better, and the nerves and muscle operate better. It allows me to think and feel on a higher level. Already the mental numbness that I have been experiencing is beginning to fade. The doc thinks that two or three more such treatments will have me back to normal or better. I am pleased.

And, just being here is restful. I am taking over the maintenance of the house and yard, which is very good mental and physical therapy. I enjoy it. I spent most of Friday working in the yard, and most of Saturday, working in the house. There is quite a challenge here. My father has not been able to do very much, so there are a lot of areas that need a good cleaning. *MAY I explain. In December 1961, my father was returning from a job interview in San Diego, and he was driving up the famous Highway 101. At first it runs along the coast. But around San Juan Capistrano it curves to the right to go inland. That section is called "DEAD MAN'S BEND."* Well on this day, there was a sudden super thick FOG BANK. My father slowed down to a creep and soon he saw he was right behind a flatbed truck. He turned his wheels to go around but then looked up at the rear-view mirror. He saw a car racing toward him, and he exclaimed "This is DEATH!" The car slammed into him, but with the wheels turned, he was shoved over an embankment and out into a farmer's field. His driver's door would not open so he dove out of the passenger side window, and realized he was injured. The car that hit him contained four teenagers. Two died instantly at the scene, and the other two died later in the hospital. It was a 17 car & truck pile up and there were *more fatalities and injuries. The California Highway Patrol was unable to cope—no accurate reports, so lawsuits were a problem. My father's muscles and ligaments were badly damaged. So Dad spent the rest of his life going weekly to a chiropractor to loosen him up. That is why he could no longer do physical work.*

And I am just the man to do the heavy physical labor. I cannot stand dirt or things in a state of disrepair. I like making them clean or fixed, and I feel a great sense of accomplishment when I am finished.

If you have ever wondered what kind of a house I would like us to have, may I say here, that I like clean and neat ones. I believe in thoroughly "Spring Cleaning," when everything gets a fresh cleaning. I don't like dirt; even in places where you can't see it, I don't like to know it is there. Like behind cabinets and couches. Or under sinks and stoves. Or up on the chandeliers and doorways.

Lest you should think I am a fanatic, let me explain or qualify my remarks. I think that when you move into a house or apartment, the whole place should be ship-shape. Then, every week when you do house cleaning, say on Saturday, one room should get a thorough cleaning, while the rest just get a routine cleaning. That way, no room is more than five weeks away from a good cleaning. Bathrooms and kitchens especially, need a lot of care, for health reasons if nothing else. When I was 27 years old, I lived with two older men, Andy 41, and Frank 43 years old, in a pent-house apartment in San Francisco. I had been known to spend a solid five hours cleaning in the bathroom; washing every surface of any kind. (We three all spent many hours cleaning the apartment.)

Well my love, enough of me and my problems. I probably have not responded to all of your questions in your letters. Of course there are so many letters, it is hard to remember each and every word. I have them numbered, just to keep track of them all. And I love each and every one of them. I literally jump for joy when the mailman brings one. I did receive and enjoy your little notebook of poetry. It is a fond treasure, which I shall read again and again.

Just listening to you outline all the work you have to do this week, just makes me tired. I am worried that you will be able to do it all to your satisfaction. I am sorry this letter probably will not arrive until Wednesday, but maybe you can use the long tape and my other letter for comfort.

Shelley, I put my hands upon your shoulders and draw you close to me. I bring my face to yours, and plant a kiss upon your lips. I put my arms around you, and squeeze you snuggly. I stand and hold you. I love you with all there is in me. And I need you. Love Patric.

Sunday, February 8, 1970, 6:45 P.M.

My Beloved Patric,

Bet you'd never have guessed that I just changed the cartridge, huh? Tonight I thought that I'd be really clever, so I came up here at around 5:30 P.M., intending to write to you as I listened to your tape. Well, it just didn't work—I get too excited about hearing your voice & I just have to concentrate & listen to you speak. I love the sound of your voice—its timbre is so mellow and soothing—even when you have a bad cold. It was ridiculous to even think that I could tear myself away from the Recorder.

7:20 P.M. Well, I got sidetracked. My parents decided to call Sally & find out why she hadn't written for so long. I only talked to her for a moment—mother used the phone in the basement & my dad and I used the other. Anyway, before I got on the line, they were talking about us—you and me. Sally told them that she received a letter from you & that you sounded "madly in love." Well! I hope so!! She sounded quite pleased. I didn't know you'd written her—you know, this whole thing in a way is quite "humoresque" as Gayle would say. Anyway, I feel sort of funny now because I haven't written her yet and you beat me to it! Did you ever think of Sally as a Sister-In-Law??

You know, it's kind of weird to think about "What If's." Like, for instance, what if you hadn't come to our house that day in September? And what if your's and Sally's visits to our city hadn't coincided at all? Or are you more of a "predestination" fan? Do you think we ever would have met if we'd missed each other in September? That's really a spooky feeling, you know?

Patric, I'm so in love with you. I sat in church today, and part of the time I daydreamed & tuned myself completely out of church. When I think about you, I get warm & tingly and sometimes I even get goose bumps. While I was dressing this morning, I turned the tape on—just at random. So of course, what I turned to was the place where you discussed being inspired by my body! I laughed—it was funny that [earlier] my finger pushed the stop button just at that spot. I have to listen as much as I can to the tape now while I still have Bryan's recorder. How wonderful it is to hear your sweet voice.

I am rather amazed that you said you don't think that you express yourself quite as well as I do. That really shocks me. Don't you believe it, darling, because you express yourself beautifully and with warmth and depth and sensitivity. And above all, with love. Your letters are treasures that I wouldn't give up for all the money—or anything else—in the world. And your tape! Well. Again, we'll just have to invent some words. It may sound funny, but one of the reasons that I love hearing this tape over and over is because I love the way you laugh on it. You have a delightful laugh—sometimes it doesn't come out as a full laugh. But I just love to hear it. It tickles me to hear you sort of burst with glee at some of the things you say—and when you do, the pictures that were probably flirting with your mind at the time that you laughed, come to my mind and make me giggle too. And to hear you sigh, well, you make me sigh too. Well, I sit with your letters and listen to the tape. And that was such a great letter that I received yesterday! I'm just all bubbly inside.

Your timing whether you realized it or not, was super terrific. I can't tell you how much I needed to hear from you.

Maybe I don't even let myself think about it, and so it's all the more delightful when I do get a letter. So, during this week of tremendous stress and strain, I will re-read your wonderful, wonderful letters and listen to this beautiful tape. I can't tell you how much they all mean to me. Thank you, Pat my love, for being so wonderful to me; for expressing your thoughts and feelings & for being interested in mine. And thank you, my sweet love, for loving me as you do.

Well, I'd say this letter is getting A BIT LONG. Have I broken my record yet? [Patric: Nope... this one is 24 pages, and another one is 26 pages!] I don't remember. It doesn't seem to me that I've said very much in here—guess it's because I've taken three days in writing it. I hope that these "books" aren't too boring to you [Patric: Nope, not at all]. My friend Agnes always comments on the weight of the envelope—when I drive, she has to drop the letters into the mailbox and I do it when she drives. Don't forget about the phone call I'm making to you on Valentine's Day. Unless you tell me otherwise, I'll call at about 10:00 P.M. my time—is that 7:00 P.M. out there?

As I sit & listen to your voice, I close my eyes and dream—envisioning you as you sat speaking into the microphone, and letting your descriptions paint pictures for me to see. You described your father's house & it sounds just lovely. I don't quite understand what the sleeping set up will be—I was under the impression that your room was the one you built (In the large garage in 1962, using your stepmother's Award money she was given after she wrote a newspaper article about the experience of being caught inside of a forest fire—$100.00.)

And I am confused as to whether you're planning on just point blank sharing the room you have with me or what. In one letter it didn't sound as if you were planning on sleeping with me except once in a while. I guess it's sort of a delicate subject, but I'm sort of curious to know—if you have decided or whenever you do. I don't want to be a problem for your father, or a source of embarrassment to anyone. Whatever your decision may be I will abide by it. This is one case where you will have to make the decision. And, I know that you are aware of my feelings about it. But I think that your father is very very important, & he has to be considered. I love you Pat.

Do you know what I daydreamed once this evening as I listened to your voice? I was at your house in California—it was this summer, I guess. We were going to get ready for bed. And so, we stood in the bedroom together & closed the door & kissed each other & held each other very tightly. Then, we stood back & admired each other, & I reached up & unbuttoned your shirt & took it off & hung it up. Then you sat on the bed as I untied your shoes & took them & and your socks off. And you let me undress you very slowly, until you stood before me nude and so very handsome for me to behold. Slowly, then you unbuttoned my shirt—it seems to me that it was my green one—& you took off my shoes and my shirt. And then you pulled my slip off and took off my hose. And you kissed my forehead and asked me to put my arms around your neck & then as I did so, you unhooked my bra & then you took it off as I let you go. And then you gently took my pants off, just as I did to you a few moments before. **You stood gazing at me, and then very gently, you began to caress my body with yours back & forth. We lay on top of the bed for a few minutes, & then I got up & went in to take a shower. When I came back there, you were, still on the bed, and sound asleep. But it was only about 9:00 P.M.! So I gently began to stroke your legs, starting with your feet. Ever so softly did I tip toe up your legs with my fingertips. And as I neared the top of them, a funny little smile played on your lips & you said, "OK—stay right there." So I played with you for a while, and kissed you, and you whispered to me after a while that you were about to climax, & I was so glad. And afterwards as you laid there exhausted, I curled up & laid my head upon your chest. You slept for a while, then & when you woke up you decided to take a shower. When you came back, I had the covers pulled down, & I was already in bed, lying there waiting. It seems to me that the house was empty except for us. And you came & began to kiss me all over. AND IT WAS JUST LOVELY.**

My gosh, Pat, are you sure you want me to "go right on dreaming!!??!!" Has anyone ever gotten pregnant from a dream? If my dreams keep going, it just may happen.

OK—you can laugh now. Oi Veh. Tell me I'm really on the 12th page. I can't believe it. Well, I promise I won't be writing before Friday probably. And if I do write before then, I should be spanked!

Whoops. It didn't burst it after all. Ha Ha, Dr. Carlson—I'm not taking an exam now; I'm still in bed with Patric, feeling his warm body shaking with pleasure. Patric, I miss you so much. I can't wait to talk to you in living decibels next Saturday.

If it bothers you to have me get carried away with my sensual dreams in these letters, please tell me. I won't stop dreaming but I could discipline my pen, but I think judging from your letters, I sort of got the idea that you enjoy expressing your thoughts & receiving mine, just as much as I enjoy expressing & receiving. Lord, even your letters *"Turn me on" as you'd say. "Gulp!"*

Back again. Now I'm in bed, for a change & I'll finish off this last page and listen to your voice for a few moments, and then try to sleep. Thank you Pat, for being so wonderful to me. Your love and devotion overwhelm me, and I pray that I will always be deserving and worthy of you. Perhaps we can't see into the future and perhaps we will change a great deal through the years.

But I can make a very solemn vow to you now that will last until our wedding, and forever after as long as we live. And that is: I promise you, my love, that with whatever source or soul I have in me, I will always love you and devote myself to you; and I will do whatever I am able to do with whatever I can give to you, to add as much happiness and comfort, and warmth and love to your life as possible. I hope I said that the way I mean for it to sound. I love you so very much, Pat. To me, we are already engaged and, as you said, we are already married spiritually. You never need to doubt my love, and you never need to question my faithfulness to you. If you ever do feel fear or worry, then come back to this letter and read this page, and know that I will never stop loving you. Thank you, my darling, for giving me greater happiness than I ever dreamed could exist. With all my devoted love, Your Shelley xxxx

February 10, 1970, 5:45 P.M.

My darling Patric,

Surprise, surprise! Maybe I should be spanked, as I wrote in the last letter. But tonight is an easy one for me, simply because I refuse to do any work. Today I had a Hairy midterm in conducting (I got a "B" on it) and in keyboard, we had a rather difficult assignment to do, so it was a taxing day, even if it wasn't a very long one.

Perhaps I should start this whole thing all over again. Typing would be faster even for me maybe, if I could just get the typewriter to work. Oh well, you'll have to put up with my illegible writing. (Illegible? Beans. I don't know). Shock of the Century: You actually may be able to get through this letter without going "cock-eyed." At least, as long as my patience holds out as I blunder along at the typewriter. Something tells me this won't last very long.

Right now, on the tape you're telling me about how you're going to get a "double bed" naturally.... Every morning as I get dressed, I turn the tape on, and it gives me my day a beautiful start. And when I come home, your voice greets me again, and whenever I come up here, I try to find a few moments to play it. I wonder if the tape will wear out? Anyway, I won't be able to listen to it for very much longer because Bryan needs the recorder back & I can't play this on my recorder.

Incidentally, I haven't finished getting all the negatives in yet, so do you mind waiting for them? I certainly don't mind waiting for the ones you have—there's no rush at all, so don't spend your money before you can afford to because I could even wait till this summer. I will try to get these back to you within a couple of weeks.

I love the sound of your voice. But it's kind of strange feeling to be listening to you and writing to you at the same time. So, I think I'll go get a shower—for a change—and then come back up & write some more, OK? 7:00 P.M. There—Spic & Span. Actually, it is a relief to be rid of that typewriter. It makes me nervous to type & I start feeling detached from the letter. Perhaps if I had a decent machine it'd be one thing. And no, I don't mind if you type because, as I think I have told you, your warmth and love just glows whether from a typed page or hand-written. Naturally, I like to see your own writing now and then. But I wouldn't want for you to feel hampered when you write to me. I would like for you to enjoy writing to me as much as I enjoy writing to you, and so whatever way you feel the most comfortable is fine with me. Honest—I love your letters, and it doesn't matter whether they're typed or written or painted or penciled. Just as long as they're from you. Because I love you.

The little Valentine's package is still sitting unopened upon my dresser. Thank you, Pat. I don't have to open it to know that I will love it, simply because it's a gift from you.

I have a problem: I have pen pal in England and she was working on a visit to my home sometime over the summer. I wrote and asked her if she could possibly come in September if she could possibly arrange this. I'm praying that she can. Otherwise, I don't know what I'll do. I can't give up living with you. I just can't if I can possibly help it. My mother is pretty well convinced that this will be OK. This summer— and my dad is certainly not objecting—perhaps not giving too much approval—but as long as he's not screaming "no" then I'm OK. (Sometimes I'm ok even if he is screaming!) At any rate, Mother's main concern now is about my pen pal's visit. It's not that she's so excited about having a nearly "complete stranger" (to her) here or anything—but I have given my pen pal the invitation. Come to think of it, she sort of invited herself—but I wouldn't have had to say yes if I hadn't wanted to. So, keep your fingers crossed. Because something tells me that if she can't come in September, or postpone the trip, that I'm about to lose a pen pal. If I were she, and something like this happened, I'd probably be pretty upset. And I myself do feel badly about it—but that's the way it goes. I mean I'm not going to "marry her." Do you think that my attitude is really wrong? I know I'm being selfish.

But I also have to follow what I believe is right. And coming to California is right. I'll tell you about the only other problem about this summer I have some other time—perhaps after we see what my pen pal has to say. Although I think a lot of her, I suppose I should admit to you (and I've never admitted this to anyone) that in a way, I've always sort of felt very uneasy about her coming here. Perhaps it'd be better if she didn't come at all. But she has her heart set on it. Well, this has been bothering me and I felt I'd better tell you at last, because I couldn't put it off any longer. It's sort of out of my hands for the moment. Remember, my darling, that no matter what, you come first. But this is going to take some real finagling (I've never seen that word written before—I hope it's right.) Well, I'm going downstairs for a while to sit with my parents—I probably won't see much of them for the rest of the week!

8:35 P.M. What a nice surprise—I went downstairs to be told by Mother that there was a National Geographic Special called "Wild River" on TV. So, we all watched it. (Pop wasn't too thrilled.) And it was marvelous. I look forward to taking short trips with you and being all alone with you and Nature. Away from the rest of mankind for a while. The mountains, rivers, trees, and wildlife; Pat, my God, how I love them. And how I loathe the way that man has tried to destroy nature— and how, if something isn't done now to stop it, man will indeed succeed in the destruction of man, animal and plant. And all of the earth will be barren stripped to nothing but a trembling, rotted skeleton, with no trace of life, no dignity in death. Nothing. That must be Hell! Well. If I got started on my love for life you may indeed not receive another letter until summer—for I would still be writing even as I got off the plane! Well…maybe I'd stop writing as the plane landed. I am not a fanatic or anything…

As I told you, tomorrow we have a big rehearsal for the BACH. Thursday—my shortest day at school, I get home at around 1:00 P.M. But that's the night of the choir rehearsal and we're having a longy this week to combine the choir with the orchestra for the Bach and Scarlatti. Then on [I can't find the rest of this letter. Sorry!]

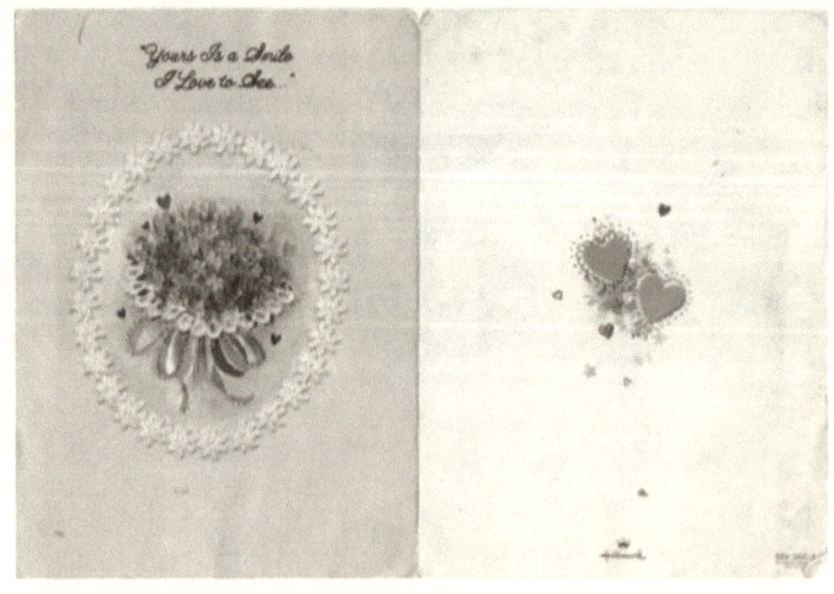

February 11, 1970 [A Valentine's Card]

My Darling Patric, [The note accompanying the card] Happy Valentine's Day to you, my love.

Today, Wednesday, I came home at 7:00 P.M. to find your lovely letter waiting for me. You couldn't have timed it better, and I want to say many things to you and I will answer when I write again. Thank you, my love.

Have a good day on Valentine's Day, and think about the magical moments when we'll talk to each other. At first, I was thinking of my call as being my Valentine to you, but I'm so excited about hearing you again that I guess it's maybe even more of a present to myself! I hope that it will mean as much to you as it will to me. This is a moment that I've anticipated for two weeks—or at least, I mean, this will be a moment I've so looked forward to. Well...I'm enclosing this note in one of the cards, because I wanted to thank you for this most recent letter. Thank you. Patric, every day is Valentine's Day—for me, because it is supposed to be a day filled with love, and each day is filled with love now that we have each other. I love you so—indeed this card is TO THE ONE I LOVE. Patric, the one I love is you. I love you in your sunny moods and stormy moods, in good times and bad. For better or worse, in sickness or in health—I DO—I love you...Bless you, darling. Lovingly, Your Valentine xxx Shelley xxx

CARD itself: Darling Patric, Bless you, my beloved Patric, on the celebration of our love's first Valentine's Day. It won't be long before we'll never have to be separated on this, or any other day. I love you, Pat, with all my heart. And tonight I will call you. All my devoted love,

Xxx Your Shelley xxx

Wednesday Afternoon, February 11, 1970, 3:00 P.M.

To My Devoted and Loving Shelley,

Permit me to release some of my tensions and depressions, by writing to you. I do not know how much my present mood may affect my words and ideas, but if you see some heavy thoughts, they are most likely the product of my depression. And, some of what I think I want to say may be heavy by its nature.

I received your wonderful 24-page manuscript today. It was most welcome and came at a time when I needed most to hear from you. It has lightened my mood considerably. I am really not sure where my down mood comes from; there could be several factors, working singly, or in concert.

One factor, for instance, is that I have not yet fully dealt with all the tensions and emotional reactions from the Graduate School situation. I left there immediately and went to our Our-Town where upon I became so involved with you, and entered a state of high emotional excitement—leaving my prior feelings "tabled," to be considered at a later date.

Well, as I recover from my cold, and all my kaleidoscopic travels, as I go to the Chiropractor and have my physical tensions released, as I become fully aware of my new situation, I begin to start thinking and remembering, and slowly the old "tabled" feelings come in. And, they are by no means easy to deal with. My experience there was a crushing blow to the ego, and devastating to my emotions and nervous system. That does not mean I am overwhelmed completely. But it does mean that it will be a while before I work through and release myself from it all; to put it in its proper perspective.

Another factor is that I am still negotiating for a job. Bank of America seems very much interested in me, and is looking to see what kind of job they can create or locate for me, that will have a reasonable salary. I had an interview yesterday with one of the directors of a regional administration. He may have room for me on his staff. But things are still indefinite at present.

Another factor is the weather: it has been cool and rainy for the past three days. We had about five inches of rain. The rain is very good for us, as we only get rain two months out of the year here. The rain we get now protects us from bad forest fires in the hot summer months. Incidentally, one thing you will not need this summer is a raincoat.

Another factor is that I have not been sleeping too well at nights. At present I am still sleeping with my father in an old double bed. We are both big people, so even in the best of conditions, there is not a whole lot of room. But, the bed is old, such that both people tend to roll toward the center! Now that would not be quite so bad, if it was you and me, but even then, one can become annoyed at the posture. Then my father does not sleep well, and he turns and tosses, so I sometimes find myself moved to the edge of the bed, or being accidentally pushed by him. Then, in his turning and tossing, he has a habit of wrapping the covers around him, or at least onto his side of the bed, so I wake up cold, with only a little cover on me. Oh well.

Speaking of bedrooms, and the like, let me explain it all. Basically, our house has two bedrooms in the house, and one out in the garage. Originally, the house had another bedroom in the house, but the people before us decided to move their kitchen into one of the bedrooms, so as to make the living room larger. Actually, the living room is very large now, measuring 16' by 32'. We intend to use one end as the dining area.

Now the room out in the garage is the one I built several years ago, and my dad finished it, after I left. Recently my dad bought some new furniture for the room, but it has to be finished with Shellac, etc. When all that is accomplished, Doc, who lives with us, will move into that bedroom. For the time being, however, he is sleeping in the other bedroom in our house. And I am left with Dad in the master bedroom.

Well, this coming weekend we are going to start work on the furniture for the garage room, and I am going to put a lot into it. I really do need my own room. Now, when you come, for however long it is, I envision that you will just move into my room with me; that is, sleeping with me the entire time you are here. Does that meet with your approval? I hope no one openly mentions sleeping arrangements in negotiating for your visit, because I would rather not say openly that you will be sleeping with me, and I would certainly not like to promise that I would have separate accommodations.

Actually, I think everyone already knows that you and I will be sleeping together. Dad, of course, knows, because I had to let him know just what your visit would mean in terms of arrangements. Anyway, the less said in negotiations, the better.

But, this all does bring me to another problem, which Dad and I touched on briefly at the breakfast table this morning. Your mother wrote me a nice note, mentioning the proposed extension of your trip. She indicated that we need to discuss it more, before considering a decision. One thing she did express was a grave concern for the sexual strain that such a lengthy visit would confront you and me with.

I let my Dad read the letter, as I want him to come to know your mother, and to be fully informed of her feelings and thinking. Afterwards, he said he shared her concern for the strain factor. He felt the tension might be more so great, as to cause resentment, anger, frustration, and the eventual breakup of the relationship.

He was not doubting that I could keep my vow about sexual intercourse. He knows me pretty well, and agrees that I could very well keep my word. As he says, I have great control over my feelings and emotions. I have had to, to survive in my environments. But he was particularly worried about you. He sees you as someone who does not ordinarily exert such control, but is very open and honest with your emotions. Which, in itself, is a highly admirable trait for any person.

My Dad is highly impressed with you, partly because of this quality, and I certainly fell in love with you, because you were able to so aptly express your feelings. He is just concerned, that with living as closely with me as you will be, that there will be times when the sex urge is just over-powering. And that even using our own self-control, the frustration will lead to resentment. He does not see three or four weeks as a problem, but wonders about two months. That does not mean he does not want you here; it just means he is concerned for our best interests, and would certainly not want us to break up over sexual frustration.

For myself, I do not share his thinking. I agree, there will be some frustration, arising from normal desires to carry through the sex act. But within me, I have several reasons why I think it would be a poor idea to have intercourse now. There are too many problems that could arise from it for us in our situation. And therefore, I would not be psychologically happy even if I did contemplate having sex with you at this time. I do have the kind of control over my feelings that permits me not to think about intercourse with you, except in fantasy fashion, when thinking of our married future.

From a physiological standpoint, I do not see unmanageable frustrations for us. I am certainly delighted to climax you whenever the need or desire arises. You know that well enough. And I certainly enjoy being climaxed by you. Once I am climaxed, my sexual frustrations drop to zero. Maybe the same is similar for you. Also, just having you lying next to me, is a release of tension for me, rather than a builder of it.

So from my side of the fence, I do not see "the sexual strain" as being an unmanageable factor. But, I think it is something that you ought also to think through. Would the strain be too much upon you? Would you resent me if I turned you down amidst the heat of passion? Can you effectively curb your desire for intercourse until the wedding? It may be somewhat difficult for you to really know, since you have only recently begun experiencing active sex. Well, do think deeply about it. It will be a major concern of your visit.

You mentioned your education in this last letter. I got to thinking about some of the possible implications of your words, and I became heavy of thought. I am concerned for you, that you should be able to continue your education. But I realize and accept that the Voice Boards may have rather rigid, and narrow-scoped standards, which may work against you. As you say, you can get all "A"s but the Senior Year Recital does not meet with their criteria, then all is naught in terms of a degree.

What immediately occurs to me, is that should you not pass on your Senior Recital, you could transfer all of your work to another school, say here in California, where the standards and concepts are broader and more flexible, and then finish your degree, after we are married. Should you not pass the Boards this coming May, then we will revise our thinking at that point. If at that time you should leave school, we might consider marrying earlier, say next Christmas. If you were not in school, or otherwise receiving a formal education, then I can't see waiting 2 ½ years.

HOWEVER, let me hasten to say that such an early marriage would be much more difficult on us than what we now have in mind. For instance, we would not have as much time to prepare for it. We would not have the finances available that we hope to have in 2 ½ years. But more importantly, I would just be moving back to San Francisco to complete my Master's Degree meaning that I would be working full time, and going to school the rest of my available time. That means 1) you will have barely more than a "weekend husband," who even spends part of his weekend studying, and 2) there would be little money, so that you would most likely have to work. The cost of living in supporting two people in an apartment is high. Two persons do not live as cheaply as one. And a married twosome lives more expensively than two singles. I know—I have been there!

And I have lived through exactly the experience I described; for that was what life was like during the first part of my previous marriage. And let me tell you, any wife gets terribly lonely, having to be alone all evening, five nights a week, week after week, etc.

At home, where you are now, you have your parents, your pets, the whole house, a yard, a familiar neighborhood and community, neighbors, friends, and relatives, all to keep you company. If we were married and living in San Francisco, it would be rough.

Tensions would run high. That does not mean we couldn't make it that way, but it would be a rough beginning to a marriage. And marriages should have a strong beginning, because that is when a major amount of adjusting takes place. You need to be around each other a lot then.

Well, I think I have expressed my concern. I hope things turn out well for you. I know you will do your best, but if your best isn't what the Voice Boards want, you and I will just accept it, and go on, seeking alternative routes. I love you, Shelley, regardless of how your studies turn out. I would like you to have a degree but it isn't crucial. And again, if the Music Academy doesn't work out, maybe you could finish your degree, or some other degree, in another school, after we are married, and before we have children.

Speaking of children, that brings me to Heather. I am glad you expressed your feelings about her. That was most kind of you. I had not taken you for granted. I hadn't really gotten around to thinking about it, particularly, only generally.

I have several thoughts on the subject. The first is, it will be a little difficult when you meet her for the first time. And I think maybe you will meet her this coming summer, if you like. Why it will be difficult is because Heather does not yet realize that I am her father. She thinks her stepfather is her real father, and she thinks I am a very good friend of hers, who does very nice things for her. She loves me dearly. But anyway, it would be embarrassing to introduce you as a future stepmother when she does not even know who I am. My ex-wife, whose name is Barbara, and I have discussed this "father situation." It was she who originally had Heather call her stepfather "Daddy." I was away for the first year of the divorce, so it was easy to accomplish. And I was hurt and upset about it, when I found out.

But since then, we have all come to an agreement, that Heather will one day discover the situation. (Heather's last name is mine, not theirs.) and then we shall simply explain the Heather has two Daddies, both of whom love and care for her. I love Heather; I'll do what I can for her over the years. But you come first. Incidentally, I pay $100 a month child support.

What is "my evening of visualization"? No, I did not plan the letter and packages to arrive together. They were mailed on three separate days!! Speaking of the tape, I am sorry it did not fit. Would you indicate to me whether you would like future tapes to be large or small—ones that you can only hear once in a while with lots of information etc. or ones that you can hear all the time, with just a small amount of information on them?

I prefer the longer, because I am long-winded when it comes to talking on tape, as you know. Whatever, let me know your desires.

No, I never before thought of Sally as a Sister-in-Law, until I met you and became so involved. I was sorry to hear about all her illnesses. And no, I hold very little stock in the concept of pre-destination.

My mother is very much of a "Fatalist," but I have never accepted such thinking. I am a strong believer in Free Will, as it is understood, and limited by the human context, in general, and a person's own special circumstances and environment, in specific.

Yes, there is a three-hour time difference. In winter, I am on Pacific Standard Time. As I travel across the U.S. next comes Mountain Standard Time, then Central Standard Time, and finally comes Eastern Standard Time, which is what your city has. I will indeed be home on Saturday, between the hours of 6 and 8:00 P.M. my time. I, too, look forward to hearing you on the phone. There were a couple of times recently, when I almost picked up the receiver to call you.

And finally, no, I do not mind reading your sensual daydreams. As a matter of fact, I look forward to them. You can enter them into your letters as often as you like. Not only do they give me pleasure and excitement in reading them, but I am most happy that you share so much of my thinking.

So many persons have been crippled, or deprived with deep rigidities about sex ingrained in their thinking. During Victorian times [1800s in England and in America] sex was a "duty" that women must "submit to," and as a result, many women grew to hate sex, and derived no pleasure. Then, through the years, various churches sought to control the pleasure of sex by limiting the coital position to one: man on top, woman underneath. They thought that was the least pleasurable. I heard a rumor that in some places they even had official spies who looked into people's bedrooms.

No, please do not stop writing about your daydreams, night dreams, fantasies, and what have you. My sex life these days is limited to vicariously thinking about it; either remembering the pleasurable moments, you and I had over Christmas, or visualizing what it will be like with you this summer. So I really enjoy reading your words and coming to know your thinking, which is as sensual as mine. Hooray! Hooray!! How about a good tongue-lashing between your toes?? Does that do anything for you? Or, how about a long slow nibble up one buttock and down the other?? Or maybe, a slow tongue washing on the back of your neck, from ear to ear??

Well, dear girl, I have had my say today. I am tired now, and I no longer feel depressed. I am lonely for you, but not depressed. I, too, hope you survive this week. Love Patric.

Friday, February the Thirteenth, 8:10 P.M.

To my Sweet, Precious Patric,

How wonderful you are. Thank you, Pat, for helping me to get through what would have been an unbearable week if it hadn't been for you. Your 7-page letter came on Wednesday—& it couldn't have been timed any better. And then yesterday I came home to find the beautiful Valentine book, and your wonderful poem. I call it a poem because that's what it is to me—so very beautiful and sensitive. Never have I received anything like these wonderful gifts Pat.

Wednesday, I think I told you that Agnes picked me up at 7:00 A.M. Did I tell you? Talk about memory—my mind is a total blank. I can't remember when I last wrote to you. It seems ages. Wednesday was such a long day—and the weather outside was so dreary! I had two classes from 8:00-10:00 A.M., and then I worked until noon on Italian, Theory and practicing voice. At 12:00, I was going to go to my English class when I ran into Lyle. I've told you about him. At any rate, he seemed to want to talk, so I decided that my class could wait until today.

Lyle and I talked for about an hour—he has a new girl and they seem very happy, and I told him that I hoped I hadn't hurt his feelings very much. Well, actually, Pat, I have to be honest with you. Lyle seemed to think that he and I were having a very involved discussion and he was impressed with the "depth" in our thoughts. Can I tell you a secret—something I feel a little guilty about? During L.'s and my conversation, I found myself getting kind of bored, and I kept daydreaming. Well, he didn't know it, but I felt a little bad about it.

Actually, I never really did get very involved mentally with Lyle (don't worry, it wasn't very physical either!) But this is the first time I've really talked to him since you and I have become so involved. And frankly, I had a hard time to relate to him. He's a nice boy, but I just couldn't get to his level—whether it was above or below my level is irrelevant I guess. I just couldn't find it! I thought that maybe that would be of interest to you.

Anyway. I worked on theory more and Agnes and I managed to get through the afternoon. At 4:00 P.M., we had rehearsal. It was such a long day. I came home, and although I hadn't eaten in over 12 hours, I took a shower as soon as I got in the house and it felt so good. Then I had some soup and pudding for supper. And finally, I came up here by about 7:30 P.M. and feeling very warm & full and relaxed, I read your letter.

It was wonderful. I very much enjoyed hearing you tell me some of your life's events. And I anticipate hearing about everything and anything that you want to tell me about your past. Or about anything for that matter. It made me feel much closer to you as I read the words that you sent to me...the feeling was one of great pleasure, Pat. I'm so happy that you wanted to tell me more about yourself. Am I making sense? If not, I apologize, sincerely.

My mind simply refuses to function properly, and from what you have told me, I guess you understand very acutely the frustration this brings. I feel as if I'm watching someone else's hand gliding across this page. I have much to say to you & I want to say things as intelligibly and sincerely as possible. So time out. I love you.

And I hope you liked the cards I sent you. I wanted to make a really pretty one for you but it just didn't work out that way. Well, tomorrow night I will have called you by this time to wish my sweet love a Happy Valentine's Day.

Thank you for writing out your Valentine's message to me, Patric. It's so beautiful. When I opened the envelope, I was thrilled to find this book of poems.... That was so sweet of you. **You know how to really pull at my "heart strings," don't you?** Thank you, thank you. I still am just speechless. As I read the book, I felt a huge lump in my throat. As I read your wonderful message, Pat, I cried. These are times when my happiness overcomes me, and then the tears flow.

You could buy everything in the world for me, but they wouldn't begin to compare with the lovely gifts that you've sent to me from your heart. And I accept your gifts with joy, because I love you. Each letter that you write to me is also a gift. Such treasures of love. I've been taking my own advice and only thinking of how much I love you.

Sometimes, perhaps, I say or write things that have been said by many other people, and said so often that they have become trite. But you know, it's kind of fun to be able to say some of these things to you, because there's so much joy in knowing that there you are, perhaps smiling at such common phrases, but appreciating them just the same.

Thank you. You know me very well, I think. I hope that I am able to show to you in one way or another how much you mean to me. I am so ecstatic and elated by the love that we share. Have I told you that I adore you? Well, I do adore you. **Patric, as respectfully and with as much dignity as I am able to, I can't imagine my life without you.**

And I look forward to the years that we will have together—the many years of sharing whatever comes into our lives. There will be struggles and hardships, and misunderstandings and problems. But there will also be great love and warmth, and strength that comes from the bond of love and friendship. I love you so much. I hope you never become tired of hearing me say that, for I will never grow tired of expressing it to you. I look forward to having your children—our children. I look forward to seeing your face when I tell you that we are going to have a child. But I also look forward to our first years of aloneness…rather… togetherness. Let's face it, I look forward to everything that life offers to me, *when I know that you will be there too.*

Sometimes I worry, and wonder if the day could ever come when we couldn't communicate; or if one day I would feel you growing away from me. I wonder too, if the two years will really go by, and if such love as ours is too big for us…if it will burn itself out? But then I remind myself to live only six months at a time. **I wonder if perhaps even at this "early" stage, I am too dependent upon you? Do I need you too much?** Well, Pat, I can't honestly set myself apart into objectivity versus subjectivity in order to try to answer that. It made me feel much better to hear you express your doubts.

When I was much younger, I had some really strange concepts about love. I always thought that I'd like to marry someone "mysterious." Well, I want to know everything about you that you want to tell me. I also used to think that it was unwise to really **need** another person. Well, I guess there was a reason for me to have to become so independent. As you probably know & perhaps much better than I—it's very difficult to suddenly realize that you're losing—or have already lost—someone whom you let yourself depend upon. Well, I admit, **I do need you**. And I do love you.

It's about 11:30 P.M. And I'm very very tired, as you may have guessed. Yesterday, I came home at 1:30 (arrived then) and worked on my theory from about 2:20 until 6:30 P.M., with about ½-hour break for dinner. I never want to see another Minuet and Trio again! Especially one in "D" minor by me! Depending upon the evaluation, I may send you a copy and show you the seemingly small results of approximately 14 hours of work! All I can say is I deserve an "A" for effort! Anyway, I received a letter from the dean yesterday.

Last night, choir rehearsal lasted from 7:45 until 10:20 P.M. or so. Today, I was in a complete stupor. And we had a long, long day—got home at 7:00 P.M. again. From 3:05 until about 3:40 P.M., I rested in the auditorium while listening to Mr. Johnson rehearse the Choral Union. We rehearsed in the big auditorium from 4:00 to 6:00 P.M. I guess I sort of was asleep as I sat in the sort of comfortable seats listening to the Choral Union. I was a bit embarrassed—even though I sat back in the shadows of the auditorium where nobody would even pay any attention. I have a lot of funny quirks, in case you hadn't noticed! (Ha ha—you can stop laughing now!) (Pretty please?) (OK—so laugh!) But I have this thing about people seeing me when I'm asleep. I really get embarrassed about it (afterwards, of course—not while I'm sleeping.) Don't worry, I wasn't embarrassed with you, I don't think. Anyway, I've had this thing longer than I care to admit—but it goes really far back into my early childhood—very far. Don't know what started it, though! Well, I'm bored with me.

And my eyes refuse to stay open any longer. So good night, my sweet love. Thank you, Patric. I love you with all my soul and mind.

Love you.

February 14, 1970, 7:00 P.M.

Happy Valentine's Day, my love!

This morning I couldn't resist opening the little box before I left for rehearsal. Pat, I love the necklace so much, and thank you from the bottom of my heart, as the saying goes. I've never seen anything like this—you knew I'd love it, didn't you? There's so much of you in it. Well, I took the shirt that I'd been planning to wear off, and instead put on my blue shell, so that my little Aspen Leaf would show itself off to the world. And so many people commented on it! It's so beautiful, Pat. I have it right here, resting on the pillow where I can see it.

Tomorrow I'm going to wear it all day—both at church and at school for the performances. Actually, I don't quite know what to say. It has already found a permanent little nook in my heart, and it will keep that place forever. Thank you, Patric. It's the loveliest necklace I've ever owned...and because it's from you, well...I don't know how to express it. Thank you, Patric for giving to me a wonderful Valentine's Day...between the book and your poem and this lovely necklace... I'm overwhelmed. **[Well, I was deeply in love with Shelley, and I wanted to give to her and do for her everything I could.]** Because you gave me gifts of love, and they all radiate the love that you put into them. And I love you.

As of now, you haven't received my Valentine to you, and that of course, is the phone call. [Telephone companies charged by the minute.] I hope that this phone call means as much to you as it does to me [Which were expensive in the U.S. in the 1960s, 1970s and 1980s.] I'm so excited to think that I'm actually going to talk to you! I realize that 15 minutes isn't a long call, but that's as much as I can afford, frankly. Oh, Pat, I wish we weren't so far apart! A friend of mine suggested that I should look into transferring to UCLA or San Francisco State University. Well, I couldn't do that at this stage of the game any way, but it's a nice thought. Well, this is sort of off the subject I guess.

Tonight, a friend of mine, Nancy, is getting married. Finally!—she's been going with this man since she and I were juniors. He's thirteen years older than she and they make quite a couple—both very nice people, but also rather unstable and very immature. At any rate, I was supposed to go to the wedding, but I was completely worn out that I just can't go. Nancy and I aren't that close or anything, but I was sort of looking forward to the wedding. I figured that since I already informed them that I'd not be able to go to the reception, no-one would miss me. If you're thinking that I'm being very selfish, you're right, I guess. But I just couldn't make the effort to get ready and eat and go just two hours after coming home from a long hard rehearsal. Not with the hard long long day coming tomorrow. And the weather is so cold out—it's snowing again and the streets are really slick. So, ok, I'm making excuses—I do feel a bit guilty. But one of these days I'll call Nancy and explain to her. Anyway, if she's thinking about me tonight, she's nuttier than I thought! It'd be different if we were closer. Well, that's all the justification and rationalization that I feel I can stomach!

I keep looking at this necklace. It's so delicate and simple and warm. And it's a gift from my darling. I don't know what I am going to say to you on the phone. If I tried to plan anything out, I'd never remember it anyway.

Do you realize that it's been 1 month, 2 days, and 7 hours since you left? In a way, it seems as if I haven't seen you in months and months. But I'll think happy about it—the time has gone by faster than I expected it to. Soon this quarter will be over. Ugh. That means EXAMS again. Which also means instant insanity for ol' Shell.

I have to discuss something very important with you now. Mother received your letter in the mail today, and I know that you wrote a lot about my coming this summer, and that she was impressed by what you wrote. She and I have been discussing this a lot lately. My father no longer objects. But mother has point blank been asking me about the sleeping arrangements. I know that you didn't want anything specifically said, and I have done a good job of sounding specific while not making any definite statements. Mother asked me today how many bedrooms there are in your house, and I said I thought there were three, and that I'd be given my own room.

She didn't realize what a spot she was putting me into today when she was asking me all these things. I didn't want to invade your-our-privacy, but I also have to give as much as I can to mother because she will do nothing but fuss and stew while I am gone if I don't give her some pretty sound reassurance. I told her that she could trust us, and she said it's not a matter of trust—but a physiological matter.

Well…Then she said something about the strains of being in bed together and NOT having intercourse. So I said, "Well, who says we're going to be sleeping together?" Well, Pat, I managed to avoid lying to her, but I did give her impressions that I don't really believe myself. I was afraid that she was going to veto this thing at one-point last week. I don't want to deceive her, but I also don't want for her to worry so much. I'm in a real pickle. I told her that I'd use my head—and if I had to, I'd even lock myself in my room.

Well, I really have no intentions of locking myself away from you now or ever. But I do intend to use my head. I know that at first when I get out there, we'll be so glad to see each other that we're getting ourselves in too deep—or rather—that we're heading for trouble, then naturally we'll have to figure something out But quite honestly, I do believe that we'll be able to "control" ourselves. I believe in you, Pat and I believe in our vow. And I think at this point that we will be able to give each other enough that we won't have to break our vow. Let me rephrase the last part. That we won't inadvertently break the vow. It's too important, don't you think? Well. I don't really know whether you're intending straight out to have me move into your room with you or what. I do think that's your decision.

And I don't know whether you are planning on our sleeping together every night—you said in one letter "naturally I would like to have my arms around you every night." I think that perhaps is possible, you should decide upon this and let me know. I know it's delicate and that sometimes it's hard to make a definite statement etc. It's your home and you will come to the most appropriate decision as you are able. But may I say that I do believe I should know so that I may prepare myself mentally? This summer will be a very new experience for me, and I'm looking forward to it breathlessly. But you and I both know that the emotional impact of seeing each other again will be tremendous.

And so I want to build up my willpower if I can. Well, I don't know if that's what I mean or not. I want to be able to accept whatever arrangements we are going to live under—and I want that acceptance to be prepared by a lot of soul searching, thinking, and building up of myself-trust.

If you don't know I really nearly gave in to myself on our last night together. Even if you wouldn't have given in to me, it bothered me that I might have let myself go in a few more minutes.

I'm not being at all successful in expressing what I'm thinking. So I better get off of this now, OK? If you haven't been able to follow me, please don't worry. I shouldn't have started in on this yet—not till I've had some rest and can think.

My mind's really murky tonight. I'm sorry if this letter really confusing etc. I'm not depressed or down or anything. But this has been a heck of a week, and I'm just all dragged out and can't think. I apologize if…Well. Forget that. Anyway, I'm trying. The word for me tonight is "incoherent" I guess.

Before I get completely off the subject, let me tell you something else, ok? Although my mother said to you (I think) that nothing's definite, please let me assure you that I am pretty certain I'll be coming. But I have to know about a job first. If I could do something with music, that'd be fine, but I don't believe there is much of a market for singers. I am really not qualified for anything. But I could work, for example, in a department store or something. I'd rather like that I think. You might laugh—but you mentioned horse-back riding around there. Well, I'm a swell stable hand. I'm a pretty good groom—though I could stand to learn a lot more about that—and I'm pretty familiar with tack and stuff. I could even be the "Exercise boy." Well, horses I can handle; you'd probably never let me get near another horse if I told you about some of the experiences, I've had with them!

I could work in a music store, or record department, etc. And any girl probably could do just fine in a clothes department. I was planning on getting a job at Lazarus Department Store or something here. I hate to sound pessimistic but I'm afraid that if I'm not there to apply, you won't be able to even get me any interviews unless you've got pretty good connections. I must know, quite frankly what the probabilities of getting a job there will be. I could, of course, work in a factory too. Forget about that. And it would be great to have hours more or less coinciding with yours. If you have any suggestions, tell me.

After that motel job I had, <u>anything</u> is an improvement; and I'm pretty much game to try most anything once. But Patric, I absolutely refuse to do any maid work again!! So if you find a needy motel management, you can "tell them to jump into the lake!!" Well, I'm going to stop writing now, probably till after I call you. OK? OK! I love you Pat, I love you, I love you.

10:30 P.M. My wonderful darling! I can't believe that already I've talked to you on the telephone. And you sounded so much better, though you were tired. I'm rather shaky still from the excitement—to hear your voice "in person" again. Don't ever believe that no one could love you this much... because I do, I do, I do, I do. God, I love you so. You sounded as if you intend on sleeping with me most, if not all of the time. And I don't have to tell you that I hope we can. Well.

Even during the very short time that I was able to hear your father's voice when he answered the phone, Pat, I sort of felt a wonderful warmth in his tones and inflections. Maybe I'm prejudice already just from what you've told me about him, I don't know. I was kind of tickled the way he relayed the "code" to me—he sounded excited. Well, please thank him for me, ok? I think I'm going to enjoy my visit to California very much. Well, that has to be the dumbest understatement anyone's ever made in the history of mankind!

I'm so happy now…you make me tingle with the glow of your love. You fill me with wonder and excitement, and hopes and dreams. You cheer me in these rather agonizing days. You strengthen my courage, and renew my confidence. I love you so much, Pat. You bring out feelings and thoughts within me that I never knew existed. You encourage me to call out the individual inside of me that sometimes tends to lurk behind the shadows of society & walls. You help me to shed my fears, and to begin to shake away the irritating complexes that try to plague me. You make me happy to be young, and happier to be a woman—a young woman.

Well, *here I am with a heart that pounds so forcefully that I can hear it.* A whole month has passed since you left. A month that's taken you far, far away from me. But also that month has found us slowly becoming closer and closer. How I love to write to you. And I love receiving your letters. They keep me going. They enable me to hold up my head and face the challenges of each new day. They encourage me to keep working even though lately I've felt as though I'm swimming in a swamp full of mud and clinging vines. They bring a smile to my sometimes-forgetful lips—and they love away the unconscious **frown that sometimes I become aware of.** They do all these things and more, Patric because they are from you, from your mind and heart. And I thank you for putting forth the effort to write so beautifully. Yours are not just mere letters. Each letter of yours is a new creation—an expedition, into the realms of your own self-expression. The soul that generates itself through those letters is so beautiful, so individual.

How lucky I am to be loved by you. How humble and privileged I feel when I am shown that here you are—YOU—Winston Patric Spencer—and YOU are

in love with ME. It's overwhelming. I pray that I am worthy of you. How wonderful you are. You are such an individual. You stand so straight and tall, physically, and spiritually. You are so graceful and charming, and so very warm and sincere. Very rare. You are sympathetic and compassionate. You make me feel secure. You are really and truly a Great Man, Patric. I mean that. You give and give to me, and I bless the day we met.

Thank you for not writing me off as just another girl. Thank you for letting yourself think. Thank you for letting me into your heart. Thank you for entering my heart. *Thank you for not fighting me too hard.* Thank you for being what you are, and the man you are. I love you.

It seems to me that there were many things that I was planning to tell you in this letter, and I don't recall whether I did or not. But I have to close it soon because it's about 11:15 P.M. and tomorrow's a full day beginning at 8:00 A.M.

I will always remember our first Valentine's Day, Patric. My God, I'm in love with you.

We will have much time to think about this summer. I look forward to taking walks with you on warm evenings; sitting in the "outdoor living room at Dad's Sierra Hills home," talking. I enjoy thinking about sitting indoors & watching rain fall, with you. I look forward to kissing you goodnight. I look forward to waking up in your arms as I did twice when you were here. I dream of you constantly— feel your hand in mine, and your lips upon mine. I think of the infinity of depth that our relationship holds, and I look forward to exploring all of the valleys and hills and plains of our souls. I love you, darling. And now I shall close. Goodnight sweet love, dear Patric. I kiss you. I miss you. And how I do love you. Devotedly yours forever, Shelley.

February 14, 1970

Patric's Ode to Shelley

On the Occasion of Valentine's Day
A time to make known your feelings for another.
It is nice to have an another.
Some people do not. They are lonely.
I have an another. My body and soul are filled with joy.
But I have waited a good many year for my friend.
Because just not anyone would do.
*Because in my younger years, I was blind and could
not receive her.*
Because we all are unique in our gifts, desires, and needs.
*Not just anyone can feel, as we feel; think as we think,
and act, as we act.*
It takes someone special; someone very special.
Last year I found my special someone, and she found me.
*My special someone holds my hand with not one of hers,
but two.*
*My special someone looks not into the passing street, but
into my eyes, and thence to the soul.*
*My special someone kisses me tenderly and fills my body
with glowing warmth.*
*My special someone teases me not, but speaks only with
words of truth.*
My special someone loves me.
*She loves me with a love that knows no limits, knows no
earthly bounds.*
*She loves me with a love that builds no bars or walls
around me, but invites me to explore the universe.*
*She loves me with a love that sets my whole existence all
that I am, into flaming ecstasy.*
*And she calls forth the golden blossoms of my soul, that
they might radiate their warmth and beauty to the world.*

My special someone is a most beautiful and magnificent human being.
My special someone possesses the attributes of the Greek Goddess.
My special someone is Venus, reincarnated.
My special someone is named Shelley.
And I love her, with all the power, with all the wisdom, with all the kindness, with all the gentleness,
and with all the humanness that I possess now, or will ever possess in the future.
For our love is the meaning of life, however short or long that may per chance be.
For our love is the highest order of achievement, available to man.
For our love is self-generating, and spreads itself to all who come close.
Without love, there is death. Without our love, life is mundane.
It is nice to have an another.
I have an another. My body and soul are filled with joy.

Monday, February 16, 1970, 7:30 P.M.

My Darling Patric,

Today, your letter came—the one that you wrote last Wednesday. Your letters are just wonderful…. I know that I must sound like some kind of a nut on the subject, but sometimes you feel something inside of you die a little bit when you are denied the realization of the dream that the one you love always feels free to turn to you in any mood. Got that? Well, explain it to me! What am I trying to say? Well, I think you already know. I want you to come to me in your times of need, Pat, because…well, because I love you. And I guess I'm feeling rather honored now because you have shown to me on several occasions that you will come. That makes me feel very good.

…Well, Death is so sad. I really get so upset about it—so many very dear people had died. My grandmother died when I was ten—and I had dreamed her death the night before. It was awful because it happened just the way I had envisioned it—For a long time as a kid, I felt guilty. My dog, Tara had died just the summer before. I adored her. And I had had a dream the night before Tara died too. I told Mary that dream just before Tara died, and we were both there to see it come true. Ever since then I've had an absolute horror of dreams about death. Not that I have them that often, mind you. I don't remember having one in years.

I'd like to be able to believe in an afterlife or something, but it's really hard for me to see it. I'd also like to think of the actual existence of God. I guess I do in a way—there seems to be some force. Sometimes I think I'm afraid NOT to believe in God. But the God of my reality is not the God in the Bible. My God is Love, and Beauty. My God is Sympathy and Strength, Courage. My God is Friendship. My God is Animals, and Trees and Grass, and Sun and Sky. My imagination just can't comprehend a God of all the Universe. So I guess that I don't really believe in God per se, but then, I don't disbelieve it in a way. However, I believe in life. And I figure that my God would want me to take and live the life I am blessed with as well as I can. I try to live by the "Do unto others" bit—I really believe in that. Consideration for others—people, animals, plants, etc. is to me one of the most important concepts in life. I figure that I will live usefully and as fully as I am able to…. I love life too much to let it slip by while I worry about death. My reality or philosophy may not be right for anyone else, but it's right for me because it gives me room to grow & change & perhaps even prove myself all wrong. And so if I figure that if I'm going to go HELL because of my beliefs, then that's where I belong, and I'm not going to make this life a HELL by living in constant fear of what I'm going to be after I'm dead. **Life is too precious to waste;** I believe that you and I will be able to put so much into life, together. Now you are a very, very large part of my reality—I guess you are first, Pat. Well, this summer I look forward to talking with you about all kinds of things! I have the feeling that we're perhaps going to learn a lot from each other. I look forward to doing a lot of thinking with you, and a lot of listening to you.

Your father is right about there being strains. But, with all respect to him and my mother (they seem to agree on the resentment possibility etc.) I really don't agree. Perhaps I am being naïve, but I do believe in your self-control, even if I don't trust mine altogether. But I promise you that I am not going to _resent_ not being able to have INTERCOURSE, no matter how completely my emotions may break down my reason—should that happen...You are probably much better prepared to control yourself than I am—I admit that. But I honestly have no intention of breaking our vow—or trying to persuade you to. It would be very sad for me now—even more than before—because I consider our vow as sacred. I think we'd be disappointed in me. I would be. Natch, all this is easy to say now. But I intend to gear myself to the facts so that I won't be a problem for us this summer. I don't intend to be the one to cause tension this summer. **I think that we can satisfy each other enough to make it easier to hold out until our "First Night."** But judging from this past holiday, on that Sunday, my inclination will be not to let my frustration turn to resentment but rather to gratitude—for want of a better term…I'm happy to be moving in with you—as long as your father understands & doesn't mind. And I'm not coming with the idea of having intercourse.

I just keep burbling on. I must have re-stated my thoughts about ten times in all that space. I hope that you can believe and trust my honesty—my honesty to myself. With you, I have been honest and straightforward. I won't talk about my past "affair" in here, because—and this may sound dumb—I don't want it recorded in a letter to you. I just don't like to see the name or memory in print now. You can read my diaries and I'll talk in person about it. This is just me that's objecting. Don't think that I want you to apply this kind of locked door to you and your past marriage and Heather! It's just one of many of my goofy notions.

Anyway—believe me, I've been successful in keeping my feelings and thoughts to myself. I kept them from my mother for two years. She never even guessed. Well. I hate to sound redundant but, I apologize if this letter's a real bomb. I wanted to reply to yours right away because it was important to let you know my thoughts. Thank you, dearest Pat, for your wonderful letter. I love you so much.

By the way—just a thought—I like to hear <u>your</u> daydreams and fantasies too! Goose Bumps, anyone?

YOU BETTER BELIEVE IT!!! Did I ever tell you that <u>YOU TURN ME ON</u>? Hey—I can't start thinking this way— I'll wake myself up. Uh Oh—there goes the blood pressure!

Pat, I love you so much. I can't believe how lucky I am. You're so wonderful. I love you, I love you. Always believe in yourself, and know that I believe in you, no matter what you do or don't do. You are a success as a man, and as a human being, and you're becoming more successful and richer in that way every day. Not many people can say that. So, when you're down, think of me, and know that I love you and I will always be proud of you in good times and bad. I love you very much, darling. Thank you for your letters. I'm thinking of you, Pat. And I miss you so. Forever in love with you, xxxx Your Shelley xxx

February 18, 1970, 6:20 P.M.

I LOVE YOU (ALL IN LITTLE RED HEARTS)

I Love You

Feb. 18, 1970   6:20 p.m.

My Darling Patric,

It's only been 2 days, but it seems as if many more than that have passed since I sat down to write to you. And as I sit here – rather, as I lie here – I'm wondering what on earth I am ever going to write about, for actually I have nothing in particular on my mind to tell you, except that I miss you, and I love you. Very much.

Today I took that Italian test – I think I told you about it. Yesterday, all afternoon and for about 1 hour after dinner, I really tried to study. But it was a nearly impossible chore, because I was too tired to concentrate. Monday night was almost totally a loss, sleep-wise. Sometimes I get too exhausted to sleep. That sounds sort of weird, but its true. 'Course, I'm sure you'll agree that I'm sort of weird! So, altho I studied to the best of my ability, it wasn't enough. If I passed the test with only a "D" I'll be surprised.. It doesn't do too much for my state of mind at the moment to go and be faced with a ridiculously hard test. Oh well. I took it and did my best, and there's nothing to do now. However, in my english class today, the teacher

My Darling Patric,

It's only been 2 days, but it seems as if many more than that have passed since I sat down to write to you. And as I sit here—rather, as I lie here—I'm wondering what on earth I am ever going to write about, for actually I have nothing in particular on my mind to tell you, except that I miss you, and I love you very much.

Tonight, I just wanted to talk to you. I wish I had a tape, but I can't afford one just yet, so it'll have to wait. Pat, I think about you so often during the days at school. Of course, you fill my thoughts almost completely here at home.

Although I'm not too well equipped to think tonight (yeah, I know—or any other either!) I think I'll tell you a bit about my thoughts about what I found in my diary last night. This was the first diary I'd ever had. It started in January 1968. And you know, Pat, I can't believe how much my world has changed in these past 2 years. I wonder if I'll think the same thing in 2 years from now?

__I guess that 1968 was the most dreadful year of my life,__ and __I almost think I'd rather die than go through it again! Luckily, I__ don't have to.

My writing—the words I mean—seemed much more eloquent then, than it ever seems now. But you see, at that time, all of my emotions were channeled into that diary. At least most of them.

…I read very quickly through some of those __tormented pages of that diary. And I could feel all over again the agony and pain.__

But, you know, it's funny, whenever I expressed joy over something regarding the affair (? with an old boyfriend? NO—maybe it was the friend CAROL who became my enemy) in the diary, the words meant nothing at all as I read last night. And that makes me feel very sure of myself. No, I haven't "gotten over" the pain yet, simply because I've never recognized it. I locked my grief away and I've never unlocked it.

As you said, regarding your feelings and thoughts about Graduate School, I've "tabled" those feelings. And I simply haven't had the courage to face them yet. And now either one of two things could happen because of you. Either my love and happiness will simply dissolve any bad feelings, or else I will be able to look at them, with you at my side. It has nothing really to do with any of the people involved—merely the feelings of the aftermath. I also thought about you as I looked briefly over those pages. *I never had the security of knowing that I was absolutely loved (I guess she means by her family?) the way you have given and given to me; I have no doubts about the quality and more importantly maybe, about the reality of our love.*

Pat, I say this to you with complete seriousness—as serious as I could ever be—I deeply, deeply love you with all my soul and mind, and emotions. *If for some reason our relationship didn't work out, I really don't know what I'd do. I don't know how much I'd care to even go on. I love you too much to even think of the possibility of losing you—would you believe that I'm fighting tears just at the thought?* I guess I'd better change subjects quickly.

Well, I became bored with my diary after about 10 minutes. There isn't room in my mind right now to cope with thoughts of the past. I am living the present, loving you, and missing you. But one day, I will no longer miss you, and then I'll not *live my past sorrows either.*

I am very sentimental, and at times I enjoy looking back. I mean really looking hard. But I love life so much that the present is too important to let slip by. For, each minute is the future, the present, and the past, all within about 70 seconds. I also love to think future. Well, I'm not in too alert of a frame of mind to go and state any philosophies I may have.

I'm going to stop for a few minutes, and will finish this up when I come back up. I love you, Pat. I hope this letter hasn't been too bad. Gee, I love you so much. **X** Keep that kiss and save it till I get there… then collect the real McCoy.

After I read in my diary last night, I picked up the letter that came on Monday—the one in which you wrote about Heather (Patric's 6-year-old daughter in California). *Your letters are absolutely stupendous—or have I told you that? I look forward to them—not anxiously, but with great excitement. And when one arrives, my heart invariably jumps up to my throat down to my stomach and out to me toes, and back again. I look forward to your letters the same way that a little kid looks forward to Santa Claus, or to a birthday party. Each of your letters is a wonderful present. Sometimes it's hard for me to read slowly because I get so excited just to see all of your thoughts. But I always do read slowly—sometimes it takes me an hour or more to read your letters. Never less than ½ hour—never! And if I say thank you again and again, please don't think that I automatically utter those two words. Thank you, Patric. I could never thank you enough; I could never tell you how much I appreciate your letters; I couldn't even begin to count the number of times I've read them all; never could I express what they mean to me. And never will I find words to adequately describe the love that I feel for you. Sometimes I sit, overwhelmed by all that you give to me, and I sort of pray that I am able, or will one day be able to give you as much in return if I haven't the dimension within me to give you as much as I'd like to know.*

I hope that I am a companion to you—or as much of a companion as distance permits. I hope that as each day, week, month, year goes by, that the love you feel for me now will be enhanced by time, rather than dimmed.

I was so concerned that you be absolutely sure before you committed yourself (to me). Sometimes I get awfully scared of this summer (When we planned Shelley would come out for a four-week visit). I really don't think, though, that I'm all that hard to live with.

Tell me honestly, please, Pat—do you think we'll make it? That sounds awful to me—I don't know how to phrase it. God, I love you so much. I know that I am totally committed to you—now and always. I'm so excited about the summer. I think that we'll do just fine if we're honest, considerate, frank, and loving. I love you, my darling.

I haven't really had any particular fantasies lately. I just keep remembering and remembering, and it's very hard not to think of you as I lay in bed. *I'm so happy we had those 2 nights together.* The other night I woke up from a very disturbed sleep, and I was completely disoriented as to where I was or when I was. And I reached over, expecting to find you there. It wasn't what I'd term frustrating, but rather, it sort of filled me with disbelieving sadness—unwilling almost to accept. But it passed quickly because I forced it to. Do you realize that we won't be together in spring until after we're married—many months? Wow—that's kind of weird to think of.

Well, love, I must go. Tell me about your job if you got it, or if you didn't [Yes, I did get the job in the Central Cash Vault of Bank of America in Los Angeles—due to having been in the Cash Vault of San Francisco for 7 years as a "Coin and Currency Verification Teller." They hired me back at a salary higher than when I left to go to Graduate School.] I love you very much and hope you are well and happy. Miss you, my darling. Think happy—think me and you! I love you so much. Thank you Pat. xxxxxxx Lovingly yours forever, your Shelley.

February 19, 1970

Los Angeles, Thursday evening, around 7 P.M.

My dearest Shelley,

Let me come and warm myself by your fires, and feel your gentler hands on my head and shoulders. I am very tired tonight, and really could use some Tender Loving Care.

Today was my second day at work. And I am exhausted. I went to bed reasonably early last night, so as to have plenty of rest.

But I couldn't get to sleep for an hour. Then, this morning, I woke up an hour before I was supposed to, and couldn't get back to sleep. All in all, I got about 5 ½ hours of sleep. That is not quite enough; I need a minimum of seven, and preferably eight hours.

Within the last three days, our weather has turned rather cool, and brought high winds to blow, blow, and blow. Wind speed varies upwards to 60 m.p.h. It blows most of the night, giving things an eerie feeling. It doesn't do much for making me feel better.

At the moment I am quite tired, both of body and mind; and probably should take a hot bath...say, that's a very good idea...I think I will and see if it helps pick me up a bit. I really hate writing when I am so weary. Be back shortly.

There, I am back and feeling a little better, but not quite like I would like to. Slowly, slowly, I learn to accept myself as I am; to realize that activities all day long take their toll of my physical and mental energies, as well as emotional.

This is really a bad night to write to you, but if I don't it will be several days until I get time again. This coming weekend is Naval Reserve Weekend, and I will be spending the entire time in Long Beach, at the Naval Base. Then when I come home Sunday evening, Dad wants to go and see the movie **_EASY RIDER (WITH Peter Fonda)_** then on Monday, the work week starts all over again. Yes, I know, Monday is a legal holiday; but I am going to work anyway, and earn time and a half. So here I am writing. Please bear with me as I struggle along, on two cylinders, instead of the usual eight.

Let me tell you about my job. The Bank of America called me on Friday and offered me a position on the Day Shift of the Central Cash Vault. I really had not wanted to return to the Cash Vault since it was in downtown Los Angeles. But I decided to take it anyway. Besides it is very unusual to have such a position open. Usually, people begin work on the night shift, and then wait, sometimes years to be able to transfer to the Day Shift. I talked to one teller today, who had waited seven years to be transferred!! So, you might say I was indeed, very, very fortunate. Luck of the Irish. I do believe there is a Leprechaun that watches over me. After all, he did lead me to you, didn't he?

Well, on Tuesday, Mrs. Jenkins, of the Personnel Office, called me and told me to come on down to fill out the papers, that I would be starting work the next day. AND, she said my starting salary would be $550.00!!! I nearly flipped, like wow…I walk in earning top dollar. Well she said, "when a person has a lot of experience like you have, we expect to pay for it." I can't believe that Bank of America said that.

On Tuesday, it took me two hours to fill out all the necessary papers and forms; I think there were at least ten of them. It was comforting to know that I already had the job, and was not just applying. The personnel interview and exchange of information took another hour. I left the personnel office at 4:30 P.M. my scheduled quitting time at the vault, and got my first good dose of commuter traffic.

Like I have really become a full-fledged member of the Los Angeles Commuting Society. It is like the Indianapolis 500 car race, except that there are 3,000 times as many cars, very few professional drivers, many unprogrammed hazards, very few rules, and lots of distractions.

From my house to the Vault, it is exactly 20 miles. And in light traffic, I can make it in 45 minutes. In rush hour traffic it takes about an hour. The freeways are so jammed these days, that I make the trip on regular streets and highways...to save time!! Only on the way home do I take a two-mile stretch of freeway, in order to avoid some small, congested streets.

The pace or speed is generally as fast as the streets and conditions will permit. You have to drive defensively; you never know when someone will pull out suddenly in front of you, or stop, or turn, or...

For those of us eager enough to get up early, there are some free parking spaces provided by the Bank. I just happen to be one of the eager ones. I may be making top dollar, but I also have a lot of plans for that money, and dislike wasting it on a parking lot. One or two dollars a day can add up to quite a bit over a month. I even take my lunch to work. It costs me about 50 cents that way. Otherwise, lunch would be around $1.25.

Anyway, I am now getting up in the morning at 5:30 A.M. It takes me an hour to wash, dress, and eat. I leave the house at 6:30 A.M. arriving at the Bank's parking lot at 7:15 and getting a free place. The Vault opens at 7:30, and work begins at 7:45 A.M.

In terms of my actual job, I again, was fortunate. They have me doing exactly what I did in the San Francisco Vault... counting currency. It is a relatively easy job, which you can do by yourself, at your own pace. There are two persons per cage, but each does his/her own work. At ALL TIMES there must be at least two persons present when money is being processed. So I like it very much.

You might just note how this affects my day, timewise: Up at 5:30 A.M., leaving the house at 6:30 A.M. Returning home around 5:30 P.M., and off to bed between 9:00 P.M. and 9:30 P.M. This is how it will be this summer when you are here. There are not a lot of hours left over. You may want to consider sharing my schedule; getting up with me at 5:30 A.M. and going to bed at 9:00 P.M. Even if you do not have to be at work so early, you might use the time to write letters, read books, or whatever. It would, of course, be nice to have breakfast with you.

About sleeping arrangements. I mentioned in my last letter that from my perspective, I would like to share the bed with you, for the whole time you are here. And I am hoping that nothing will interfere with that idea.

I can well appreciate your present situation with your mother.

I hope that your present replies will satisfy her, or, that you can continue replying in such a way as to not lie to her. I am apprehensive that if it came down to hard bargaining, and your mother made it a stringent condition that you sleep alone the entire time, my Dad would be a stickler about it. For he would have the responsibility to your mother to chaperone us. And he takes his responsibilities seriously.

As it stands now, he knows we want to sleep together and as long as no one else says anything, he won't. Personally, I would be upset if I had to vow not to sleep with you. There would be far more tension and irritation that way, than by sleeping with you. I really do not like to contemplate not sleeping with you. UGH! For need of facts, we do have three bedrooms, and you will be given your own room, closets, bathroom, etc.

As far as the sex question goes, there is no doubt, whatsoever, in my mind, that we will keep our vow. If you want, just rely upon me to uphold it. Don't be upset with yourself. Just don't resent me for upholding it. The truth is, I don't "lose control." I am actually over controlled, in the sense of keeping an iron grip upon my feelings, when it is important to do so. And I feel this is very important. Besides, I really think that **the** physical closeness we already share, will be plenty to satisfy our needs and sexual tensions. You may, however, want to think about this some more, for your own self.

Forgive me, but I got depressed at the thought of not being able to sleep with you. All my life I have been responsible for my own behavior and standards. And, all my life, I have resented any external authority who tried to exert unwelcome control over me.

I know that may sound a little immature, perhaps it is. But frequently, when people control others, they, the controllers, are forcing the controlees, to live by the controller's standards and viewpoints and not by the controlee's own viewpoint. And often what is beneficial for the one, is detrimental for the other. We all view life from our own peculiar standpoint. Well enough philosophy.

If you would suggest we sleep separate, I would. Because that is different. You are an important part of the "we" that is involved. On the other hand, your mother does have a legitimate concern…the sexual strain, which is normal. *And it would be hard, if not embarrassing, to tell her that the strain is greatly reduced because we both caress each other to climax.* So without this knowledge, she is arguing from a valid position. My, what a problem! Let's hope it will pass quietly. I feel my physiological condition (tiredness) has affected my mood and thinking; and thus, my sentiments upon this subject. When I stop and think about it, it is like asking for the moon, to expect a well-meaning mother to allow her young 20-year-old daughter, to leave home, perhaps for the first time, to travel 2700 miles, and to sleep with a 29-year-old man for twelve weeks!!!

But, I say, this is a very special occasion. We are different.

Do the best you can, and we will ride the waves as they come.

I know I have not responded to any of the lovely communications we had in relation to Valentine's Day. I did very much appreciate everything. But this evening, my responders are depleted of energy. If you will forgive me, I will respond at a later date, when more of myself is alive and functioning.

Right now, I am in the emotional throes of re-adjusting myself to my new life. There is a lot to contend with, and it consumes a lot of energy. My father, also, is working through some of his problems, and they weigh heavily upon me, as I am his confidant, and listening post, as well as "advice giver."

And now that I have a job, my transition is almost complete; and a new routine begins to form around my daily habits. And at times, Graduate School seems far back into the past. There is still a great deal of house and yard work, which consumes my every spare minute and ounce of energy. So please bear with me. You did ask to know me in my down periods, as well as my up ones.

It is hard to be highly romantic and all excited when you feel tired and down. But what would be welcome would be to sit or lie quietly next to you, and feel your warmth, your closeness, and your arms around me tenderly. To sleep, knowing that you were near, I can do the same for you. An hour's worth of hugging and holding will go a long way toward smoothing the trials and tribulations of the day.

So may I take my leave now and thank you kindly for all you have given to me this past week, including the wonderful phone call.

Lots of Love, Patric

Feb. 24, 1970, 9:00 P.M. Tuesday

[I can't figure out why this scent (Chanel #5) smears so much.]

My Dearest, Darling Pat,

Forgive me for writing to you while I'm in this present state of mind. Perhaps by tomorrow night, I will look at this feeble beginning and frown—and then tear this up. But at the moment, I feel a very strong need to simply write to you, if only a few sentences. Because I need you now, Pat.

I received your letter today, and since you told me about it, and because of your obviously much happier mood on the phone, I didn't get too upset over it. Naturally, I am in complete sympathy with you in your downs and ups. Perhaps empathy is a better term. And, so I must turn the light off very soon. May I just briefly tell you some of my feelings now?

Since Friday, perhaps even before then, I have felt like a nervous little mouse in not one but two cages, with a brief tunnel connecting the two. One cage is the "school" cage, with all of the anxieties of term papers, theory assignments, lab-tapes, books that must be read, practicing, etc. forming bars of the cage. The other cage is of course, my home.

HERE I AM UNDER CONSTANT EMOTIONAL PRESSURE OF A DIFFERENT SORT—MY MOTHER TO BE EXACT. No, I don't mean for that to sound cruel. Actually, the bars which are imprisoning me here in a way, constructed by her love, strong will, determination and "self-righteousness" of sorts. The tunnel is in a way, my freedom, & it is of course, the roads I travel each day from one "cage" to the other. And like the typical nervous little mouse I rush blindly from one side of each "cage" to the other, batting my head, falling down & picking myself up again, only to fall down again. When I'm in one "cage" the other "cage" seems more peaceful to me— "surely it can't be as bad as this one?" But as I move from one to the other, there is no relief. The anxieties of each are carried over into the other.

There is one more factor involved, and it not only makes the mouse's plight more frustrating, but it also is the only element that adds blessed meaning and comfort over it all. That element is the Sun, with its warm, inviting, rays, always reaching for the mouse & asking it to come

out of the cages, always assuring the mouse of beauty and peace and freedom. Frustration, comfort.

Love. For I, the mouse, seek you, the Sun. I love you Patric. Please send your rays of light and warmth and love. Please send them to me, burning brightly, and forever. I love you. Goodnight.

11:40P.M.!!! Phone call!!!

Wow!!!! This has got to be the shock of the century!

I'm so excited now that I really don't know what to say, Pat. I'll tell you a few of my thoughts:

- my mother mentioned yesterday that it'd probably be better for us not to "elope" this summer…because perhaps we'd be rushing into it and because it's so important for you to be absolutely positive.
- Mother would probably object strenuously to having an actual wedding in '72 [Shelley's graduation.]
- Certainly, it would be totally inappropriate for me to wear a traditional gown then.
- I am totally against marriage as an escape to the problem of this summer [Intercourse]. But actually, I really can't see us being together only two months out of the year, and perhaps less often than that next year, should we not marry.

Well, those are a few of the negatives—as a matter of fact, in my state of agitation—excitement! Of the moment, I really am not equipped to think of the negatives. But, before I turn off my light (It's nearly 12:00 midnight and I have to get up at 6:00 A.M.) Please let me add one more thing: I don't want you to be rushing in to this. I don't want you to be as frustrated and a chance that you will not be totally satisfied and happy. I must go to bed—not that I will sleep, of course.

This may sound funny, but it is an important factor: I will have to start taking the "PILL" (Contraceptive birth control) in the relatively near future, if we are going to get married. I'm not sure how much of a period of time it takes to regulate my system to the PILL, etc., but I know it's at least a month—probably two or more.

After I've thought this over more carefully and I'll talk to my mother—she'll know about the pill bit.

Pat, I love you so much. I will try to make you the happiest man in the world. No matter when we marry, I know we'll have a wonderful life together. Boy, I'm all excited in every way—I just had a thought and I'm all "Turned On!! (Betcha can't guess what I was thinkin'!) (Ha Ha.)

February 25, 1970

Patric, you are the dearest, most precious person in the world to me...

Oh yes. It occurs to me that perhaps on the tape I sent you yesterday, I made it sound as if I do want very much for us to get married this summer. No, I am not trying to push it at all, but it's not because I'm not sure of our love. Rather, it's because I think that we should go into our marriage with as few "disadvantages" looming before us as possible, whatever they may be. At times, I wish very much that we could marry before I *graduate*—not meaning that I wouldn't graduate in that case, of course.

But I want you to feel as happy and free as possible when we marry, and I don't want you to feel cramped or rushed in any way. There would be many frustrating moments in our future separation if we were married this summer—but there are also many such moments now. Well, I guess that if you wanted to get married this summer, I'd be very happy to. But, I'm willing to wait too because I love you, and I want you to be happy. If I do give you the impression on tape that I want to get married this summer, don't get upset ok? This past weekend for me was a living aggravating HELL, and I do mean HELL!! It was the worst few days for me since you left. And when I made the tape, well anyway. I'm not going to think of it now.

Pat, when you feel little doubts going through your head, I hope you'll feel free to ask me for encouragement and reassurance if you think it will help you. Do you ever worry or wonder whether I'll change my mind? Or, do you ever think about...well, I don't know. There is nothing in the world that you should be afraid to tell me... always remember that. And there is nothing that you should feel you must unwillingly tell me either. If I need to know something, then perhaps, you could think about it & then tell me—well, I've lost my train of thought. It appears that I've also lost any ability to write legibly, too (if I ever could do so!)

May I tell you one thing that keeps popping into my mind?

On tape, you said, "As I sit here now, there is no one in the world whom I'd like to be married to as much as you." Something like that. I don't know, but that NOW sort of shakes me up at times. I guess I figure that I'd rather find out NOW whether or not things weren't going to work, because I can't stand the thought of our love diminishing—Well I'm sorry. Believe me, I do have faith in you, and I trust you. And, God, Pat, I love you so. At times, I also become rather wary of the possibility of your becoming tired of me, because

I write too much—both in content and number. It seems as if I haven't been writing as often lately, but perhaps that's because I'm losing my marbles.

Again, I ask you to please not become upset with me for writing this way to you. I really am not feeling these doubts NOW, but they have pricked my mind in low tides of spirit, and now I must write them to you when I have the courage. I suppose I'm really going crazy for missing you now. With Exams & all this mad rush work in the last two weeks of the Quarter, I always go insane.

Fortunately, so far, I've been able to enjoy lucid moments in between exams. Somehow, that just isn't a bit humorous—it isn't even in good taste maybe. Well, forgive me. I'm becoming a bit antagonistic with myself at the moment because of the tone of this letter. Forgive me Pat. But in these few moments, in this week's evenings, I really do feel a very strong need to communicate to you. I think I must be wanting to honestly show you my thoughts when they're frustrated & nervous & depressed. I want you to know me. I'm not particularly happy with myself in these moods, but since they do occur, I sort of feel a need to show them to you honestly. I do want you to be sure. I don't particularly want to surprise you after we're married—I mean surprise you in a negative way.

You've had one bad experience in marriage; and I want this experience, our experience to be a wonderful, rich and rewarding one…that will not only last, but perpetually grow and expand. And so, because I love you so much, I want you to know me, all of me. I love you Pat, with a love so deep that I can't even find an end to its great expanse within me. And I don't think that I ever want to find any limits upon my love for you, because if I don't, it will mean that we have indeed achieved and blessed one another with the richest, rarest gifts in the world: the limitless, boundless, endless gift of pure, infinite love. Let me grow with you, Patric, let me follow you, and lead you, through all the paths our love may take us. And let me love you, my darling, Pat. And please love me too....

Again, good night xxxx...Shelley

What a darling you are! Thank you so much for the wonderful letter that you wrote on Monday night. As tired as you were, to take that precious time and give it to me was the kindest and most thoughtful gesture in the world. Thank you, Pat, for putting a smile to my lips; for stirring my heart into a pounding laughter; for tickling my imagination with a few of your "visions," for thinking of me in my time of great need. **And most of all, Pat, thank you for once again replenishing my soul with the joyful encouraging reassurances that you do love me.** I wasn't expecting a letter today, and was overjoyed at finding it when I came home. I have all the pages spread out before me as I write. Thank you. I am so happy right now...I guess I needed your friendship, your love, your strength even more than I let myself think. And now, you have happily shouted to me "here I am!" **And it means everything to me to know that I have your love and thoughts and encouragement.**

I brought your letter—unopened—upstairs with me and as I finished my term paper; your letter inspired me. For, I held your letter next to me as I wrote the last pages, and the warm thoughts from the letter jumped through the paper and envelope straight into my heart—just as they were written not from your hand, but from your heart. And by about 3:00 P.M., I'd completed my work, gotten my shower and was ready to sit down and read your wonderful words.

I love you so much, Pat. I have more or less resigned myself to the probability that I will not be allowed to stay with you for the entire summer. If I can get a job here, there will be no more "if's" about it. But if I can't, then I will have to try and get one out there. It was a tremendous ordeal—this weekend I mean. That my mother agreed to wait for a while on making a definite decision is, I think, a very good thing—even if she does say "NO" in the end. Anyway, as I see things now, it appears that there are already 2 ½ strikes against the whole summer bit. Well, I don't particularly feel like going into it all now. I'm not thinking too clearly and I don't have the time.

Sometimes, though, I do wonder if we would have a bad time this summer. I really can't see how things could go as sour as everyone says they might. **My father's being a real prig about it—but my father never has taken too much interest in anything I've ever done except the TV bit.** [Shelley had already been a guest soloist on the opera TV programs.] Remind me to tell you someday about some of the discussions that went on this weekend. Discussions that I wasn't supposed to hear, but that were too available for me to stand and listen to. I guess I was "eaves-dropping;" but I sure wasn't intending to—you know how you will start to go into a room and interrupt a conversation and suddenly stop when you hear your name…Well anyway. My Mother's had a hellish life and she doesn't want me to have one like hers.

Pat, I love you so. And yes, I do accept you. I feel that you are honoring me by offering so much of yourself for me to accept. You are a fine human being, a very complicated personality, and a wonderful and very rare man. One line in particular of one of your letters keeps going through my head, and it cheers me when I'm blue. Never have I received such a compliment in my life as the one you gave me when you let yourself fall in love with me. You said in one of your letters:

"If what I have done with myself can make me into the kind of person that draws your love and respect, then I am well proud of myself!"

Thank you. That is a very great honor—But you have every reason to be proud of yourself! I feel very humble when I think that I have somehow earned your love, for I look up to you and respect you so much that I feel very small when I think of you. You are a giant in my eyes...you are a king, you are a very great man, Patric, and I am very very proud of you. How on earth I was ever blessed with qualities that attracted you, I'll never know. But I constantly thank God that you did find something in me that you want and need. **I pray that I'll always remain attractive to you—that you'll always want me for your own. I really don't think that I deserve you, but I'll certainly try to be worthy of you, now and always.**

My heart contains a home that will always welcome your soul to come in and inhabit it forever.

This home contains a room that is perpetually full of sunlight—it has windows and is always full of cheer and happiness.

Another room is rich and full of quiet strength—oak wood, many books, deep, thoughtful tones and colors.

Yet another room is in this home: It has a warm friendly fireplace and a rug and a rocking chair— this room is always lighted by the glow of the fire and it is warm and friendly and comfortable.

And there is another room, the bedroom, in which all of the desire and fierce passion of your body and your soul can find their fulfillment.

The rooms of this house are always open to you, Patric. You cannot buy this house, because I have already given it to you.

You need no key to enter this house, because there are no locks, no doors.

There are no walls that bound or limit you in this house. You can always find shelter here, without the need for a roof; you can find privacy here without need of doors.

There are windows in this house. They are for you to look through when you want to peer into my soul.

There are no curtains, no shades at these windows, because only you can see through them, and you will always be welcome to look through.

This house is unique because you are unique. For this house only exists for you. You may enter whatever room you wish, whenever you wish.

You may create more rooms and my heart will grow and carry them for you.

You may choose the room which best suits your mood at any given time.

And thus, out of complete love, I offer this house to you, Patric. It is my mind, my heart, my soul, and my body.

Only you will ever know how to find this house; only you will ever enter it. You have already found it, you have already entered it.

I offer you a home…a home for your heart and mind and soul and body.

And you may do with it as you wish.

If you cannot take this home, or if someday it no longer seems your home and you leave it forever, —if someday you should reject it, then this home will then become full of walls and locked doors, and shaded windows. And no one will ever enter it again. Because it belongs to you, and it will always welcome you, and accept you with a smile and with tremendous warmth.

You are free to do whatever you want to in this house, with no fear of society's disapproval within.

You may laugh in this house, or you may weep—and the house will laugh or weep with you.

You may dance or sing.

You may talk, and the house will listen; you may roar, and the house will accept.

You may quietly seek silence in the house and you shall have it.

You may do whatever in the world you wish.

You may tremble and shake and find the limitless ecstasies that passion offers you.

All the house needs is to be loved in return, and cared for and appreciated.

For the house is my soul and mind and heart and body. And now the house is yours, Patric.

I love you very much. Thank you. Lovingly, devotedly yours, forever, your Shelley.

February 27, 1970

To My Dearest Precious Patric,

As I thumbed through many pages of poetry searching for a text to use in a song I had to write (theory), I came upon this anonymous verse:

> *"Western wind, where wilt thou blow?*
> *The small rain down can rain*
> *Christ, that my love were in my arms,*
> *And I in my bed again."*

It made me think of you, and I wanted you to see it....

It is Friday night about 10:00 P.M.—a bit later that that, actually. I want to say many things to you, but somehow, in this time of need for them, the words are being very stubborn and playing "hide and seek" with me. So I will probably stumble and trip through this letter, but perhaps as the thoughts come tumbling toward you, you will be able to reach out and catch them.

As you probably expected, today my thoughts were totally full of the idea of our getting married this summer. And, I've been very frank and honest with myself: I've been thinking con as well as pro, believe it or not!

Right now, I am wondering and wondering about the thoughts—whatever they may be—going through your head. I'm wondering if perhaps you're discussing this with your father. And I'm wondering what kind of frame your mind is in, as I sit here. In the letter I mailed today, I briefly outlined some of the negative aspects. I want you to be absolutely sure that you are not only ready to marry, but that I'm the one whom you want to marry. If you feel that you don't know me well enough yet, and if you feel uneasy about getting married so soon, then it's worth it to both of us to wait a longer time. You must not feel obligated to get married, Pat. And we must not get married at this time if it's merely for the purpose of escaping this sex problem. We would be giving up the traditional–type big wedding (if we do marry now) but we could have a celebration of some sort (with a Wedding cake and all, if you wish) at a later time. I don't want for you to blindly go into marrying me. We will have problems at times, naturally.

But I don't want you to feel that we're "pre-maturely bursting a bubble," as you said on tape. And I don't want an anger or frustration to work itself up within you when we're apart (after being married). It will be of most significant importance for me to be sure—positive—that you do want to marry this summer, before I can give an absolute "YES."

I guess that's the most important issue now. I would imagine that your father would be very concerned about this, and with very good reason. I don't want you to feel regrets, Pat. I love you too much to put you through that.

My darling, it's only about 10:40 P.M., but I'm so tired that I can't think. I do hope I'll be hearing from you soon on this matter. And thank you for calling me…you're so wonderful. I ought to spank you for spending so much money on me! But…. Oh, I love you so much. I miss you. Good night, my sweet darling. Sleep well—I'm with you.

Bless you, Pat. I love you. I love you xxxxxxxx

Saturday, February 28th, 1970, 8:00 P.M.

[Shelley was working on a school assignment to write a piece of music.] So, it was kind of hard, kind of fun Natch, the **words gave me fits; I've been working on the music for a week now! All I have left to do is copy it over on good paper. The music is sticky sweet, so I made the song a lullaby. Mother keeps ASKING ME "ARE YOU TRYING TO TELL ME SOMETHING?" Yeah, sure.**

I thought you might like to know—my dad is completely in favor of this marriage bit—he's thinking only of the sex thing though.

My mother is stewing about it of course; she says:

- that I've probably been pushing you…
- that we ought to learn to use our self-control…
- that really she can see no point in it yet…
- that you wrote in a letter to her only a couple of weeks ago
- that you wanted a chance to get to know me better (and vice versa) before we get married.
- that it would certainly solve the sex issue…
- that this is the damnedest thing she ever heard of, and WHY can't I be just a "normal" kid—and be like all of her friends' daughters?
- that it'd probably make more sense to stay the whole summer without getting married even though she's all but vetoed it…
- that we'd be damned if we do and damned if we don't because she's not too excited about my staying the whole summer either way; but she knows how

unhappy or restless I'd be back here after a short visit with you…

- She even suggested (in a way half-hearted, you'd better not! – way) that I take the pill and then for us not to get married.

That idea I vetoed—even though it sounded rather attractive. But I've not only made a vow to you, but also to myself. I'd be very disappointed resulting from breaking it too.

Well, I'd like to stop for a while. My pen's almost out and the scratching of it is driving me Looney. My darling, what are you doing now? Now I'm the one who's having a hell of a time not to pick the phone up and call you. It is now 10:00 P.M. Actually, when I sit (lie) down to write in this letter, my mind just doesn't function. Maybe if I just start in on my feelings then the thoughts will flow out. If I could only figure out what my feelings and thoughts <u>are</u>.

I wish that I had a letter from you right now—I mean one continuing your present thoughts. It would make things easier now—I mean, if I could see more of your thoughts on the matter so that I could agree or disagree and explain in here. Well.

Right at the moment, **I feel a rather burning hope that we will marry this summer.** But let me add, I also feel a hesitancy and almost a kind of old fear. I love you so much, Pat. I think that a very small wedding of this sort would be very lovely because it'd be so intimate and personal. Of course, it'd be nice to have our closest relatives, but anyway. In a way, I'd prefer not to get all tangled up in a very large wedding, first of all because of the expense. And, it's getting so that people tend to lose sight of the purpose of the big wedding or any wedding. I don't like weddings that look like stage-productions for an off-Broad-way play. That really "turns me off." That's one of the reasons I didn't particularly want to attend my friend Nancy's wedding. I've **come out** of some weddings feeling **nauseous**. I simply can't stand pretense in place of ceremony, pomp instead of celebration.

Well. I really didn't intend to get into that. [Long discussions about the pros and cons of getting married this summer.] My fear is based upon the feeling that I was the one to suggest getting married this summer. I think I was because my dad suggested it ages ago. But when I mentioned it to you—I guess in a letter—it wasn't with the intention of encouraging you to start contemplating it. I'd feel just awful if you thought I was "throwing myself at you" as mother would say. Actually, until last weekend, I never seriously thought about getting married this summer—and I certainly didn't think too much about it then because of all the negative thoughts that you expressed on tape…you keep talking about the importance of our getting to know one another as well as humanly possible before marriage. This is a very important consideration.

I have had a very strong intuition about you, as you may very well know by now, from the beginning. It may sound dumb, but I rarely feel anything as powerful as this intuition about you. If I never knew anything before in my life, & if I never learn or know anything again, *I KNOW THAT YOU ARE THE MAN I WANT & NEED AND LOVE FOR MY WHOLE LIFE, IF I AM GIVEN THE CHANCE. I AM VERY DEEPLY IN LOVE WITH YOU, AND I HOPE I DON'T SOUND TOO YOUNG AND NAÏVE,—BUT I AM SURE OF YOU now—I really am. It would be a big mistake to get married if you aren't just as sure about me.* **Naturally, I** *can't deny that I don't know what would happen to me if something ever came between us—if we broke up. But I love you too much to be selfish enough to want to imprison you—to bind you to me—when you don't want me, if that time ever came. I would rather see that one of us could be happy than to see you unhappy because of me.*

In other words, I would have to say that I believe I'd place your happiness before mine if you wanted to break off the relationship now or ever. **You know, Pat, it's killing me to even write this.** All kinds of memories are popping up—not of people, but of my feelings. Old feelings of pain. I can't think of ever losing you. I couldn't bear to hear the echo of the words "YOU CAN'T LOSE WHAT YOU NEVER HAD" AGAIN. I couldn't bear to wake up in the morning **feeling** blissful, if only momentarily forgetfulness, only to suddenly remember that there would be no less emptiness this day than the day before. I guess the reason that I'm saying all this—and tolerating the painful lump in my throat—is because I would rather have these thoughts remain thoughts, than to have them become realities.

I went through it once, and I don't think I could again. Because you are...so...well... *I never really KNEW WHAT LOVE COULD BE—WHAT POTENTIALS IT CAN HOLD, WHAT BEAUTY THERE COULD BE when there is love. And if I was so crushed and heartbroken when I gave up what there never really was—what I never really understood—well, I just don't know what would happen if I lost you, Pat.*

And so, you have my fear. My fear that you will find qualities in me that you can't take. Fear that I am not all that you think I am. And that I will disappoint you somehow.

...My God, what am I saying? That I'd rather find out now if we're not going to make it? You of course, know how I adore life—how I love living. I love the adventure of watching flowers grow, or seeing children play, or watching a puppy stumble haphazardly. I adore seeing the rainfall, and hearing, breathing, and watching a summer storm. I love to see the first streaks of sunlight, and hear the very first bird sing. I love to walk at night and listen to the peaceful silence. I love looking at the stars, and gazing beyond them into eternity. I love to see my dog, Sarabel, joyfully run to the door at the sound of my voice. I love to see her sit in the front yard, and watch her as she witnesses life around her. [And a whole page of poetic thoughts.]

I love to see the tiny beginnings of a leaf on a tree. I love to smell the first breath of spring. I love to kick up the powdery snowflakes from the sidewalk. I love to feel the muscles of a horse as I ride bareback through the fields. I love the wind whistling in my ears, and stinging my face as I fly over the land on my horse. I love to feel the heavy breathing...that pushes my legs as the horse rests. And I love the feeling of the complete oneness of myself and the horse as we go flying over a wide ditch or log—neither of us earthbound, both of us together with nothing between our spirits but our bodies.

Yes, my darling Pat. I worship life. But now that I am in love with you, all of my feelings become intensified and endless. *AND IF I LOST YOU, I CAN'T IMAGINE EVER LOOKING AT A FLOWER AGAIN WITHOUT GRIEVING. OR ANYTHING ELSE. I DON'T KNOW HOW MUCH ANY OF LIFE WOULD MEAN TO ME. I CAN'T GUESS.*

So what is the point in all this? Only that I want you to be sure. And if you're sure enough, then I want you to be more than sure. Would this be the best thing for us to do? Could we manage it?

Pat, I very much want to be married to you. I never told you, but I think that **being married would help me through these lonely nights. I can't explain that. It's just me.** But now that I've admitted it, I want you to know that if I—you—we—should decide not to get married this summer, I will accept that too. In a way, I wish we could decide soon—because I don't want to get all excited & then postpone my excitement than to make a hasty decision which you—we—may—regret. I love you so much. I love you so deeply.

I'm sitting here wondering if I've said anything that is relevant. Have I even given my opinion? I really don't know.... Yes, I do want to marry you. But only if you honestly think that this is the right time and way, etc.

I NEVER, NEVER WANT YOU TO BE HURT AGAIN, PAT.

And so, I guess that I'm hoping that you will take what I've given you—and whatever else I can give if you ask—and that you will somehow make your decision. I do want to marry you—you know. I dreamed this letter before. I have written this letter in a dream—many years ago. When I put that "I do want to marry you" it bit me. But I don't remember the dream too well. This is an odd feeling in more ways than one. OK—so I'm saying "YES" if you decide you want to go ahead. And if you don't want to, then I'm saying, "I accept."

So right or wrong, young or no, that's it for tonight. Bless you, Patric, I am with you, in thought and feeling. You are with me. I kiss you, I miss you. I love you. My God, I love you **so**. Good night, my love. My warm, tender, kind, beloved Patric. Goodnight.

Sunday, March 1, 1970, 9:35 P.M.

A while ago, I skimmed through some of last night's "entry" in this letter, and I feel somewhat apologetic about the tone of it.

I must sound like some sort of nut, always making poor excuses for what have seemed to be very depressing letters lately. Well, I must warn you my love, that during the last few weeks of each quarter, I go really berserk with all the pressure. And these last few weeks have been the worst of any since I started school. There has been tremendous emotional and mental stress and I'm just knocking around doing the best I can—which may not be very good at all. Do forgive me, Pat. I promise that I'll probably be in much happier and lighter spirits as of March 16th—when my last exam is over.

It's unfortunate that we can't talk about this marriage idea—in person I mean. Pat, this is a very strange feeling. This whole letter just hasn't been "right." It is the first time since you left that I just have been completely unable to express my thoughts accurately. My mind is on you all the time, it seems—and I promise you, I HAVE been doing some "VERY HEAVY THINKNG" as you would say. But I can't seem to grasp at the ideas that are constantly in my mind. It is a very disarming feeling…. Don't think that I'm using you as a slapping post, Pat. I just get frustrated, and if I don't let you know what's up, then you may wonder about the weird tone of my letters….

…Do you want to hear something that's going through my mind now? I'll tell you—I'm afraid to mail this letter to you. I don't want you to be upset. It seems as if this whole thing is one big negative. **Well, I guess you're getting a chance to see part of my icky side.**

I hope I receive a letter from you early in this week, because I may get a chance to answer it.... Look into my heart—look at the pictures of me and search my soul. Please try to be patient with me a little longer. I love you so very much, Pat. I love you for what you are, for who you are. You are Patric Spencer, a very fine man, and I love you. I think and think about the possibility of marrying you this summer. But it isn't enough—I want to know YOUR feelings. I wish I were with you now. I need you so much, and miss **you.**

Thank you for letting me give my love to you. Thank you for loving me. Do I deserve you? You are wonderful to me. Bless you Pat. Always yours, Shelley.

Monday, March 2, 1970, 6:35 P.M. [same letter]

"So what's this?" She muses curiously.

Well, I'll tell you. Last night I got this letter all set to mail, but this morning I just couldn't bring myself to send it to you. Perhaps I have nothing more to say. I really am not too sure....

My friend was telling me: "He'll be home in ten days!!!" She was so excited. Her husband was in Viet Nam for 10 months—flew helicopters and with his being in the service I guess they haven't seen too much of each other for ages. I was so happy for her—wow! I thought about how I'll feel when the time comes for us to at least come together and live together forever.

But I'm happy for us too, Pat. Yes, it'll be a while before it's time for us to settle down together. But in the meantime, we're communicating and relating with one another, and perhaps we're both growing—I know I am. And although it becomes frustrating at times not to be with you, I know we can bear it. Because we love.

Pat, I've been doing so much thinking. Actually if I haven't said so, I am—even if a bit hesitantly—in favor of getting married. Hesitantly because I don't want you to think that because I think it could be a good thing now that you should agree with it for this reason alone. Somehow, I just have the feeling that that sentence simply doesn't make sense.

I am hesitant to express all of my thoughts at the moment because I don't want them to come out wrong, and also because I don't want to have to eat my words later on, depending upon what the decision will be about this summer. *FOR MANY YEARS, I HAVE BEEN VIOLENTLY DISCOURAGED OF EXPRESSING MY OPINIONS and I WON'T SAY BY WHOM. AT ANY RATE I FIND IT EXTREMELY DIFFICULT TO NOW EXERT MYSELF WHEN IT COMES TO A CONTROVERSIAL ISSUE. I SUPPOSE THE CHILD IN ME IS STILL AFRAID OF THE CONSEQUENCES.*

The feelings that I have now are somewhat confusing, Pat. All of the sudden, little thoughts are popping through, and I hadn't realized their somewhat uneasy existence before.

I suppose what I'm getting at is this summer—as unmarried. I am becoming somewhat wary of spending the summer if we're not married. Not because I think we'll get into all this tension toward one another, and certainly not because I am afraid that I'll resent you in any way. *I AM NOT EVEN TOO CONCERNED ABOUT WHAT MY FEELINGS WOULD BE IF WE DID HAVE INTERCOURSE. THE PROBLEM IS THAT I AM REALIZING MORE AND MORE HOW VERY DIFFICULT IT WILL BE TO REFRAIN FROM HAVING INTERCOURSE—AND I AM THINKING THAT IT WOULDN'T EVEN "BOTHER" ME IF I WEREN'T A VIRGIN: EXCEPT FOR THE FACT*

THAT WE MADE THIS VOW. I want to be responsible for my own doings—I will not have you carrying all the responsibility on your shoulders. It isn't fair to you—it isn't right. Just what I'm trying to say becomes clear as I write.

I guess I'm thinking that it will be difficult to live together—you and I—as man and wife—when we aren't man and wife. I couldn't stand not sleeping with you. But I'm wondering if deep inside, you might rebel just a little bit against the idea of it.

With you, I have thrown a tremendous amount of what used to be my "morals" right out the window. Simply because when a person's ideas don't fit with his/her situation, then the person has to decide which is more important—his/her ideas, or his/her situation. Well, my choice was YOU, Pat. My ideas didn't fit, and so, I let them go **and found new ideas.**

But I certainly wouldn't feel the same way about any other person. I'm sure you must understand what I'm clumsily trying to say.

I feel no guilt, no regrets about "how far we've gone," so to speak. I can't respond to anything if I'm having doubts inside.

And so you ought to know that I feel no doubt. I hope that our sexual experiences have been exciting for you. You are not naïve, and I am (or was?). I love you, Pat. Last night I couldn't sleep because I started thinking about us—from the first kiss at Chamberlains *up until you left.*

We went farther and farther—and I remember feeling a sort of fear that you would respect me a little less the deeper we went. But I had that intuition and knew it was right.

And now, I have an intuition also. But I want to know your thoughts more before I express it. There's not that much to express and you may be able to guess what my "intuition" is.

There are times when I think that I'll go crazy if I have to be without you for another minute. Physical separation is difficult. To me, it seems more difficult perhaps because I am aware of **how much I desire you—and if we aren't married, I will not break our vow because there's a great meaning in it for both of us. It means the ability to stick to our promises to ourselves more than to each other.** I don't believe that by marrying we would shirk our responsibility—I mean that we'd merely be running away from self-control.

I don't want to have this whole idea based upon the sex issue, even though, for now sex is of course, a major issue, simply because of the strain of physical separation.

This feels incomplete, but I'm going to end here anyway. Think hard, my darling. I need to hear your thoughts. I need your love. You're so wonderful to me. And please let me say once again that I love you, Pat with all the love my soul and body have to give. Bless you. Take care. I love you forever. Shelley.

Tuesday, March 3, 1970, 6:00 P.M.

My most beloved Shelley,

I truly hope that your answer to my proposal on tape, is yes. Yes, that we will have our regular wedding this coming June. I want you now, more than ever. There are no doubts in my mind, whatsoever, about wanting and needing you as a life-long partner. And if I can extend this, may I say to you: have no fear, have no doubts, that I love you with all the capacity I can draw upon, that I am firm in my desire for you.

If we can give each other the kind of love you speak of, in your "Home of the Heart," and I think we can, all else is secondary. You have faults, so-called; and you have moods, and down moments—moments when you feel very small and insignificant. And so do I. Please do not forget that I am human. I make mistakes. I have short comings. I am sometimes thoughtless. I have my fears.

But the love we seek, and in good measure have already attained, will provide for us, so that we can face ourselves unafraid, and so that we can work toward making ourselves into more aware and sensitive human beings.

As far as I am concerned, you need not worry another day about whether you deserve me, or are "good enough," or can "perform" well enough for me. With the love and acceptance, you offer all you have to do is to be you. The rest will take care of itself. Your home within me will serve you well.

It is a heavy burden to always be wondering or worrying if what you have to offer, or can do, is good enough for the other. Let us just concentrate on increasing our love for each other, and what we do for each other, will come along naturally.

I am deeply moved by your "Home Within My Heart." How long I have wished for just such a place. How saddened I have been over the years, not to have found such a place. But it is so rare. So few people will offer, or know how to offer that much love to another person.

At the same time, I am awed and concerned; concerned that I can give freely of myself to you, as you have to me. I want to, with all my heart, soul, and body. And if you give me the chance, I think I can. *What gives me cause for concern, is that over the many years of my life, I have often felt that I had to withdraw my feelings, in order to protect myself against emotional hurt.* No one, save my father, has come close to giving me the kind of unconditional and warm acceptance that you have. When the rays of your love strike upon me, I open up like a blossom. I come out from my shelters. I could feel this happening to me at Christmas time.

I could see the beauty of it then. But, I know also that it will take a while to tear down many of my defense mechanisms. I am hoping that you will understand. You mentioned once in a letter, how you went looking for something warm and secure to relate to, and when you didn't find it, you began to develop defense mechanisms, to protect yourself against future disappointment.

I know that you cannot see from my eyes, but can you not see how over many years of many such disappointments as you had, that I would become increasingly protective of my feelings??

I am trying to say something. Something like: your tremendous love and acceptance is a great challenge to me. It has been a while since I have been so challenged. I will meet that challenge, and open my soul as you have opened yours. But I feel a need to ask your patience as I struggle to do so. I guess I am apprehensive that I will make mistakes along the way, and I am hoping like hell that those mistakes don't hurt you.

Maybe I am making a bigger issue than is necessary; know that at Christmas Time I was very much myself, giving to you as I could. Know that all the letters, tapes, phone calls, and gifts etc. have come from the deep love I have for you. Know that I have done everything gladly, with joy in my heart. I have only begun to give and share with you. I want to do everything in my power, to meet your needs. You are someone I look up to, I admire, I bless.

You have said that you and I are much alike. I think we are. And I am pleased when I contemplate that I can be your "SUN", shining and radiating warmth to you. Neither of us stands very well alone, but together, we can build towers to the heavens. Love is a very powerful force.

I used to think it was somewhat of a weakness, to really "need" someone else, or to depend upon them. And I took pride in "my independence." But what it really was, was self-protection, avoiding vulnerability. I am not that kind of proud anymore. I NEED YOU SHELLEY!!! I need you, if I am to grow and expand, and become what there is within me to become.

And I think you need me, in the same way. I am very glad you need and want me. What could I really do for you if you didn't need me?? Sometimes I won't quite understand what it is that you specifically need. I hope that your love will always allow you to verbally express to me what it is so that I can meet it. I am very poor in recognizing subtle hints. I am naïve in some ways. I think differently than many people do. Please let us not have any hidden agendas between us. If we would like the other person to do something, let's sit down and discuss it, so that both of us know what the situation is.

It is perhaps an inappropriate time to include this, but my first wife had a way of saying, *"If you don't know, I'm not going to tell you; it's for me to know and you to find out!!"* It was a hell of a position for me to be in. And it occurs less obviously, all around us. People have expectations of others, but rarely or never expressing what those expectations are; but yet, having hurt feelings, if the expectations are not met. I will do as much as I can for you, Shelley, but I must know what you would have of me. OK??

May I say here, please do not burden yourself, worrying about what expectations I may have of you, in our married life, whether it be during this coming June, or five or ten years from now. I am marrying you for your love, for my home in your heart, for what I can become, by having the benefit of such great love, by what it does for me to have someone to whom I can give all my love. I am marrying you for what I can do for you. You are a most beautiful spirit, and I want very much to contribute to the growth and enhancement of that spirit. You have very deep needs, and I want to fill them.

So, please, think not of how you will measure up in marriage. We will work out structures, roles, agreements, arrangements, etc. as time and circumstance seem to require. Do not be concerned over some shortcoming. If you haven't had much experience cooking lately, then we will learn together. Think of our marriage as the beginning of a learning process; do not think of it as a test of what you might have learned already. And I will do the same. Hand-in-hand, heart-with-heart, we will walk the unknown paths together. Both guiding, both following, both comforting, both being comforted.

I used to think that when I became an adult, (whenever that actually is supposed to happen) that I should then be "completed," or perfect, or something of that order. And it was indeed distressing to keep discovering imperfections in myself. Now I see how deadly such a concept was. Life is a continuous process of growing and changing; otherwise, you start dying inside.

Know that you, Shelley, are very much accepted just the way you are for those things I know of, for all of the things I don't know of, for all of you, in every respect. You have a home in my heart, too. And it can be expanded to become whatever you desire.

I thank you for your acceptance of me. Can you not see that we need each other now? That there is so much more we can give to each other by being married? Yes, there may be separations, lonely times, but yet, shorter and richer. My heart, soul, and body want no more barriers, to prevent them from sharing in the world's most beautiful love. Love, Your Devoted Patric.

March 7, 1970

My Beloved Pat,

Thank you, a hundred million times, for sending me these pictures. Especially the beautiful enlargement. What a lovely surprise! And how I love to sit and look at the way you're gazing at me in the picture.

Only one more week of torture and I'll be finished with this quarter—exams and all. This tape may be totally full of nonsense—I don't know because I haven't really listened to it. If you can't get much out of it, I apologize, ok? Please excuse me and keep that love a 'comin'! My mind is in such ecstatic (oh yeah?) delirium (try again!). I'm so glad that we're going to go ahead with the wedding. Just so glad, I can't even tell you. You're the most wonderful man in the world to me, Patric. And I'm the very luckiest and happiest girl. Bless you. You're so sweet to me. Welcome to my home, Pat. You have entered it, and I can feel your warm, quiet presence. I can feel my love expanding for you. And I can also see and feel myself entering your home. I will treat your home with great care and consideration. I will let my soul soak in all of the warm affection and love that your home floods me with. And I will try to help your home for me expand to new depths and dimensions from the love I feel for you, in the same way that you're expanding my home for you.

I love you so much. Don't be afraid of your barriers that you've built to protect yourself through the years. Don't be afraid to reveal these barriers to me. I think I understand how you feel, and I accept. **You need not fear me, Pat, for I will never try to force you to tear down any barriers that still are useful to you. When you no longer need your self-protection, then and only then will you be able to let the walls fade away.** But you are the only person capable of letting go of them—I can't do it for you, and I know that you don't expect me to. If we run into problems because of these barriers, then we will have to sit and talk about it. I'm not afraid of the barriers, Pat. I love you so very much. You've had such a hard life, and you've done a tremendous job of making yourself into one of the finest human beings in the world. <u>The finest</u> to me. If you ever hurt my feelings, I'll let you know. And if I hurt your feelings, then perhaps you'll be able to tell me. I don't believe we'll have any "hidden agendas" between us if we give each other the trust and acceptance that we both need so very much.

Never be afraid of being yourself before me, Patric. I love you as you are now, and I love you for whatever you have been and will be.You are my friend, my love. And soon you will be my husband.

We are betrothed to one another now. Our souls are betrothed to one another now.

I miss you so, my darling. But my loneliness is full of expectant joy, and I can't be sad. To be loved by you, Winston Patric Spencer is the greatest gift that life has ever given me. It is the greatest privilege and joy in the world. Thank you, Pat. I love you.

Later, 9:45 P.M., after a telephone call.

I'm so excited to have talked to you!!! Pat, I love you so very, very much.

About the wedding ring—the more I think of it, the more I know that I want you to buy the band that you like best for what you can afford. Actually, I never really thought about a ring much, but I know that I will love whatever you pick— not only because you have such wonderful taste but because whatever you pick out will be with care and love. I want what you like—because I know I'll like—love—it. Ok?

I realize that I may not be making much sense, but is any bride-to-be, only 98 days away from marriage, supposed to be coherent? And I never have been coherent to begin with!

Pat, I'm so glad to hear you say that you're absolutely sure—and that you're very happy.

My heart sings, my soul burns passionately, lovingly. Very soon, we will be completely together. When I think of you at times, my desire becomes so great as to send longing flames of passion throughout my body.

I am yours, Pat, and no one else's. I love you so very very much. I look forward to hearing your visualizations, should you write them down. And even more, I bless the fact that very soon we will indeed be no longer visualizing, but rather experiencing each other. I love you. Thank you so much my darling for the pictures, for your love and for being the man you are. With all my love, Shelley.

Monday, March 9th, 1970, 7:30 P.M.

"June 13, 1970" all in tiny XX kisses.
"Mr. and Mrs. Patric Spencer."

Monday, March 9, 1970 7:30 p.m.

XX XX XX XX XX XX XX XX XX XX XX XX XX

To Patric, my dearest Darling.

Today my whole being has been so completely filled by your presence that everything else has seemed rather pleasantly vague. It's been a long wearing day, but my thoughts of you have filled me with such happiness that I've enjoyed the day after all. This evening I feel very much like writing to you — altho I haven't anything pressing to say. Perhaps I just want to see if some of the exuberance I feel will come through this letter and smile upon your eyes and let your soul know that you are joyfully ecstatically, and very deeply loved.

I feel so good tonight! Several mysterious little occurances (sp?) have happened to me. Well, mysterious isn't the word at all. At any rate... Today in my Traditions class,

To Patric, my dearest Darling,

Today, my whole being has been so completely filled by your presence that everything else has seemed rather pleasantly vague. It's been a long wearing day, but my thoughts of you have filled me with such happiness that I've enjoyed the day after all. This evening I feel very much like writing to you—although I haven't anything pressing to say. Perhaps I just want to see if some of the exuberance I feel will come through this letter and smile upon your eyes and let your soul know that you are joyfully, ecstatically, and very deeply loved.

I feel so good tonight! Several mysterious little occurrences have happened to me. Well, mysterious isn't the right word at all. At any rate...today, in my Traditions class, I really wasn't there. It was a rather strange feeling because I wasn't really thinking of anything in particular. Usually, daydreaming is a result of guiding one's mind into certain channels & letting imagination take its course. But today was different. I sat there, aware that the teacher was talking about Emily Dickenson, but that's just about all that I remember. I don't even remember sitting there through most of the class—in all, I lost about 30 minutes I would guess. As far as I know, I could have been laid out on the floor in a coma, or dancing a jig on a desk & I never would know the difference. It was mysterious. My soul was completely separated from my body, and my consciousness was separated from my soul. I know that your soul was with me—at least as I reflect upon it now, it seems as if part of your soul must have been there. I have never had anything like that happen before. It was very beautiful, I think—I mean, as I think of it now, it seems that it was a beautiful thing that happened. No drugs or artificial stimuli could ever bring that inner peace.

Yes, I think that that must be the word for it. It was because of you, Patric, that this happened to me. You were a very big part of it. It was as if my soul were released from my physical being, and it was set free from earthly thoughts connected with words. It was filled with the peace that you send along to me from your soul. I don't know where my soul went—I don't know what I did while it was gone. It was like waking up in a strange place and not remembering anything for a moment, when my soul came back into my mind. And I was filled with a radiant warmth & I felt like laughing and singing and dancing. It was as if my soul was for the first time, completely free, and when it came back to me, it was refreshed and happy. I think that my soul must have paid you a visit today, Patric.

As I think about it, this may sound really weird to you— No, I'm not cracking up. I think that it must have been just a split second that I was really unconscious of everything. But the rest of the time was the drifting of my mind once again, containing my soul.

If it sounds strange to you, well, don't get upset. I don't pretend to understand what happened but it was very beautiful because it started out with thoughts of you, and it ended with thoughts of you. So, you must also have been there in between.

Well, enough. Perhaps you've had things like that happen to you. Perhaps inner peace is something so rare and fleeting that people become afraid of it. But it makes me feel as if our souls do indeed have the capacity to lend peace to one another. And when we're together or apart, our souls are free and happy because they are always together; for they love and want and need one another, whether they're within us our without our bodies. And perhaps your soul did commune with my soul today—and maybe without you even realizing it. Thank you, Patric, for giving to me all of the love that you do. You have released my soul by calming it with peace. And I hope that I may do the same for you. I love you very much.

And so I sit here, very much taken by the immensity of our love. I am very touched, and very awed. Your soul is so very beautiful, Pat.

You overwhelm me. And that you love me is the most profound blessing that could ever be bestowed upon me. I love you.

Tonight, as I read my book [for school] I suddenly felt the urge to just sit and look at this beautiful photograph. And as I sat there, I saw the serenity upon our faces, and I was kissing you once again. Rarely have I thought so hard about your kisses or caresses. Like you, I begin to miss you so very much. But I gazed at the picture, and it disappeared, and everything else disappeared. I was with you, kissing your lips, feeling you kiss mine. It was beautiful and I felt warmed. For, it won't be so very long until you'll come driving up to the house, and I'll come running out to you. And whether it's at night & I'm in my robe, or whether it's in the day, when all the world may see, I will kiss you a welcome kiss as soon as I see you come. I love you so much. I think I'll stop for a while. *My head is pounding as __agitatedly as my heart.__*

My precious Patric. Bless you, my darling. Always know that you are needed by me; that you are wanted and desired by me; that you are forever mentally, physically, and spiritually loved by me with a love that will never remain the same from one moment to the next—but that continually, perpetually grows and expands and deepens with every beat of my heart, and with every beat of yours.

Well, Patric, I'm kind of all tired out now. I was thinking that perhaps I could begin a spontaneous visualization here in this letter, but, as tired as I am, I need sleep. And if I start working on my imagination & and let my desires start to burn as fiercely as they do when I write to you at times—well, I just may never get to sleep. Believe me, I know!!

....Gayle's young brother is such a honey, and so are you. I look forward to our years of just togetherness—the two of us. And, I also look forward to bearing your children. It gives me chills to think of it. My husband. My love...

Thank you again for the pictures, Pat. You're so wonderful to me. I'm so very lucky. And happy. I love you so very much. Take my love to bed at night, and take it to work with you in the day. It's yours, Patric, to keep forever. I love you, or have I already said that? Take care, my love. Drive carefully each day. My sweet wonderful Patric. Mein freund. Miss you, I love you. Devotedly, and happily your xxx Shelley.

Los Angeles, Tuesday Night, March 10, 1970

To my dearest, and beloved fiancé, Shelley, (That lucky girl!)

I have run short of time this evening but did want to get this off to you. Just this morning at 8:00 A.M., my boss at the Bank of America approved my request for leave of absence, during the middle two weeks of June. So I immediately began planning the honeymoon, or at least coming up with ideas and suggestions.

Let me outline my idea, so that you will have a chance to think about it, and let me know if you approve or disapprove. Anything can be changed. All you have to do is to let me know. OK?

Here goes: I thought we might be married somewhere between noon and two P.M., so that we could be on our way from "Our Town" somewhere around five or six at the latest. The First Night (the big night), we might drive to a nearby city to the west and stay at one of the nicer Holiday Inns (near the airport). We could eat a nice dinner, and then retire to our room for the celebration. The drive to that city would not be too much, or too hard on us, but it would give us time to take cognizance of what had just taken place, and prepare for the evening. Also, it would give us a fair boost toward our trip.

We could get up, whenever, on Sunday, and make our way across Indiana and Illinois to Moline, Iowa, or wherever your aunt lives. If it were not desirable to stay there, we could drive on to a motel or something. Any way the second day would be a short driving day.

On Monday, the third day, we could get a reasonable start, and drive across Iowa (Stopping at the Amana Colonies—and stay at Die Heimat [German for The Home Place] motel, if you would like), and up towards Sioux Falls. We could camp out somewhere along the way, if you like, or, find a nice motel. Whatever.

The fourth day, Tuesday, would be spent driving to the Black Hills of South Dakota, and then enjoying Mount Rushmore. (That is where the heads of Washington, Jefferson, Lincoln, and Theodore Roosevelt are carved into the side of a mountain.) It is a beautiful area, and great for camping. When I say camping, I mean sleeping out in sleeping bags. We would not do any cooking.

On Wednesday, we could enjoy the Black Hills some more, and then, when we are pleased, drive on toward Yellowstone National Park. We would not reach Yellowstone that night, but we could stay in Cody, Wyoming at Buffalo Bill's Hotel—the Irma—named for his daughter.

On Thursday, we could drive into Yellowstone, and begin enjoying our country's oldest National Park, and I believe, one of its finest and most exciting. I have already made reservations for us at the Old Faithful Inn, for Thursday and Friday nights. (We can always cancel them, if you don't want to go to Yellowstone, but if we do, it would be necessary to apply for them now.)

I thought that on Friday, we could spend the entire day, sightseeing in the Park. There is quite a bit to see. The Old Faithful Inn is a beautiful large old structure, built in 1904. It has charm and quaintness, and puts us near the more exciting part of the park.

According to my planning, Saturday would be our hardest day of driving. We would leave Yellowstone quite early in the morning, and drive all day to my cousin Ruth's in Reno, Nevada. Something like nine hours of driving.

On Sunday, we could take the scenic route, U.S. 395 into California and down to Los Angeles, arriving around 7:00 or 8:00 P.M. Home at last!! Of course, I would have to get to bed early, and be up at 5:30 A.M. the next morning to get to the Bank on time.

Well, <u>what do you think</u>?? <u>What are your feelings</u>?? Do you have other places you would rather see?? Would you want to camp several nights, or stay in a motel most of the time?? In addition to being fun, camping saves money: Camping costs upwards to $2.00 per night. Motels cost between $8.00 and $12.00 per night. But whatever you desire, we can do. After all, it is our Honeymoon.

[Actual costs for the entire trip, from carefully kept records, were: $207.46!]

You will never guess what I did today. I went out and bought your Wedding Ring!! I won't tell you very much about it, because I want it to be a pleasant surprise. I think it is very beautiful and really is appropriate for our needs. The jeweler was very nice, and suggested that I take the ring I want, put it on your finger at the wedding, and then when you get back to Sierra Hills, he will measure your finger for proper fit, exchange rings if necessary, and then engrave it, as I would like. I am buying a size six, as per your instructions.

I am also making plans to buy a new suit for the Wedding. And I really could use a new suit. But I think I would like to be married in a Tuxedo—white coat.

My darling Shelley, I am way past bedtime, now, and regret it, but my days are hard if I don't get the right sleep. So I shall close for now, and write again tomorrow night, when I hope to have more time, and hopefully, will have received your tape, and can comment.

WEDDING NIGHT SCENARIO

Now may not be the most ideal time to give forth one of my visualization, since I just got home from work, feel a little tired, feel a little rushed for time, and had bean soup for lunch. But let me give it a try anyway.

Our wedding night: I see us arriving at the Inn around 7:00 P.M. We check in, move our luggage into our room, freshen ourselves, and go to dinner. Perhaps we will have a very delicious steak…filet mignon. Afterwards and quite satisfied (food-wise) we will return to our room. We will unpack. Then I will use the bathroom first. Shower, shave, and "get ready" in general. Then, it will be your turn in the bathroom. I will wear just my Japanese Kimono

(bathrobe). While you are preparing, I will make things in the room ready. I thought we might have candlelight. And bring a bottle of Champagne with us from the reception.

When you are all ready, I will welcome your entrance into the room. I will gaze upon you admiringly and bring you slowly into my arms, for a loving hug and kiss. Then we will drink a toast to each other, and ourselves together. If we have not had sufficient time earlier, then I would like to spend a little while "collecting ourselves together" mentally. Talk for a while about the day's events, reflect upon them, and express whatever significance we find they have for us at the time. And then slowly bring our minds and souls to the immediate moment.

I would ask you to stand. I would kiss you, and then very slowly walk us over to the mirror, where two candles are burning. I would have you face the mirror. Then very slowly I would caress your body (I would be standing directly behind you) with my hands. Slowly my hands would find their way to your breasts, and slowly and sensuously caress them. In a while, my hands would begin to move down your body and clasp your thighs. Then ever so slowly, I would begin to remove your negligée. Eventually, we would both be standing nude together, before the mirror, enjoying our nakedness before and with each other. I would pick you up into my arms, and carry you over to the bed. There I would lay you down gently, and lay down beside you.

With all the time in the world, I would begin loving you and your body in whatever way occurred to me at the time, or using whatever fantasies you chose to express to me. After an hour or so or maybe even shorter time span, I would eventually kiss your vagina a most passionate kiss, and perhaps you would desire to kiss me.

Then our very personal ritual would begin. Ever so slowly and gently (with the help of K-Y ointment) I would begin to enter you, listening every moment for your responses, so as not to hurt you or cause undue discomfort. There would be all the time in the world. Penetration might take up to a half an hour, or, several tries. Once in, I would come to a rest position on top of you, caress you, and once again reflect upon the great and wonderful lifelong adventure we are now beginning.

Shortly thereafter we would begin the rhythm (we both can move, not just I). At first we would explore to find out how deep I may penetrate without hurting you. (Vaginas come in several sizes and lengths.) You would probably still be quite tight inside, so we would be extra slow and gentle. We might thus for a half hour or so. If you felt that you might be capable of a climax, we would work toward that, however long it took. When you were fully climaxed, then I would begin to work toward a climax (simultaneous climaxes are too difficult, usually) at this stage. (And it is much better that I go after you.)

Upon my climaxing, I would sink into your waiting arms, to be held, and covered. It would be a non-verbal time, but of just opening all our sensory awareness receptors and just enjoying the sensations our bodies gave to us.

We might then shift to sleeping positions, and sleep for a while, or, if we were so inclined, begin the foreplay all over again, and climax a second time, or a third time, or... well anyway, the evening is ours...whatever comes into our minds, souls, and bodies.

In the morning, we would shower together; and I would wash your entire body with just my bare hands and soap, and your mind. (And if we were so stimulated, we might retire once more to the bed.)

March 10, 1970, Tuesday, 11:05 P.M.

My Dearest Darling Patric,

Surprise, surprise! Since I have no classes tomorrow, I decided that it'd be nice to sit up a few more minutes & send my thoughts to you.

Today, I drove downtown because I went to drop off the ***ENGAGEMENT ANNOUNCEMENT—WOW!*** *At the Society Desk of the morning newspaper, as per your mother's instructions. [Mother—who was part of high society— arranged with the Society Editor to place the announcement in the weekday morning—where it will be seen, as opposed to the Sunday edition.]* Did I ever feel excited? I stopped for a moment & looked at some wedding bands in a store window, but I got so excited that I had to quit looking. My mother wrote the announcement & I'm not even sure what it said now; we sent no picture. There is a deadline & it'd be such a mess to have tried to get a picture in. [*But they were able to supply a beautiful picture in time.*]

Perhaps you could inquire of some of your friends and acquaintances as to whether anyone knows of people who would be interested in taking folk-style guitar lessons this summer. If I could manage to find about 15 people or so, or even 10, perhaps it'd be possible for me to teach a while each day that I'm out there this summer. It wouldn't be much money, but it'd help. My mother is really very skeptical of my getting a 9-5 type job in my first few months of marriage—as unusual as our first months will be.

What do you think, Pat?

My darling, I've wasted much time chattering, and now I'm so very tired, so please excuse me now. I must sleep. Last night I had a strange but very warm dream about you, and I woke up with a feeling that you have been with me in my sleep. And I felt at once both mortified at the three remaining months, but also, very sure that the time will fly by & we indeed soon will be together. I love you so much. Goodnight my sweet love. I love you, Pat. With all of my soul. Xxxxx

Wednesday, March 11, 1970, 8:40 P.M.

[same letter continued]

Good evening my love. How are you tonight? Perhaps you've just gotten home since it's about 5:40 P.M. there [in California]. Are you tired now? Did you have a long day? Soon, perhaps, I will be waiting at the door for you as you come home, and I will kiss you hello and tell you that I'm so glad to see you, and that I've missed you all day. And then I will sit with you for a while and ask about your day, and tell you about mine. Perhaps you'll want to rest in a rocking chair for a few moments & maybe you'll ask me to sit on your lap. So, I sit on your lap and gently massage your forehead & stroke your neck & rub your shoulders and chest. And you'll smile contentedly perhaps, and tell me that you like for me to do all these things, and perhaps you'll give me a gentle loving kiss. And then I'll put one of my arms around your neck, and rest my head upon your shoulder perhaps, hold your hand. Perhaps we'll just sit quietly for a few moments, rocking peacefully. **And then, I will get up to put dinner on the table.**

Well, I have so many visions in my mind, waiting for me to call upon & recognize them. I do hope that if I get a job this summer, that I may perhaps be able to be home before you…

Wedding dress plans…But I sort of don't want to tell you about any of it in detail—because I want you to be surprised if possible.

I know a fellow who passed out when his bride got up to the altar. I certainly hope you don't do that—if you do, who's going to hold me up???

[*Actually, Patric was the one who was emotionally overwhelmed and cried during the ceremony.*]

I guess the big news of the day is that your mother, Elinore Harrington, telephoned. She and my mother talked on Monday and mother felt good about it. Today, your mother called my mother (I was home) to tell her that mother's friend Mary, from the Society Page of the newspaper called her. Mary saw the announcement I took in yesterday and when Mary noticed Patriuc's mother's name [mother was well known in local society] Mary called. So I guess that's what your mother called about the first time today. Then, she called back to tell my mother that she had talked to her friend Mary, again, who said that the Newspaper wouldn't put the announcement in on Sunday, but rather, on a weekday—which is quite a privilege. So your mother and my mother chatted about reception etc. I don't want to talk about the reception in here—I want to discuss it with you on the phone. OK? Ok. Well, at about 6:00 P.M. I was telling my mother that I had the feeling that somebody would call tonight—if not YOU, then someone else. About 5 minutes later, the telephone rang and I answered, thinking it's Bryan or somebody. "Hello?"

"Hello, Shelley." "Yes." "Well this Mrs. Harrington!" Boy, Pat, I nearly fainted on the spot. There I was in a pair of old tan jeans, a mucky orange shirt with holes in it, no shoes, my hair up on top of my head with little pink rollers in it so I looked like a Martian about to take off...And I was TALKING TO YOUR MOTHER!! & clutching a glass of milk so hard that it might have curdled! [This was a rather odd reaction on Shelley's part because this was years before any kind of SKYPE or video phone!!!]

Nervous? Who said anything about nervous? All of this self-conscious once-over my appearance and circumstance took place in between the first and second syllables of her name, of course. So I tried to gather my wits then. Your mother was, of course, very nice to me, although we really didn't know exactly what to say a couple of times there. I hope I didn't sound too foolish—I do get nervous talking on the phone anyway because I have a thing about liking to see a person's face when I talk to him/her. But anyway. Of course, this is a rather awkward situation now—typical of the type I have a knack for getting into. I hope that your mother will like me—or at least, just tolerate me. I know that for a while there, things were really miserable between Sally and Clifford and their in-laws on both sides. I hope that it won't be like that for us. Your mother wanted to tell us about another detail of the announcement business. But, if she's anything like my mother, she purposely chose to wait to call until the dinner hour when it'd be likely that I'd be here. Women have a way about things like that!

She told me that I'd be a "very busy girl" from now on till the wedding, and I said that the excitement of first announcing the wedding would make my exams a bit difficult to study for, but that it'd be good practice for the next time when I'll be taking exams a week before the wedding. She said she had not realized that I'd be having exams that close and I told her that you'd suggested having the wedding the first week in June, and that I'd told you I'd never make it. So she said something about handling men, but I forgot exactly what she said. By that time I'd gone into shock, you see. She said that you'd told her that you and I get along quite well in having good conversations, etc. and she said how you and she often have deep philosophical discussions. Well, it was all very pleasant and I'm very glad to finally have spoken to her and heard her voice. I guess you probably realized by now that I am very sensitive to a person's voice. Well.

So that was the big event of the day. I'm still a little shaky. If you were here, Pat, I'd feel so much more at ease. But as things are, I'm not very sure of myself. Naturally, I do want to make a favorable impression upon your mother. Well I'm a big girl (yes, in more ways than one.) and can handle myself I guess. [I know Shelley worried about her weight.] At least your mother isn't on the Voice Board at school too. Now then, I'd really tremble!

Let me hasten to say that I do have an open mind about your mother. I have formed no opinions about her, naturally, since I haven't even met her. So, please don't be upset with me if I admit my nervousness to you. OK?

I hope you realize how very grateful I am for the many ways in which you show your love to me. You are such a rare kind person, Pat, and I'd be so upset with myself if you didn't know how very much I appreciate you and everything you are, and everything you ever have been or will be. I wake up in the morning feeling warm and happy as if coming out of a beautiful dream. But, whether I've been dreaming or not, the joy that I feel results from the knowledge that the reality that I open my eyes to is the reality of love. The reality of your love. And when I see the empty pillow next to mine, it is lonely. But my loneliness is your loneliness too, and thus we share our "SADS" as well as our "HAPPYS."

Lately, I've been so filled with emotion—emotion awakened by you, Pat. I feel like running through a park; I want to stretch my arms to the sky & sun and spin around till I become dizzy. I want to laugh and cry. And, I want to be near you. I can't wait until you drive up to my house. I'll be so relieved to see you safe, for one thing. As I think about your homecoming, I really get all choked up—and if I ever cry tears of joy, it will probably be when you come. I cry happy tears more easily than sad ones.

Pat, my beloved Pat. I am so very lucky. I am so very happy. Ours will not be an ordinary, dull, unexciting life together. We shall explore every aspect of life that we are able to. And the love and very deep devotion that we feel for one another will carry us through hardships & problems.

It seems as if each day, I love you more than the day before. Each day, I feel a new depth expanding in our love. With each letter or tape or phone call, or note from you, I am shown more of your soul. Sometimes, you reveal totally new elements within yourself. Sometimes you show me more of a part of your soul that I have already seen. I love you so very much, Patric. I hope that I will always be able to retain this mysterious element of inspiration for you which you say I now possess.

My darling fiancé. I want you so much. My desire for you burns very warmly and brightly. My passion stirs so longingly for you. I am yours, Pat. Completely yours. Soon, you will have me, and I will have you. Soon you will come

into me, and our bodies will join & strengthen the union
which our souls have already begun to form.

Soon, our physical needs and desires for one another will
be fulfilled, and we will be at last able to encourage and carry
out all of the passion and love for one another & go beyond
physical pleasure, spiritual love, and on into an infinite realm
of love which no words will ever limit or label.

Yes, my darling, I am yours. So whatever you wish to
dream, do so. Whatever I am able to give you, I want to do.
Let me turn your fantasies into realities, if I may. **Yes, our**
sex life will indeed enable us to further commune together.
We are very sensual people & we need each other's physical
love to enhance all of love's other elements.

So, I ask you now, before we have engaged in intercourse,
to please talk to me always. If you are not satisfied with me,
sexually or any other way, let's talk about it, argue anything.
But let's never let silence build a wall between us. I want to
give you as such pleasure as you can ever know. So, perhaps
sometimes I may need your help that I may fulfill your desires.
I will always want you to be happy in every way. I love you
so, Pat. I love you...Lovingly, Shelley.

Friday, March 13, 1970, 10:05 P.M.

To My Very Precious Patric,

Thank you. Thank you for the card that I received
Wednesday. Thank you for the lovely maps that came
yesterday and the pictures too. I love maps, & I'm so happy
to have these. And, my darling, thank you for the very special
map that came with your letter today.

How wonderful you are to me. I told you that I needed to
hear from you this week, and you've been so very thoughtful.

My poor darling—you stayed up so late writing that letter and my sympathetic heart is so very appreciative of your kindness. You're so good to me, Pat. And you're so good FOR me. Thank you. I trust that when you know you are heading into a difficult time, you will let me know so that I can "be there" to encourage you, just as you have encouraged me. That's a wonderful kind of relationship to have. You're a wonderful man to love. Goodnight, Pat...three months from tonight we'll be together.

Saturday, March 14, 1970, 6:30 P.M.

[same letter continued]

I can't tell you how much it meant to me to come home today from a rather tiring exam, and to find your tape waiting for me; I was so excited! Actually, I had a feeling that there'd be something waiting for me. [**Shelley truly had ESP.**] You said in the Tuesday night letter that you'd write again Wednesday, but I just had a feeling anyway that you'd send something— whether a tape, card phone call, etc. It was awfully nice to come home to a letter, rather a tape, Pat. Thank you.

First, I want to make a few comments. The perfume [on the letter] that you spoke of is _CHANEL #5_. I wore it during the holidays for you, and when we went to bed together that last weekend. Of course, I'll wear it on our honeymoon!! I wish it wasn't so expensive—I could spray more letters with it. But...

I will look at silver now and send whatever I can to you. Most silver I've casually looked at in the past really doesn't do too much for me. I don't know—I just don't care that much about it. Maybe that sounds awful. However, I do know how nice pretty sterling can make a table look for special affairs. So, I'll be a good kid and start looking. But here I come again with my "Scotchness"—because silver's so darned expensive, we may not receive much. So, I'm going to get the cheapest that I can find—that's half-way attractive of course. I do prefer very simple designs—this elaborate stuff just doesn't appeal to me.

Boy, I didn't intend to go into all that much detail. Don't get me wrong—I will enjoy looking at silver and registering, etc. But I'm not the type who gets all ecstatic every time a beautiful fork comes in front of my eyes.

As for stoneware, for everyday china—I really don't know about that: Bryan and Theresa have stoneware and Theresa says that it chips just terribly. I think it best to hold off for a while on that—we don't need it yet and I wouldn't be registering for it anyway. _"It's just not done."_ Ha, ha.

Crystal—although eventually we do want to obtain some nice glassware, I think it would be unwise to register for it now. The main reason is because it'd be such a headache to try to transport any crystal we receive. It's really difficult. So, unless you feel very strongly about obtaining it now, perhaps we could wait on that too?

Not to put a damper on or anything, but I was reading the etiquette book a while back and it had a section on gifts to the bride and groom. It mentioned that if it is not the first marriage for either party, then friends and relatives who've given wedding presents once before are not "obligated" to give again (if they ever were obligated...) So, I don't know how your family feels about it, but I thought I'd better mention it in case you didn't know. I'm also sure that you're far better informed on these matters than I. I'm a genius at faux pas

(there: big words—I've just got to start learning what they mean. But it sounds sort of nice, huh?)

Another thing: have you chosen your ushers yet? That's kind of important. And, your Guest List! I know you're so busy, but please when you can, do send your list. We can't order invitations yet because we don't know how many we need. OK? Love, your devoted Shelley xxxxx

Monday, March 16, 1970, 5:00 P.M.

[same letter]

Naturally, I forgot to mention ten billion things at the closing excerpt of the tape:

- does your mother know that I will be coming back here in September?
- does she know that Sally and I are sisters—would that make any impression upon her for better or worse?

OK. Now. You asked me to list some of my favorite flowers. Outside of roses, it's hard for me to think. I like Lilies of the Valley. And I think Gardenias are lovely to look at, but the fragrance has a tendency to make me sick…awfully nauseous. For my senior prom I had gardenias for my corsage, and it was really a trial—my date was so pleased with them and so I decided to suffer rather than disappoint him. I love pansies because they're so velvety. I like carnations. And I like violets. So, after roses, I guess they'd be: Pansies; Lilies of the Valley; Violets; and Carnations.

Then, there are all kinds of mums too. I really never thought about my favorite flowers, after roses. Oh, I like *Snapdragons too. Let's face it, I like all kinds of flowers!* I have the flowers for the wedding in mind—am I supposed to get them ordered? I just assumed I was.

Now – Guess What? *We're engaged!*

The announcement is in this morning's newspaper. I'll send you one when I get a copy, ok?

Pat, I love you so very much. My longing for you becomes more intense with each new day. I need you so. My dear, dear Patric. By the way, I didn't send you a St. Patrick's Day card. Know why? Because ***EVERY DAY IS SAINT PATRIC'S DAY TO ME!!*** Sure, an I luv ye, darlin', whatever where ever, and whomever you may be. My precious Patric. Miss you.

Forever devotedly, lovingly Yours Shelley.

Envelope: Help!! There's a blizzard outside!!! If it would start melting right now, it might be all gone by June, but I wouldn't count on it...? Would you like a winter wedding?

Includes a detailed drawing of a Snowman groom and a Snow woman bride in wedding clothes.

St. Patrick's Day, March 17, 1970, 8:00 P.M.

To the most beloved woman in my whole life,
That is you, Shelley!

I don't know quite how this letter will turn out. I feel very tired; my back muscles are aching; and in general, my spirits are medium to low. So the tone of this letter may be a little on the down side. Then again, by writing to you, my spirits may lift. It just seems these days, that I am running, running, running but not quite getting everywhere I want. During the week, work, the preparation for it, the relaxation afterwards, and the commuting, just takes a huge bite out of my time, and energies. In the evenings I don't feel like doing much at all. Like tonight: I wanted to write some other letters, and a few notes, but my mood is just too heavy at the moment, and bedtime is only one ½ hours away.

My weekends are full too; either with the house, car, yard chores that I have been putting off, or with trying to rest up from the previous week, or with traveling. So they are not much relief these days.

On the emotional side, I think there are at least three major factors influencing me. One, is of course the forthcoming wedding. There are a lot of details to be thought of, and taken care of, such as writing to several relatives, making up a guest list; making arrangements for the trips across country, thinking about the wedding, preparing a budget, trying to get the house, here, ready for you, etc. etc. etc.

On my 29th Birthday, I went down to the Ocean, and spent the day meditating. One of the biggest thoughts that came to me was: "A person must be in possession of his own soul, if he is to enjoy, and participate fully in life. Therefore, I am going to go out and wrest back my soul from all of the 'funny' places that other persons have seen fit to take it." And ever since, I have been doing battle, to regain my full and complete soul. Shelley, I hope you don't mind that I tell you all these things. But they are a part of me, and I want you to know me. I am very pleased that you admire and appreciate all my efforts to become a worthwhile, loving, and experiencing human being. But all persons have their weaknesses too, and I certainly have mine.

Can you see, all the more clearly now, how much your unconditional acceptance of me, means to me?? How beautifully my heart and soul expand and grow because of the warm radiance of such love?

Because of your acceptance of me, especially as it is so well expressed in "My Home in Your Heart" you have won my eternal gratitude and devotion. All mountains become mole hills with a woman like you by my side. Shelley, I love you.

And maybe you, too, are seeking such acceptance. You shall indeed find it with me. It may take me a while, sometimes to know and understand just where you need such acceptance, but as I do become enlightened, you shall have what you see—forever.

Yes, I am feeling better now. Thank you.

Your mother mentioned two O' Clock in the afternoon, as the possible time of the Wedding Ceremony. That is fine with me. Love, Patric.

March 18, 1970, 6:40 P.M.

To My Most Darling Patric,

I sit here and can't really think of an appropriate beginning. Your letter arrived today, and I am so touched by the love that you have sent me. What can I say? Thank you. Thank you so very much my love. You're wonderful to me. And I love you so...

Bryan is a fine person, but he and I are very different from one another. He is a very strong and domineering man, and I become tired of having him stomp upon my personal opinions. He doesn't seem to realize that I'm not the child he thinks I am—of course, I realize that I am young yet. But, I'm not all that dumb. Well anyway. I'm glad he's my brother—but I could never live with him as husband & wife. We just don't get along well enough among other reasons. I shrink back & let him have his way most of the time. I either shut up and take it, or walk away in anger, as I did tonight. First, he was talking about how much hell he and anybody who'll join him are going to raise when you get here & especially on our wedding day (or the night before).

Anyway, at 8:00 P.M. I took a shower & it felt so good. I guess I am a fanatic about personal cleanliness—in case you hadn't noticed. Simply can't relax if I am dirty, or if I feel dirty. And I could never go to bed without having had a bath!

Your letter today did me a world of good. I was worried about the phone call—I knew you wouldn't have forgotten, and so I knew also that something must be amiss.

We have found a fellow to do the photography on the wedding; I don't think he'll ask too much. Frankly, Pat, we're pinching pennies wherever we can.

Do save whatever money you can, wherever you can. You mustn't spend too much on the honeymoon, Pat. OK? Don't worry—I'm not used to extravagance. Of course, it would be nice to spend our first night in a kind of special place. *But after that, we can camp all the way if you'd like to & it's safe. Weird things happen these days, & we'd have to make sure we could safely camp. And, if we found some nice spots along the way & we could be pretty much away from people, I think it'd be lovely to sleep with you in the open air.* **After all, sleeping bags aren't straightjackets! I'd love to have intercourse with you under the stars.**

...When I was going through exams and studying etc. I couldn't let myself think much about fantasies—not even at night.... You helped me through it with your card, and maps [for the Honeymoon] and the tape, all the love you let me feel. It's such a relief now to be able to lie in bed and think of you—remembering our past experiences and visualizing possible future ones. I love you so. In every way I long for you. I can't wait until the moment when we'll be together again—till I'll hold you once again, and you'll hold me. Well.

I sent a rather 'crude' pen-sketch with the letter and tape I mailed today. I certainly didn't mean for it to be vulgar, or what some people would label as "dirty." I saw a picture in my mind, and my pen wanted to show it to you, even roughly. I explain it to you here because I guess I feel a bit insecure about having sent it. I've never drawn anything like that before, and of course I'm no artist anyway. I hope you don't mind the picture—I hope it doesn't bother you to look at it. The picture in my mind is so peaceful and so full of warmth and love; and I don't know whether I communicated those important dimensions into that sketch. Please tell me what you honestly think—not of the artwork, but of that expression. If you don't like the idea, that's ok. I have the feeling that I'm letting my fear rise above the knowledge of your acceptance of me. Forgive me, if I am.

I guess I was a bit surprised at that sketch. **It came out somewhat the way my songs do—as if I'm not really there—as if I have my eyes closed and someone else is guiding my hand or voice or fingers.** Actually, I didn't mean to make this big deal out of it. I seem to be rambling on about everything tonight.

It's nearing 11:00 P.M. and my hand is very cramped from writing—especially since I peeled and diced two bags of carrots today, and about 6 or 7 potatoes for a stew. That's always "crampy" work. And, my eyelids are drooping. I'm still recovering from a great loss of sleep from the past three weeks. So I'll go on up to bed now.

I look forward to evenings when we'll read together (perhaps read to one another??) and then retire early, together. When I won't go to bed alone. I love you so, Pat. How I miss you. And how happy am I that soon I will be your wife. To love you, and stand-behind you and next to you through bad times and good. To be your companion, your lover. To be your friend, ever devoted. I will be a good wife to you, Pat. I know that, because I know you will be a wonderful husband. I love everything about you. I accept everything about you. I am privileged to have the honor of being able to accept and love you. Shelley xxxxxx

THERE WAS A SENSUOUS DRAWING INCLUDED IN THIS LETTER:

My love, Yes, I guess it may be a bit sensuous, but it is one of my visualizations. Perhaps on our first night [after the day of wedding], at one point you will lay exhausted, your head pillowed by my breasts, your body warmed by mine & mine by yours, our legs intertwined. My pen just began to sketch, so I played along with it.

Yes, it's a very crude reproduction of one of my mind's eye's pictures. I send it to you, with the hope and trust that you will overlook my artistic incapability, and that you will see beyond this, perhaps in your own visualizations.

Our visualizations may be amusing at times, and very lustful, but nonetheless, as lovers we should perhaps show our visualizations somewhat of a reverence. For we see them not from our mind's eye alone, but also from our souls. One day soon perhaps we will sleep in reality as my pen has imagined here. I hope so. I love you so very much, Pat.

Only to you would I ever give such a sketch as this—only for you would I feel as much love, and only by you would I ever be inspired to make such a drawing. I love you. I am totally yours, my darling, body and soul.

Take them. Keep them. Love them.

Sketch of Shelley and I after we have made love.

Thursday, March 19, 1970, 5:30 P.M.

My poor darling! How I longed to close my eyes last night, and then to immediately open them and find myself by your side, holding you, comforting you. You sounded so sad on the phone, and I felt so helpless. I wanted to be there so that you could crawl into my arms and cry, if that's what would have made you feel better. I wanted to pet you and pamper you and sooth your tired eyes and heavy heart.

Bless you, Pat. Your sensitivity and compassion for others brings you much grief and sorrow. My darling love. It won't be so long before I will be there with you, and you'll be able to turn to me for whatever spiritual or physical comfort you may need. I will give you all that I have. I hope it is enough. I love you so…. Enclosed is the engagement announcement… what would you like to register for wedding gifts?

Mother is in one of her moods tonight—I know she's tired and worried about money. But then, sometimes she depresses me so much when she starts harping at me about the kind of person I am, etc. etc. Tonight, she didn't harp very much—she merely shut me out—she acts as if I've done something awful, but she won't let me in on it.

Well, I'm not going to take it out on you. I know what's the matter with her, and I understand it. But I can't help it. Poor mother. I'll only talk about it in person to you, OK?

Pat, I love you so much. You are under stress now, and so am I. I hope you'll be all cheered up by the time this letter arrives.

…Yes, of course you must stay here on the first night you're in town. I should've said something before. I can't wait. When you come in that night, you'll be so tired.

Friday, March 20, 1:45 P.M. [first segment]

I must ask you something, and I'm not going to be diplomatic or anything—I'm just going to ask: May I make a suggestion about your ushers? I think that it would be very appropriate to have Bryan as one of the ushers, and I hope you don't mind my saying so…

I hope you and your Dad are both pulling out of your depressions. If you should need for me to tell you, Pat, then let me say that you can always come to me for comfort or whatever you need. And when you feel low, remember that I love you and always will. Close your eyes and think of me, and feel my heart and love within you. I love you so much. I'm so sorry that I haven't been with you physically in your times of need. But you have my thoughts, Pat, and my acceptance. Your devoted and loving Shelley.

Friday, March 20, 1970, 10:00 P.M. [second segment]

To My Beloved Pat,

Your letter came today but I didn't even know it until 5:45 P.M.! The mailman didn't come till after 3:00 P.M. & mother and I had gone shopping by then. I'd given up on any mail, because it usually gets here before noon. When I let the dogs out this evening, I looked at the mailbox and got a really strong impulse to look inside of it—it was weird. And when your letter looked up at me, I was really surprised. "A bit of ESP?" I don't know. Maybe the love from your letter called to me.

What a beautiful letter this is—yours—and how melancholy. You had me in tears, Pat. I read it ever so slowly—absorbing every thought as fully as possible. I am so impressed by your self-expression. You are an extraordinary man, Pat. Don't let anyone tell you otherwise.

My eyes are very sore and tired tonight. I've been using them far too much. First, with all the reading and studying for exams. During vacation I'd planned on letting them rest. But I have letters to write and books to read. I suppose I'll have to slow up a bit…. Pat, one of my main philosophies—if not, the only specific philosophy I have about life and people is the Golden rule— "do unto others as you would have them do unto you." I believe implicitly in this, and actually when you give it some thought, it is a very "heavy" statement.

I'm bringing this up in regard to my acceptance for you that you value so dearly. When you first began to let me know how profoundly my acceptance of you affects you, I was rather taken aback. I hope this doesn't burst any bubble you may have about me, my darling. You see, I never really thought about how completely I accept you until you pointed it out to me. I guess that you might say that it is sort of natural for me to accept. I realize that that's a pretty strong statement, but I don't mean it to be.

Well, I sort of got side-tracked. I realize that there will be times when you and I disagree, and maybe we'll have arguments & the whole bit. I detest arguing and I'm not very "good" at it. But anyway, I hope that when we do argue, Pat, that you will not feel that I am rejecting you. Nothing could be more inaccurate. **You are the person I accept. Whoever you are, I accept you. Every single quality—all of your weaknesses, as well as your many strengths, I accept.**

Pat, don't hurt yourself. **You don't have to "improve" yourself for me.** Please don't force yourself to call upon haunting sorrows and fears. I fell in love with you when you were here at Thanksgiving—more than I let myself think or admit. And at Thanksgiving you certainly were not at one of the high points of your life. (Struggles in graduate school.) **You don't have to change for me. I don't want you to.** Whatever you feel you need to change within yourself must be for your own peace of mind. Your defense mechanisms seem to be plaguing you rather than protecting you.

Relax. Your mind is really a wonder to me. Sometimes I sit and marvel at you—I really think you must be a genius— whatever that may be. You have such tremendous depth and compassion, and you are not afraid to think your own thoughts, feel your own emotions, and share the feelings of others. *Please don't be afraid of me.* I am not afraid of you… competition may be the key. Well, I do not intend to compete with you, my darling, because there is no reason or need or desire to. In fact, the thought of it leaves me blank…. You must love yourself in order to love others, and what is life if it is not love?

Oh, I'm saved. I know I said one truth—one reality that I can and do live up to: I said "I love you" and Pat, there's nothing more true in this world. Good night. Your Shelley

Saturday, March 21, 1970, 6:00 P.M. [same letter]

You asked me once what I thought about living in California. Well, here goes. Right now, I'm going to exclude every pro-or-con but this one point.

Pat, I am a coward! I have a terror of disasters such as fire, tornadoes, hurricanes, and earthquakes…But I did live through that tornado here in town this summer, and it was a horror. I'll never forget the sound of that wailing wind as long as I live. Bryan went to Alaska on the day before that terrible earthquake (in Alaska) took place. It was five long days before we had the vaguest notion whether he was dead or alive. I couldn't stand not knowing about you.

I hope you are getting a picture of the "real" me through all these letters. Anyway, I'm a number #1 coward & I admit it. Well, that's my only thought on the matter for now. I'd rather discuss it with you. [About staying at Shelley's the first night back in town] I'm sorry you worried about that—I should've said something. We sort of assumed that you'd stay the first night & I should have invited you. Forgive me, I'm sorry.

Another thing. You had that "fantasy" about my career & not being home for you, etc. First—remember that you always come first! Nothing and no one in this world even come close to meaning as much to me as you…. **I am yours alone. I won't desert you, and I won't neglect you. I will try to meet your demands and needs, and I know that you will be a very wonderful husband to me…. I do love you so much. I am thrilled that you love me, Pat. Never, never could I have imagined in my most wonderful dreams as fine a man as you are. That you love me is the most amazing, joyous thing in the world. And that you want me for your own is a wonderful gift to me. Well, I am yours, my darling, Pat.** You are Love. Bless you. I love you.

Sunday, March 22, 1970, 2:15 P.M.

I hope this "entry" doesn't take on a depressed tone—I'm not depressed! But, since Thursday night, I've been having a bad time with my head—my parents say it is NEURALGIA—& it's all due to my stupid sinuses. I switched on the recorder, on which I had excerpts from your first tape playing. I had to lie down for a minute & I thought about how much better I would have felt if you were with me, *just holding me in bed....* *Pat, whenever I feel bad, I just close my eyes and think of you and how much love you have for me. And then my love for you shuts out the bad feeling of the moment.*

[Shelley has been talking with a close girlfriend] ...Of course, when I hear her talk about never having an orgasm during intercourse with her boyfriend, I become a bit afraid myself. I haven't experienced what you might call a total or complete orgasm (I'm sure you know!) And I sometimes worry about it. I know that it could be a big problem in married life for the man and wife not to climax together. And, I wonder if I will climax with you. Pat, I want to give you all that I am & want for us both to be satisfied. Well, I guess it's normal for a girl to worry about it. You and I have been pretty darn frank about our sex fantasies, etc. You've taught me a great deal, whether you know it or not. I'd just die inside if I didn't...well...I don't know how to finish that. I guess I'm afraid, & I need to let you know that, because I need your reassurance. And so, I ask you ahead of time to help me if I do have problems, OK?

Suddenly I realize how much it may have affected me to have had any mention of sex—so suppressed around here. I don't even like to think about how naïve I was, experience-wise when you came along—but I'm glad I was now! So, if I do have some kind of mental blocks about sex, please help me. I guess I remember some pretty bothersome thoughts I had a couple of times there back at Christmas time. I found myself <u>thinking about you</u> & not <u>feeling your caresses or kisses at all.</u> Guess it might have had something to do with an anxious fear that someone might come into the living room and there we'd be in the nude. I guess that it was mainly the first night you asked me if you could kiss me that I felt that fear. Of course, I'd never been kissed like that before, so I was kind of feeling a little strange I guess, wondering if I was doing the "right" thing, etc. And I kept wondering what you were thinking as you kissed me, and I watched your face in a sort of awe. When we were on the floor, I was less afraid than when we later were up on the couch where you again kissed me. I kept wondering what it was that you seemed to enjoy so much about kissing me. I worried about what you thought of me—whether you were wondering how many other lips had caressed this private little world. And I was feeling my nakedness before you and all of my stifling modesty was about to choke me. And in the meantime, my love for you was growing with each caress, because I came to realize that you did enjoy kissing me, as strange as it then seemed.

Pat, I've never played those funny little games with you that most girls & women seem to think are clever. I have to tell you my thoughts because I want you to know them now. I guess that I'm blowing all the rules of feminine flirtation & coyness sky high. But I can't see the point in a relationship if I can't be honest & express myself...I trust you and I love you. And perhaps you'll have some thoughts & reassurances for me.

You might laugh at this & I wouldn't blame you! You asked me to kiss you on that night too—remember? That was the night you proposed to me. Well, I wanted to give you so much pleasure & I was so afraid. Natch, I'd never kissed anyone else either, and I'm sure you're aware of that. I was embarrassed because I was so acutely aware of your experience and my inexperience. I felt clumsy and inept and I really didn't know what to do!!! I don't know whether to laugh or cry at that—maybe I really shouldn't be letting you know what a dumb-dumb I am. I have no way of evaluating my own "sex-appeal" and I have no way of knowing whether I please you unless you show or tell me. I was so afraid that you'd be laughing at me on the inside because I knew you had every reason to. You could probably sense my fear because you whispered, "Don't be afraid." Of course, I don't mind being laughed at when it's open and direct. I don't know. I wanted to give you pleasure and excitement. And, in spite of my worries and fearful thoughts, I did enjoy kissing you; Pat, I love to touch your body everywhere, and I love to feel your erection…. And how I look forward to having you <u>inside</u> of me! I can't tell you how thrilled I became each time your penis grew, so full of potent energy.

And I also can't tell you how I wanted to pull you toward me, and let you come into my open, desiring body that was stirring so wildly with the passion that you aroused.

My thoughts about you "turn me on" and I hope you don't mind my talking this way. Maybe it isn't very feminine or appealing to you—but I really don't think you object do you? At least, judging from some of your very exciting letters, and your comments on a few of mine. I would guess that you don't mind.

I just love you so much, Pat, I could never think of any other man. If I've never told you, let me tell you now that my life and love will always be devoted to you—my faithfulness to you will always be complete and willing. I have never had intercourse before, and so you will be the only man ever to "HAVE" me. That means a lot to me. Perhaps it means something to you too, I don't know.

Boy, I just read over what I wrote & I certainly am kind of dumbfounded at my BOLDNESS. I sure hope that you're not upset with me. My insecurity perhaps?—is leaking out all over the place with every stroke of this pen. I'm almost afraid to mail this…. Please don't be, well, I was going to say <u>mad</u> at me, but I don't think that's what I mean. I don't mean to be erotic. I was just saying what *I* was thinking, OK?

Of course, there's no point in denying that I think about you that way and often, too. But my thoughts always have a rich, warm, aura of love permeating them. I love you so deeply, Pat. And when I'm 80 years old, I'll still be courting you and flirting with you & putting your favorite perfume on just for you.

I love you, Patric Spencer. You're the dearest person on earth & if nobody in the world knows it, I do. But I'll bet that <u>everybody</u> who knows you sees that you're a rare kind of man. And how lucky am I that YOU love me! Wow! Take care my darling. Are you thinking of me? Love you xxxxx

Well, I went downstairs at about 4:00 P.M. and fed the animals, etc., fed myself. It seems that we all pick different times around here to be hungry. I don't like that, but…

The damned head business is starting up again—I was free of any pain almost the entire time I wrote to you this afternoon. It's been a cold, rainy day today, very dreary and dismal. The weather has been absolutely unreal and everybody's sick it seems. Too bad well, I'm thankful for this cold vaccine so that I don't get a cold. It takes my voice usually three weeks after I've recovered from a cold to get back to normal. That's a bad deal and I'm not taking any chances for my boards. I'm going to stop now. I'll finish tomorrow and mail it. I love you, Patric Spencer.

During May we in the Chorale, are singing "Carmina Burana" with the symphony at Music Hall (It's a ballet) … Do you realize what a hell May will be? I have, on the 24th of April, to sing in a big concert that our church and another church are giving. Then we have a big concert at school. Of course, exams are the first week of June, and during May not only do I have voice boards, but also piano boards. Oi veh, oi veh, oi veh.

Did you say you know someone who's getting married in June? Who? Me??! Mr. and Mrs. W. Patric SPENCER—or Shelley Spencer.

Love Shelley

March 23, 1970, 1:15 P.M. (Monday)

This morning I finished washing down the remaining cupboards, drawers in the kitchen—that's really tiring. As for me head, don't worry about it because it's getting better. Last night it was really bad—I felt like crying not only because of the pain but because it was so frustrating. But today I've have very few "attacks" and although they're severe and longer lasting, they're so infrequent that it's really not too bothersome at all. Boy, is my poor ol' head ever tender! I don't think I'll have any more trouble with it! Hooray!!

I was looking back at my diary entries from Xmas time, and I really feel that our love has grown tremendously since then. That's very exciting because sometimes people can't seem to communicate when they're <u>together</u>, let alone more than 1000 miles away from each other. I don't feel as far from you as that, Pat. I feel very very close to you spiritually—a very rare kind of communion within our souls has started to take place I think, and the closeness of our minds and hearts—souls—makes the physical distance between us seem less. Just think of how our love will grow when we are together!

Your letter to my mother came today (the note). And your letter came to me today also—the one you wrote on Thursday. I feel so much better after having read it, Pat. I was so worried about your low, low spirits. Thank you for the wonderful letter, Pat. Your letters are so warm and loving. You communicate your feelings and thoughts beautifully, and my heart sings the song that you create in my soul. I love you so much. My Pat.

I knew I'd receive something from you today, for I dreamed it last night. Pat, you spoil me with all of your attention—and I love it! But don't wear yourself out by staying up late writing to me, and don't neglect other things that you want to do, ok? You're so very precious.

I took the wild flowers that you sent and pressed them between wax paper (you know, with the steam iron) to preserves them. They're so <u>YOU</u>, and I love them—that's why I pressed them.

I have to stop for a moment. Well, I was going to clean the bathroom, but it's occupied so I can't! Of course, I'm <u>terribly disappointed</u>! Pretty soon, I'll take this out and mail it.

Pat, do take care of yourself. You don't have to do anything extra to prepare for my arrival! I love you so much. I guess I've said a few things in this letter that I've never told anyone—talked about things that I would discuss with no one but you. I trust you, Pat. I really don't know what to say to close this. I hope you haven't minded going through this <u>manuscript</u>—I hope that all the sex talk hasn't disturbed you. I hope that I haven't brought a frown to your face by being so bold.

I need your thoughts, Patric. You don't have to hurry them to me or anything. I promise that I won't worry about your reaction, OK? I miss you terribly, and how I long for you—of course, I'm so discreet about it (that's supposed to be a joke). Bless you, Pat. Thank you for putting up with these long letters. I hope this hasn't been too boring.

Take care, my darling. I miss you. I think of you day and night, always lovingly. My Fiancé, my Patric. Think of me, Love. Thank you, Pat, for being you. I love you.

With all my love, your ever devoted Shelley xxxxx

Tuesday, March 24, 1970, 8:30 P.M.

My Dearest Shelley,

Tonight I received both **your 26-page letter,** and your 16-page letter, along with the silver brochures and wedding announcement. I have only an hour before bedtime but I felt like making some kind of reply.

But, I must warn you, I have a strange mood surrounding me. I feel like a pilot of a jet plane: flying upside down through a twisting canyon; my mind is running like four computers, trying to handle a whole array of inputs, and attempting to do it logically and efficiently. Go, go, go, it says...Do, do, do. Run, run, and run. Look here, look there, look everywhere. Watch out to your left, to your right, now behind you. Now this way, Run, Stop. Duck. Jump. Close your eyes, keep alert!! Get the feeling??

Let me handle as many of your inquiries as I can. I will put them in no particular order. I admit it is a hasty way of writing, but things are moving so fast these days, I worry if I don't do them now, I don't know when I'll have time to get to them.

I don't have time at the moment to discuss Mary's problems. Maybe in a later letter. Personally, I think she is headed straight for trouble of the kind you mentioned. But it is wholly understandable. Her behavior is quite typical of the behavior of children from strict and repressive homes.

About Bryan, Yes, as I mentioned in the letter previous to this, I definitely would like his assistance, valuable assistance, as my head usher. I have no qualms about his appearance. He can be himself. I wouldn't think of asking him to be any other way. If he feels more comfortable with a haircut and beard trim, fine. Yes, I had thought we would wear white jackets during the ceremony. I hope this will not be a burden to anyone.

Flower suggestion. 1) With reference to a going away corsage, a bridal bouquet can be made in such a way as the center part can later be detached, used (or is actually a corsage, and the remainder may be thrown, as is the custom). 2) I can sense your mother/parents are concerned about financing this venture. Therefore, I recommend a) I have an account with Louis the Florist: have all the floral arrangements charged to me, and I will pay it off on time. A) Argument: your parents will have to support you when you return to Our Town. Fair is Fair. B) My mother is not rich, but she is more than willing to assist financially with the reception …particularly the Champagne. Talk to your mother into letting my mother help. C) If it can be arranged, put the photographer on account, and I'll pay for him too. Remember: this wedding should be an enjoyable affair for your parents too; not a financial crisis.

Sex. With you Shelley, there are no ideas, no visualizations, no words or phrases that are not fitting and appropriate. You have all the freedom in the world you need, to say whatever you wish at any time. I fully accept your thoughts, and am actually quite pleased to have the benefit of them. I realize, more and more, that in your life, sex was a repressed subject, and that you are hesitant and somewhat apprehensive to deal so openly and boldly as we have so often, in such a short span of time.

I can no more tell you to stop worrying about your future sexual performance, than you from my perspective, that I will certainly help you in overcoming sexual difficulties, and/or learning what I know about the sexual world. Orgasm, a really deep one, is something that takes time and patience to develop. Six months is certainly not uncommon. A year is still average. And for many couples, it takes years. I don't think we fall into that category: our communication is too open, honest, and direct. I should estimate between one and six months for us.

For your information, it has been quite a while since I have had any real intercourse worth mentioning; so it will take me some time, also to readjust to the new situation. Just don't expect too much from our first few experiences. Then, if very little happens, like orgasms, you won't be too disappointed. And, if everything goes well, we will be extra excited.

Frankly, I sense that you have a very strong sexual instinct and warm orientation toward sex, even though you were so "naïve" until a few months ago. You turn me on more than any woman I have ever met. So, just give us both, you and I, a chance to develop sexual harmony. It rarely happens overnight. But, I am confident we shall one day so experience sex such as very very few couples allow to themselves; key: love, and extremely effective communion, and communication.

With reference to sexual fantasies, I am afraid events are moving so fast and in so many directions these days, that I have almost no time, no proper psychological mind set, in order to conjure them up. I know though, that once I am with you, my mind will utilize its full powers of imagination.

A thought: My friend Betty Barton is getting married on June 19th. That means I can leave Los Angeles, immediately after work on Friday, June 5th. It is therefore possible I might arrive in Our Town late Monday night. If so, could I stay over at your house both Monday and Tuesday nights?? Please? I could really use that kind of relaxation after such a hurried trip of 2400 miles. I don't need to remind you of how little I am able to relax once I move over to my parents' apartment.

Thought. I was with you today, during the hours I speculated that you and your mother would be having lunch with my mother at the Play boy Club. I hope all went well. I didn't sense any negative vibrations in my thoughts as I thought of you.

Thought. Thanks for your suggestion regarding future telephone calls. I will have to wait and see. It does seem that since we decided to get married (this summer), that the more expenses keep popping up from the woodwork. And, it will be just a little tighter to cover everything we have planned. However, there is great need for overtime work at the bank, and the Navy has scheduled extra Drill Weekends, during April, May and June. So, I have a fair chance of earning a few extra hundred dollars. Most of the Honeymoon Trip can be charged on credit cards, if need be, such as gasoline, motels. Actually, the trip will not be particularly expensive. Gas will run about $40.00, food about $50 to $60.00 dollars, motels: $40.00 or $50.00. **All told maybe the trip will cost $200.00 or $250.00, which is cheap. [The actual cost, from**

carefully kept records, was $207.46!] I know—I have driven across the country 36 times already! The enclosed drawings are from my sister Leslie, age 9. I thought you might like to see them, and then return them to me. She has been asking all kinds of questions about you and the wedding.

About last week's depression. I am feeling quite a bit better this week, thanks to you. I feel so good, that I sometimes wonder how I can fall so low during other periods. Your love and comfort was of great help to me. Thank you, a thousand times. Dad is much better too, and seems quite elated to have his children with him again. (During one of their visits— usually about ten days.)

Speaking of the children, they are having a wonderful time, and are happy to be here. I am very happy too. I love them, and like having them with us. I feel more like a second father, than a brother. Tonight, they all went to a movie. On Thursday evening, we are all going down to Disneyland. I just love that place. I think you will too.

Each night the kids compete to see who gets to sleep with me. The first night it was Leith, my brother. Last night it was Leslie, my sister. Tonight it's Leith again. When they are in bed with me, then I really feel like a father. I enjoy doing for them, and talking with them, now that they are older.

I am sorry that you have had such pain in your head. I am really a coward when it comes to pain. It hurts. When I am with you, I will give you lots of Tender Loving Care, like holding you, rubbing your neck and forehead, if that seems to help, and kisses. It may not make the pain go away completely, but it may dull it, and make it more tolerable.

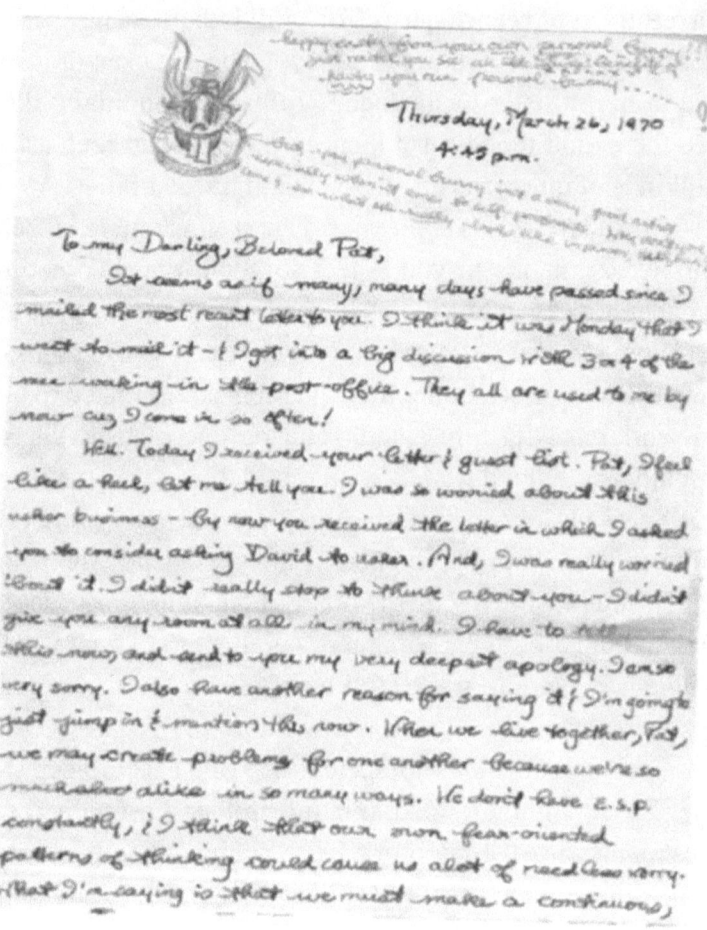

Beautiful pencil drawing of an Easter Bunny's head

Happy Easter from your own <u>personal bunny!!</u>

Just wait until you see all the "Fringe Benefits" of having your own personal bunny, and saying: "but, your personal bunny isn't a very good artist, especially when it comes to self-portraits. Why don't you come & see what she <u>really looks like in person, huh?</u>

<u>Huh?</u>

Thursday, March 26, 1970, 4:45 P.M.

To my Darling, Beloved Pat,

It seems as if many, many days have passed since I mailed the most recent letter to you. I think it was Monday that I went to mail it—& I got into a big discussion with 3 or 4 of the men working in the Post Office. They all are used to me by now because I come in so often!

Well, today, I received your letter & guest list. Pat, I feel like a heel, let me tell you. I was so worried about this usher business—by now you received the letter in which I asked you to consider asking Bryan to usher. And, I was really worried about it. I didn't really stop to think about you—I didn't give you any room at all in my mind. I have to tell you this now, and send to you my deepest apology. I am so very sorry. I also have another reason for saying it & I'm going to just jump in & mention this now. When we live together, Pat, we may create problems for one another because we're so much alike in so many ways. We don't have E.S.P. constantly & I think that our own fear-oriented patterns of thinking could cause us a lot of needless worry. What I'm saying is that we must make a continuous, conscientious effort to communicate the little doubts, fears, & tensions. We may surprise ourselves. Well, for example: you were evidently very worried about the first night that you arrive in our city, and you wanted to stay at my house but you took a while to ask. In the meantime, you worried & had bad daydreams about it. And all the while, I stupidly put off inviting you—very honestly I now admit—because I was a little bit anxious as to whether you'd think me too bold. So there we both sat ignorant that we both were worrying about the same thing. I apologize for not inviting you sooner. This time, it's my fault. But, do you see what I mean? We can't let these little things occur, because they're unnecessary.

And, if we're really hesitant about something, let's give one another at least a <u>hint</u>—sometimes I can't communicate a fear or worry unless someone actually coaxes it out of me no matter how much I may have wanted to talk about it. That's insecurity! For a while we might fool ourselves into thinking that our very <u>real</u> and deep love for one another will be a magic cure-all for our little quirks (?)—but there is no magic remedy. As soon as we become blind to the reality of our own limits—as well as becoming blind to <u>each other's limits</u>— well, we're heading for trouble. We just can't take things for granted. And I know myself well enough to know that sometimes you might have to remind me of this paragraph. Please do, when you feel that you need to. OK?

I guess I just want to thank you, Pat, for showing to me (without your realizing it, I guess)—that I can be really unfair at times. There's a word for that—I think I'm calling myself a jerk. I realize my mistakes; I apologize for it. And I promise that I'll try not to let it happen again.

Thank you for your list & for the information about the ushers. No, I don't mind that you have four—I think it's very nice—and I deeply appreciate you for having asked Clifford, too. What a love you are! My precious Patric.

I was thinking about perfuming your dad's letter— Somehow, I just couldn't because I was afraid that if the letter turned out to be a dud, the scent wouldn't help matters. Anyway, he'll probably be grateful for having no perfume now—& he'll remember back blissfully when he could actually smell food & coffee in the morning rather than Pat's wife's Chanel # 5. Don't worry—I don't use that much…. At any rate, I'm glad he liked the letter. Thank you for mentioning it, Pat, because I was pretty anxious. The letter never seemed to express what I wanted it to.

I guess you're wondering about my impressions of your mother. Well, I had a very nice time—the 3 of us (my mother too) went to the Play Boy Club [**PB's were very popular in the 1970's; mother's office was in the same building, and the boss had a membership card**]. and it was nice—I enjoyed it. I don't really know what to say—your mother was very nice to us & I appreciated her apparent ease at keeping the conversation going. She & my mother did most of the talking. By the way—if your mother comments that she's not sure whether you're marrying a girl or a <u>mouse</u>, don't get mad at her. I hardly said a word & I felt like a real dumb-dumb. I felt very shy—I usually do around new people, especially when the person is important. Well, it isn't <u>every day</u> that a girl meets her future mother-in-law. I hope we'll get along. I hope I didn't make too bad an impression. But, well, I'm not the type who worries about "spilled milk" most of the time. I was excited to be in her presence because she is attached to you—I mean she's a part of you (or vice-versa). I felt close to you—as if you were looking over my shoulder, quietly giving me encouragement & friendship. I guess I miss you very much, my darling.

Do you want to hear something funny? This quarter, (I mean this past quarter) as you probably know, was a very demanding one, and for me, was extremely trying, emotionally. Patric, you keep calling me away from my studies! And I love it!!! However, I got really nervous about my grades because as hard as I worked, I just felt very apathetic just the same. Well, I ended up pulling a 3.52 score—the highest quarter average for me yet! I'm still laughing—got my grades yesterday. I brought my accumulative grade point average up to a 3.48—last time it was 3.47. I think it's really funny. This quarter will be a real trial.

My parents are arguing again. It's been so pleasant around here lately (sarcasm)....

Gayle came home Tuesday afternoon—a very exciting surprise! So we're inseparable. She went to school with me today to see about transferring to school here in the autumn. I'm so thrilled about that. She'll go with me tomorrow—I'm only going to chorale.

Forgive me for not sending you anything—even a card—for Easter. I didn't know about the mail, etc. I'm not the most conscientious person about sending holiday cards either (like Easter, Saint Patrick's Day, etc.). I am sorry. I think I might call you. Have to count me money. Please forgive me. I do have your birthday present ordered. I sure hope I get it soon so you'll get it on time! My darling, I love you so very much.

I can't tell you how excited I am about having Gayle here. We're so very close—I guess she's getting used to the idea of having her best friend being a "married lady." Pat, I have something very very important to say: We've changed our plans drastically, as you know. But, I'm telling you that we can't change one plan, no matter what: I have to come back here to school in September. This is more important to me than our vow that I'd remain a virgin—so you know it's important.

I also know that I'm not going to want to leave you. But I'm asking you—if I'm not quite firm enough with myself when the time comes for leaving comes close, please, my love, be firm with me. It means so much to me to finish here—I'll go into all the somewhat incredible reasons when we're together. You mean the world to me, Pat, and you're the main reason I <u>have</u> to come back. So, I'm saying to you now that I do have to come back—it means too much to both you and me to give up. OK? OK? I'm going to close this soon—yes, I know I always say that 13 pages before signing off, but I mean it now. I have to go to choir after while & I really haven't finished my dinner yet. Are you in shock over the length of this letter?

I hope that the children's visit there is going all right. Are you enjoying them?

Pat, I love you so very much. You mean everything to me. If you ever need something from me that I'm not giving, please come to me. Don't suffer inside—I couldn't bear to hurt you because you are dearest person in the world. You've had such a hard life, and now I want to fill your life with as such happiness and contentment as I can. Help me to do so, my love, by always feeling at home with me—by helping to build your home in my heart into whatever you need it to be. And I will do the same.

Truth and honesty are so very important. Let's never talk about things that bother us about each other to anyone else before we talk it over with one another. Let's never stab one another in back. Let's never let problems drive us apart—but rather, let's permit problems to drive us toward one another. Pat, I can't even bear the thought of life without you. Never worry about my fidelity—you have in me a wife who will be true to you in <u>every way</u>. I love you so.

As the days become fewer until we shall be with one another again, well, I miss you more & more. My thoughts are always with you—my love & my concern for you. I smile when I think of you—even if a vagrant tear manages to fall at the thought of my beloved Pat, I smile. I will always love you, my darling, no matter how far apart we may be. Perhaps your past sorrows will help you to appreciate your future joys all the more. I pray that I will always possess whatever it is about me that inspires you, which draws your love. I am not lonely, Pat. Loneliness, I think, results when a person has no-one, near or far away to love—I mean in a man-woman relationship. **Well, Pat, if this is so, then I can say to you that no matter how many miles separate us, you have my deepest love—and so, my beloved Patric, you'll never be lonely again.** Because I do love you so very much. Take care. Lovingly, Yours xxxx Shelley xxx

April 13, 1970, A Card

"I don't know what's with you!" followed inside by: "But I wish it was ME! XXXX" Inside: My Darling Patric, when I went to buy a book just a few minutes ago, this card said, "Hey, send me to Pat." So I am. It's 2:00 P.M., Thursday, and I am in the library—with all my books staring at me. But I miss you very much right now, so I wanted to talk to you.

I hope that you're feeling much better now. I've been thinking about you all day, and last night I dreamed about you. Heather was in my dream—the three of us were at your father's house. And when I woke up, you were on my mind. I love you, Pat, and today is a very lonely one. But I have your picture with me, and your love for me keeps me going. Bless you, Pat. This is probably confusing for you to read.

There are so many things going through my mind now. What are you doing, as I write this? We have a beautiful love, Patric, and nothing could ever change my feelings for you—unless of course, the "change" was loving you more each day. And I do. Think happy, my darling, for you have my heart and my love with you always. Lovingly Shelley.

Monday, April 13, 1970, 6:30 P.M.

Patric,
Seven letters upon a piece of paper can mean the world
when they symbolize you.

They symbolize Love, Beauty, and Life.
They symbolize Peace, Quiet, Joy, Excitement, Love.
They symbolize Friend, Companion, Comfort, Love.
They symbolize Husband, Partner, Mate, Love.
They symbolize Father, Love, Life, Husband, Man.
Patric. You, my darling. And how much I love you.

To my Beloved Patric,

Two short months from today, you will be a Married Man. And I, a married…uh, and I will be married to you. Actually, I didn't really intend to begin this as a comedy, but when I came to that part above where "woman" should have been the next word, I had to stop and think. Somehow, it didn't really seem to fit me as a description. Well.

I've been thinking of you so much today, in a rather vague, indescribable sort of way. "Two months" kept running through my mind. 61 days, 56 or 57 days until you get here. I wonder which day I'll be more excited—the day you arrive or the day we marry. I guess in several ways, it's a toss-up because I'll be so excited on both days in rather dissimilar ways. Well, I'm sure you may understand what I'm trying to say.

I have been thinking about coming home and writing to you, and so here I am. One letter is on its way to you now. But I feel bad about the number of days that have passed since you heard from me, and so I suppose I'm trying to do both apologize and make it up to you.

But my mind isn't functioning appropriately for letter writing. In my mind are extensive impressions that are accompanied by no words. I think about our fast-approaching wedding day. I think of your arrival. I think of our First Night. I think of our Honeymoon trip. And of course, I think of California.

I am also thinking of things between now and your arrival—the addressing of invitations; finding a minister (!); having the picture taken for the paper; ordering flowers; buying gifts for my attendants; money (!); catering; not to mention the big program the choir participates on April 24th; May Festival, the big spring concert at school; piano boards;

<u>voice boards</u> (gulp); exams; recitals; etc., etc., etc. Plus, all the reading for Traditions I have as well as Theory assignments... Well, I guess that things will all work out in the long run. Right now, I'm fed up with school as a matter of fact!

I just realized, in thinking about all that I have to do, that I do have several duties to attend to yet this evening. So, I think I will stop this for a while.

First—how was the wedding you were in—wasn't it this past weekend? Or is it this coming weekend? I've forgotten. I also have to add something to the last letter: I told you that I really got out of the mood to write last week, and I gave you the reasons regarding all the tremendous emotional stress.

But I neglected to mention something— *"your <u>letters</u> really affected me deeply. Friday's letter was beautiful. But in the first days of the week, it was the other two—those that arrived Monday. They are so beautiful, Pat, you really swept me off my feet, love! I don't exactly know how to explain this. Naturally, I <u>know</u> that I would have been able to respond to your letters had I not been under such strain. Well, I guess that amidst all the strife and conflict, these two letters came to me and sparkled in the night, brightening the darkness that surrounds me in the day. I clung to them, and they became so precious because they were <u>you</u>, Pat. They smiled at me, and promised the soon-to-come reality of your fantasies."*

My darling, I really don't know how to express my feelings. It's not that I wasn't just as sure of your love—oh boy—that's not what meant at all—let's try again. My pen's not doing so well. Neither is my brain.

Let's just say that although I felt no insecurity whatsoever, your thoughts <u>reassured</u> me in a time when I needed extra love. You gave to me so much, Pat; you constantly give so much more to me than I would ever dream of asking you...

than I would ever think of myself. I am unaccustomed to being so showered with affection and attention. You are more than kind to me. You are…I don't know why I never can come up with the words to describe what you are to me. Can you imagine what you mean to me? I really don't know whether, from your point of view, you could really fathom how much I adore and love you, Pat. My darling. I love you so much.

My darling, I must stop now. I don't know whether I'll write more tonight—I really don't feel up to it now. I am disappointed—I thought that perhaps the expressions would begin to flow again, as they frequently have before. But I have sat here and pondered and fumbled. And to no worthwhile end, it seems. I'm sorry, Pat. I hope these two letters—the one I mailed today and this one—haven't been too disappointing. But I think they have been. So.

I am soon going to bed, although it's only nearing 8:00 P.M. I'm tired. If you can, try to imagine the depth of the thoughts I'll be thinking of you. Try and feel the love I send you, not only tonight, but as you read this. Think of how much I love you, Pat and when you're in bed at night, let the kiss of peace softly caress your cheek. Peace—the inner peace that comes from knowing that you—YOU, Pat—are loved deeply, freely and perpetually. Each day I love you more. And so good night my precious love. Sleep well, my darling. I am yours. And I love you very very much. Xxxxxxx.

I've been thinking of you ever since I stopped writing, and I am in the mood to write some more.

Lately, many thoughts have been going through my mind. For some reason, a great deal of that thinking has been about life, and the meaning or purpose of life. I suppose I have been influenced by the books which I've had to read for Traditions, such as "<u>Winesburg, Ohio</u>," "<u>Snows of Kilamanjaro</u>" "<u>Uncle Tom's Children</u>." There are others, but I haven't read them yet.

Life and death are constant topics in each of these. What is death? What is life? And how can people take them lightly? Well, I don't know. Sometimes a person must corner himself and force himself to face questions in his mind. And I don't like to think about death—who does? I have to be honest— when I think about death I do feel a fear inside. But that fear stems from the hope within me that my life will have been as meaningful and as <u>full</u> as possible. Too many times young people die—babies, children, young adults, etc.—before they've really had a <u>chance</u>. And yet, they still manage in many instances to have lived full enough lives so as to have made some sort of impression upon another person. I had to stop for a moment. I haven't read what I've written, so I'll just keep on going. I can't seem to grasp one idea and complete it—I just keep floating...

Although I feel a rather doubting fear sometimes when thinking of death, I usually don't sit around and let myself get all "hung up" over it. I <u>never have</u>.

I love you so very much, Pat. When you have trouble sleeping—when you miss me in bed—close your eyes and lie there for a while. Pretend that you are not alone, but rather, that I am near you, watching you as you begin to drift off to sleep. For, you really won't be pretending at all, my darling. I love you with my heart and mind now, even if I am unable to love you physically. Let me gaze upon you in your mind. Let me hear your breathing become relaxed with sleep. Let me look at your face as you sleep. Let me smooth your hair and touch your hand ever so slightly. I will do all of these things in your mind with my mind, if you will let me. And very soon, you shall have me near you physically as you slowly fall asleep. I very much would like to sooth you into slumber when you come back in June. I love to watch you sleep, Pat.

Life is so precious, don't you think, Pat? Life. To me, life has too much to offer; it is too blessed to waste. I will never know the answers to the questions in my mind, and it is better that way. I do not have the security of a religion which binds me to questions, which forbids me to doubt. That kind of security is a prison. I will not sit around and worry about whether or not there is an afterlife, because if there isn't then all these moments of worry have been wasted; if there is, then I may go into "afterlife" with the full benefit of having completely lived my precious life. In a way, I cannot believe that there is afterlife; in another way, I cannot doubt it. Soon, too soon (whether it may be 100 years or 10,000, it is too soon) I will find out what death is. God help me not to ever discover what living-death is.

I guess that through the years my ideas will grow and become more concrete concerning religion. I hope I always leave enough for myself to question my own ideas. I suppose that many of my friends think that…well I lost that train of thought. Excuse me.

I don't believe in allowing fear to dominate me. I am basically a "good" person, I suppose, and I let my "conscience" guide me. I do not base my actions upon a fear of supernatural retribution. I do believe in an existing something that I call "God." I look at this "being" as a friend in a way. I don't fear it any more than I fear my own conscience. If I am "wrong"—if there is an Almighty God that rules overall and sends people to hell or heaven—well, I really can't see myself fearing this God either.

I live by the Golden Rule—I believe in it implicitly, but I'm not fool enough to carry on about how I <u>always</u> follow it because I know very well that I don't. But if I am to be damned because I cherish life too much to worry about heaven or hell, or because I am not a believer in one specific God to whom I must kneel and worship and pray humbly—well I guess I've damned myself. Pray-yes, I do that I think. I am seeing more and more and more that I am becoming strong enough to stare at fear and study it. In ways, I have been afraid to doubt the existence of God. But that's me—a long story, I guess. (?) I figure that if God's Perfection, then he not only understands doubt, but also encourages them. Well, anyway.

I don't know how I got into that. I guess all this time I've been thinking about the new meanings—or newly fulfilled dimensions—that my life has been taking on. Pat, you have added more to my life in a few short months than I've ever had in my whole life. I love you so, Pat. My darling. **Sometimes I am nearly overcome with awe...that you should love me makes my life more meaningful in these early young years that I ever thought or dreamed it could be in a whole lifetime.**

Together, we can explore all of the dimensions which open themselves to us. We can seek together. We will find means of communication that will unite our souls more deeply each day. Our home will be filled with the peacefully quiet overtones of our love's harmony.

My darling Pat. I do love you. Never doubt that. Please never fear me, or what I will think of you if you displease me. We will disagree, and perhaps you will be angry with me at **times**, and I with you. But anger does not diminish love—it doesn't have to. I will never desert you, Pat. I will never betray you, or deliberately hurt you. I am prepared to <u>work</u> toward making our relationship full and complete. I will try—I will do my very best. I have so much love to give to you, and I need so much in return. You give so much to me, Pat, more than I ever dreamed existed.

My darling, you have in me love to last your lifetime. I love you Pat. Thank you for letting me love you. Thank you for loving me. Take care of yourself, please. I love you so very much. And now, I will turn out the lights and close my eyes. And you will be with me, watching me sleep. I love you; I love you. Good night, my wonderful friend. Goodnight my sweet love. Goodnight my Pat xxxxxxxxx Your Shelley.

Wednesday, April 15, 1970, 7:00 P.M.

My Beloved Patric,

How are you, my darling? Thank you so very much for the telephone call last night. I knew the minute the phone rang that you were calling. But I feel so guilty because I think that if I'd written to you sooner, you might not have needed to call. I am sorry. I was hoping that you wouldn't worry or get upset, but I certainly can't blame you for doing just those things. At any rate, I hope that you felt as wonderful as I did after the call. I love you so very much Pat, and I miss you.

Things are really moving around here-I told you about all the housework I did Thursday (yard work, rather). Last night by the time I went to bed, I had addressed about 64 envelopes altogether—and had "stuffed" and completed about 44 of those, I think. It's a job, but I enjoy it. I've been using this pen—black ink, you know.

Yesterday my mother waxed the living room floor, so later on, I polished it with the floor-polisher. It looks lovely! It's kind of a long job to polish floors like that, but I really enjoy doing it because of the fact that the work really shows itself off beautifully.

Today, I drove to school and parked way down the street to save the parking money. I was very pleased to find the place. Then, Agnes and I cut our 8:00 A.M. classes and went up to the Bookstore and killed a whole hour. It was great fun—I love to look at cards and books etc. I bought my parents and Bryan and Theresa's anniversary cards. April 16 is the date of both anniversaries. It's Bryan and Theresa's seventh and Mother and Pop's 31st! That's pretty good, I think! Since my Dad works tomorrow, they celebrated tonight while he's home—and I could kill them because I didn't get their present yet and they didn't tell me they were gonna do that!

Well. When we celebrate our 31st anniversary, you'll be 61 and I'll be 51. My parents are 59—their birthdays are three days apart. At 10:00, Agnes and I went back to the car—about a ten-minute leisurely walk. It was gorgeous day out! The trees are blossoming, etc. and it's all so beautiful. How I love to see the leaves come back.

Just had an interruption—Mary called about the slumber party Friday night (at which I can't stay past midnight because I've got a heavy schedule this weekend.) Mary has shingles! I told her not to have the party, but she is determined. She is trying to see if she can postpone it.

Anyway, Agnes and I drove over to General Hospital today to "donate" our blood—for $15.00 [Shelley had a very rare type—I think O +]. I really felt guilty about taking the money but...We went in and they had to take a little sample to check on the iron content. Agnes passed with flying colors. They took our temperatures—hers was 98.6 and mine was 98.2 (pretty good for me—it's usually lower!) The lady also took my blood pressure and both my parents and I were surprised to find out that my pressure is low—100 over 70. (Normal 120/80.)

Actually, there's really nothing to be done for that—it's nothing of any great importance in my case. But then when she tested the iron content, the blood got **all** goofed up in the solution which means there's something amiss, so she took another more accurate test in a little machine. "Just like on TV" I said, and she agreed.

Everybody was really nice. When the test came out, she charted and checked about three times and told me that I'd just barely passed. She said, "Are you sure you want to donate?" so, now my parents are aggravated because my iron content is "so low."

And they're saying I have to start iron tablets and special vitamins etc. which is a bunch of bull. I told them that it couldn't have been all that low or they wouldn't have accepted it!

But, I have been getting too tired lately and so I'll probably have to get it back up there. But I really enjoyed that experience today—it was very interesting and I about drove everybody crazy asking questions! I had to lie on that darned bed so long and suddenly all these TV guys were in there, talking about putting me on TV. I was so embarrassed! But luckily they wanted a shot of the blood coming from the person and I was already finished. So, they took a shot of the guy next to me and took pictures of my feet! They were from WXEK and I'd seen them all before [Shelley had made several singing appearances on that TV station] but I'm sure they didn't know me. I was kidding around with them—so embarrassed because I couldn't get up. I had a great time and everybody laughed at me because they kept making fun of my soon to be "famous" feet! When I tried to get up, I got pretty woozy so they slapped a wad of smelling salts on cotton in my hand and told me to take an occasional whiff. Ugh. I really had a great time goofing around with all these guys! **The director sat on the bed with me—are you jealous? I wish it'd been you. Of course, in that case, you wouldn't have been sitting very long...**

I got a terrible craving for meat after that—minced ham of all things! So, I bought some (and some salami) on the way home. Natch, I came home to find that mother for the celebration, had bought the best steak I've ever had—rib roast. Boy, was that good! Anyway, I really ate meat tonight as if it were going out of style. Me—the pro-vegetarian. Oh well.

9:20 Mary called back and she's going to go ahead with the party—just 5 of us will be there. Mary, her roommate Libby, Mary, Charla Anne, Darby, and I. It will be the last slumber party I go to as a single girl! How about that! ….

I'm quite tired tonight—poor old body's trying to figure out what happened to that blood today! I'm so glad I did it. If I hadn't needed money so badly I wouldn't have "sold," but would have given. As a matter of fact, I overheard Agnes talking to a nurse and I thought the nurse said she never heard of paying students for the blood. So, I thought I was "giving," after all. Until it was all over and I was told where to pick up the money. At least I know I would have given anyway for free. That reassures me.

My darling Pat.

Do you know that last night on the phone you said something to me that you never did before? The very last word you said, as a matter of fact, so I couldn't even show you my appreciation and recognition of it. You called me "Hon" [short for Honey]. I really was surprised—I didn't expect it. I liked it—it sounded nice the way you said it. I like the way you say everything.

My beloved Patric.

How do I respond to the three beautiful most recent letters? Where can I ever find words to express my feelings? Where can I find an extra hour to relax enough to write that way? I want to make an appropriate reply to these letters as much as I feel you would like for me to.

Know that I cherish these letters beyond description; know that I think replies in my mind that never want to be expressed verbally. And above all, my darling, Pat, know that when I am with you, you will find my responses and replies waiting to bestow themselves into your heart and soul and body. To look at you, to touch you physically right now as much as I do spiritually. We will provide a union for these two kinds of loves, so that they will not have to remain separate any longer.

I love you so very much, Pat. When you have trouble sleeping—when you miss me in bed—close your eyes and lie there for a while. Pretend that you are not alone, but rather, that I am near you, watching you as you begin to drift off to sleep. For, you really won't be pretending at all, my darling. I love you with my heart and mind now, even if I am unable to love you physically.

Let me gaze upon you in your mind. Let me hear your breathing become relaxed with sleep. Let me look at your face as you sleep. Let me smooth your hair and touch your hand ever so slightly. I will do all of these things in your mind with my mind, if you will let me. I love you so very much. And now, I will turn out the light, and close my eyes. And you will be with me, watching me sleep. I love you; I love you. Goodnight, my wonderful friend. Good night, my sweet love. Good night, my Pat. XXXXXXXX Your Shelley.

May 4, 1970, 8:35 P.M. (Monday)

To my Darling Patric,

Well, how's this for elegant stationery? Hope you don't mind too much. This is what you call desperation! You see, I have a term paper coming up in Traditions, so I need the notebook paper for that. I'm sure that the paper doesn't much matter to you—at least you've never indicated displeasure at some of the junk I've used so far. Well, variety is the spice, and all that rot!

Today, your note came—the one you mailed on Thursday. Thank you, Pat. I do hope you're feeling better now. Take care of yourself!! I love you.

The week promises to be the beginning of the mad rush. In the next four weeks, I can't believe how much has to be done. Saturday morning, there's a two-hour rehearsal for Chorale—we're giving a concert Sunday night. Then, Friday the 15th, is my conducting final which I don't care about but have to do well on. Monday the 18th, there's a big paper due in Traditions. And I think that we have another Italian test on the 15th too. Piano Boards are somewhere during those last two weeks and voice boards are on the 25th, 26th, and 27th—I don't know when I go. I also have 9 ½-hour-long sessions of Italian lab to go to. I wish I could audit Italian this quarter—it's going to wipe me out at this rate. The last week of school we'll be having Theory Exams—2-year Comprehensives of all things. Besides the fact that on the 22nd is the May Festival program that we sing in, and there are three extra rehearsals that week for it, involving, I think, 7 or 8 hours. Pat, I tell you, as I sit here, I become panicky thinking of it.

You asked me to tell you what you can do to help me now. Well, I think what I would most appreciate would be your understanding. I really don't see how I'll ever be able to sit and write to you from now on. And that's pretty hard to accept for us both. Well, I'm not making any definite statements about writing—I seem to contradict myself most of the time anyway. I have a half notion to stop now so I can start my term paper. But I guess I'll keep this night open. I only wasted an hour at school—but I need a break from work, too. I went with my friend Diane to lunch—I didn't eat though (natch). Well, so much for school.

You can wear white jackets by the way. The etiquette book says it is ok. But we'll call the Tuxedo Rental Place to make sure.

My mother is unreal. Pat, I won't mind if your moods change quickly...but I hope that when you become upset or angry with me, you will talk to me and tell me so that I don't feel as if I'm talking to a brick wall of silence. That absolutely infuriates me.

Well, anyway. I also hope that should we argue and say things in a fit of anger, that once we apologize, it will be done with. I don't know whether you hold grudges or not, but I know what a hell grudge-bearing can create, both for the bearer and the object of the grudge. So, there's just a bit of what makes Shelley mad, for your "useless or useful" information book, whatever the case may be.

Forgive me. I'm taking the frustration I feel, out on you. I'm so sorry. Today, started out wrong and I'm quite tired (for a change). I've owed Gayle a letter for almost a week; and I still have unfinished invitations to do. I have to call Gayle's mother about the shoes. I have to call about renewing my Driver's License (I'm making use of the 30-day grace period). I was supposed to order some music two weeks ago and I forgot, so now it is useless. Things to do, do, do, to do.

I'm going crazy. And when the gifts start coming, I think I'll move to Alaska and hide…I'm sorry. This must be one of the bitchiest letters I have ever written…no?... well…it's pretty bad. I was in a fairly even mood until I started thinking about school. If I could audit Italian, I'd be I good shape. However, as a matter of fact. Well.

The pill [Birth-Control Pill] isn't giving me much grief— sometimes I feel a little "morning sickness" in the middle of the night…I'm ok. I sure hope that this has no bearing on children. I'm really a "fraidy cat" I know! I'm sorry.

I hope you can forgive me. If there's one thing you don't need now is for me to yap at you about…what a time I'm having. Actually, if you were here to see me, you would observe that my bitching is really just a sort of a stream of monotone rattling…. I'm going into shock… Thank God, I'm in pretty good shape for the voice boards.

I love you so very much, Pat. I want you to know that things would be almost as hectic without our wedding plans too—so don't think that I'm complaining about the early date of our wedding. I can't think of a more wonderful "release" to look forward to…If I don't have a nervous-breakdown before it. Actually, I lost 1 ½ pounds; only 290 to go…Joke!

Damn. This letter is so negative that it's getting on me nerves. So, I can imagine what it's doing to you. Please forgive me.

Pat, I love you so very much. I must turn to you now, for I have no one…Lord knows, mother has too much on her mind. So, do you, but at least you can put away a letter, knowing that it is a testimony of my relief, just in its existence. That don't make sense, do it?

I love you—and that <u>do</u> make sense. By the way, Burt told me that the definition of a nightgown (not a tired one): what is "a nightgown? That's the thing you hang at the foot of the bed in case of fire." Amen...!

Please take care. I think of you so much—you help the smile to come to my face in time of confusion. I love you... hey, Pat, did I ever tell you I LIKE YOU? Well, I do. I like you VERY MUCH. After all, how could I love you very deeply without liking you too?

And now, goodnight. Sleep well...maybe you can dream of me. Tomorrow I must tell you about your Birthday Present. Goodnight. I love you, Pat. I love you. Love Shelley

This is Tuesday, May 5, and it's about 9:15 P.M.

Today, was lovely weather-wise. There was a student strike at school. Classes were canceled Officially. But I went to my two classes anyway...

I'm so upset about your Birthday Present. I've had it on order over a month and I found out that it would cost me as much to mail it to you as it did to buy it. Would you mind receiving a certificate for it or something, telling you what it is? [It was a beautiful American Heritage College Dictionary which I still use to this day!] You could open that on your birthday. I'm sorry—I really should've thought about the mail cost. I have a little thing to send too—and I'll be calling you. Thing of it is, I just can't afford to send it. So will you be really disappointed? It's really a weird birthday present for a fiancé. I realize, but it's nice and useful. Tell me what you think—Honestly! I'm sorry.

This letter seems to consist mainly of bitching and apology! My darling, Pat. These two days (Monday and Tuesday) have been strange for me, for my family, for the Music Academy, and for the world. So, please pardon this icky letter. I love you so. I guess I'm giving you a good look at me in an extremely disoriented state of mind. I also guess it must be awfully boring to read this letter. I apologize, but really, I feel incapable of improving. If I ended this way, I'd feel bad, so I'll keep this one more day and see if things aren't looking up tomorrow. I love you so much, my dearest Pat. Do take care and think of me often. I love you. Goodnight xxxxxxxx Your Shelley.

[Same letter but now it is May 6, 1970.]

My darling Patric, in these times of violence and strife, I look to you for peace and security. [Shelley was alluding to all the student unrest across the U.S.]

As you've heard by now, four students at Kent State were killed yesterday [By the Ohio National Guard, called in by the Governor]. And now students all over the nation are on strike, supposedly to protest the deaths (and the Viet Nam War).

But how can they hold the deaths against anyone else more than themselves? Everyone is to blame as much as anyone. They say that the four students had nothing to do with the violence on campus that resulted in their deaths. And so how can strikers cry this in good conscience, knowing that by striking, they are opposing the beliefs of the four who died.

Today I was accosted I don't know how many times by students— "peace-loving" students—who became irritated, even angry, when I either ignored them or refused to join them in their strike. To one boy, I said "I'm sorry, but I just can't afford to strike." "Well, can you afford to die? You could be next."

He didn't mean it as a threat, I'm sure, but I couldn't help but feel a rather numb pity for him, and the others. God forbid we should become a nation of "human beings" thriving upon death—the living death of hate. Somewhere, there is reasoning left in this country. Somewhere, love exists and grows. I pray that "somewhere" finds its way to the campuses soon. Before it's too late.

I don't think anyone in this country wants Peace any more than I do. But how are we to achieve Peace abroad when there is such turmoil in our own country? [Shelley continues with two pages of discussion concerning her political views and attitudes.]

Well, I just stopped for a few minutes, and I won't read what I've just written. I guess I got carried away. I'd been thinking for a long time before I sat down to write to you and the tension within my brain built up to the point where it simply had to be released. My thoughts are probably unorganized, but I hope they—the words—expressed some of what I was thinking.

Today, we received our second gift from a longtime family friend. It's a silver gravy boat on a tray (one piece) and I guess it's solid silver (not plate, but not sterling), It's just gorgeous and impractical but you'll love it.

Tomorrow, I'm going to register for stainless steel—we have to. I'll try to get something close to our silver pattern. People should have a choice and Lordy, we <u>need</u> stainless steel! I finished all my invitations. (Except the ones you'll send me.) Hooray! Today I worked so long on Italian that I'm turning into a pizza.

Pat, I've got to talk to you—I'm so upset. You know what I go through about weight, etc.—well, I've started gaining weight with the pill. I've gained 3 pounds and so I'm really going strict on my diet to see if that'll help. I've been so bothered thinking about it. "What would

Pat think if he came back and I was fatter?" I can't stand the thought. I'm going to crash and don't tell me not to because I won't listen.

Please tell me what you think. I don't want to gain—but I guess I can't help it with the [Birth control] pill. Will you mind that much? I have to know your thoughts. I don't want you to be ashamed of me. Maybe the weight won't even show, I don't know.

Another thing—Doctor Girard said that he wants me to tell him every reaction to the pill. I'll probably go sometime after next week for the blood test. But he said that if I get headaches from it then he'd take me off! What am I going to do?? I had a headache all day and have had a bit of one nagging for days, but how should I know it is the pill—more likely, it's tension! But another reaction is that my breasts are swollen and pretty tender—just like they get right before my period. That's kind of uncomfortable, but certainly not unbearable. Theresa hates her diaphragm and says they're hell. I don't know; I'll see what he says. Whatcha think? Don't tell me I'm a neurotic—I already know that!

Pat please excuse me in this letter. I really didn't intend for it to be so damn bitchy. I love you so very much, and hate to make you suffer through this. Life is pretty hard now and I'm going crazy for a change. But I love you and miss you, and so I keep going o.k.? I feel fine, so don't worry. And I'll feel even better after getting some sleep. I wish you were here to lie naked with me now. I'm sending you a lot of love now. Take care, my darling Pat. Don't get upset about this letter. I love you so much. Devotedly, your Shelley.

I'm sorry — I meant for the note to be cheerful.

I love you so — just think, we're only 38 —no— 37 days away from being "Mr. and Mrs." My beloved Patric.

I do hope you're feeling much better and that you're taking good care of yourself. I miss you. Perhaps one of these days you'll get into the mood to write again.... But in the meantime, please think of me often so I can feel your love coming to me. Bless you, Pat, you're the dearest man alive. I love you so much. Remember that, always. With all my love,

your Shirley
xxxxxxxxxxxx

To my dearest Pat,

I felt like saying hello to you, and sending very warm love to you tonight. At choir, the Wedding Cantata by Pinkham was rehearsed; it's very nice. Dr. Whikehart had us rehearse part of a piece that he wrote on marriage (for our program MAY 31).

And I like that more than the Pinkham. The words to Dr. W.'s piece are written by Kahlil Gibran from the book *THE PROPHET* (Lebanese mystic, poet, and artist).

And Dr. Whikehart's piece was included in our Wedding Ceremony!!

THE PROPHET
BY KAHLIL GIBRAN, 1923

"His power came from some great reservoir of spiritual life else it could not have been so universal and potent, but the majesty and beauty of the language with which he clothed it were all his own."
—Claude Bragdon

Then Almitra spoke again and said, And
*   what of Marriage, master?*
And he answered saying:
*   You were born together, and together you*
shall be forevermore.
*   You shall be together when the white*
wings of death scatter your days.
*   Aye, you shall be together even in the silent memory*
of God.
But let there be spaces in your togetherness,
*   And let the winds of the heavens dance between you.*

Love one another, but make not a bond of love:
*   Let it rather be a moving sea between the shores*
*   of your souls.*
Fill each other's cup but drink not from one cup.
*   Give one Another of your bread but eat not from*
*   the same loaf.*
Sing and dance together and be joyous, but let each
one of you be alone,
*   Even as the strings of a lute are alone though they*
*   quiver with the same music.*

Give your hearts, but not into each other's keeping.
For only the hand of Life can contain your hearts.
And stand together yet not too near together:
For the pillars of the temple stand apart,
And the oak and the cypress grow not in each other's shadow.

Well my love, how are you feeling now?

I have three envelopes to send you, and they are marked "Do Not Open until May 13," so look for them, ok? I did want you to notice the "Do Not Open" signs.

Bad news—my two new bras don't fit now—guess who's getting bigger because of certain little pill? Please do something—say something to help me overcome this fear I'm feeling. I don't know, I guess my inferiority complex is placing not a material, but a <u>weight</u> value upon your love—it keeps telling me that you won't love me anymore past such & such a weight. Don't let that hurt you, Pat—I know it's stupid, but it's sort of like that dream you had that one time that you weren't allowed to be alone with me and the other one that I put my music career before you. Well my complex says you put weight before me.

I'm sorry—I meant for this note to be cheerful. I love you—just think, we're only 38—no, 37—days away from being "Mr. and Mrs." My beloved Patric. I do hope you're feeling much better and that you're taking good care of yourself. I miss you. Perhaps one of these days you'll get into the mood to write again…but in the meantime, please think of me often so I can hear your love coming to me. Bless you, Pat; you're the dearest man alive. I love you so much. Remember that always. With all my love, your Shelley xxxxx.

This was the last letter either of us wrote. Shelley became totally consumed with end-of-the-year exams, mixed in with wedding preparations. When we needed to communicate, we telephoned each other.

Patric had been working steadily with the Bank of America Central Cash Vault in downtown Los Angeles. He put in a request for two weeks off in June for the wedding and honeymoon. The request was granted. One day after the last working day, Patric began a quick cross-country drive to Our Town. The wedding plans came off without a hitch, and in June Shelley and Patric were married in a fair-sized wedding and reception. It was lovely. Around 4:00 P.M. Patric and Shelley left town on their honeymoon (and their vow of virginity honored right up to the wedding night), which naturally included a car trip back to Los Angeles, with stops and visits to the Amana Colonies, the Black Hills of South Dakota—home to Mt. Rushmore, where four presidents' likenesses are carved into a mountain; Buffalo Bill's town of Cody, Wyoming; two days in Yellowstone National Park— staying in the original Yellowstone Inn, on to Reno and an overnight visit with a cousin, and finally down the backside of the Sierra Nevada Mountain Range to Patric's father's home in Sierra Hills. [Note: This was a great adventure for Shelley as she had never been away from home, let alone driving 2000+ miles through ten states.] And here, after an intense six-month courtship, in the Sierra Hills, Shelley and Patric began their new lives as Mr. and Mrs. Spencer!

Does one say, "Mission Accomplished"?

Dr. Patric Leedom's Biography Sketch:

Dr. Patric Leedom received his doctorate in Curriculum and Instruction right here at UC in 1992. Prior to shifting from teaching K-12, to teaching College students, Patric Leedom was a founding team member of the New School Montessori in North Avondale, and a founding team member of Sands Montessori School for Cinti Public Schools.

After receiving his doctorate, Dr. Leedom joined the Department of Teacher Education at Shawnee State University. Over the years, Dr. Leedom has taught a variety of courses, but focused more on: Introduction to the Teaching Profession, Math and Science Methods, Senior Seminar—A Capstone Research Course open to the whole university student body, AND, when Ohio switched from Certification to Licensure, Dr. Leedom created a course titled "Guidance and Classroom Management" but a better descriptor would be: How does a teacher take a group of students and create a very positive educational atmosphere where: every student wants to be there every day, every student feels welcome and respected, every student feels SAFE, not only from fellow students but also from the teacher—not embarrassing him/her in front of other students, and finally, every student feels that there is a positive relationship between that student and the teacher.

Parallel to his teaching, Patric Leedom had a career in the U.S. Navy Submarine Force. He was a "Quartermaster" responsible for the safe navigation of the ship. Patric stayed for 24 years, was submerged on 23 different submarines (they always needed help with navigation), was on the Submarine Admiral's Staff for 11 years. In 1983, he returned back to active duty for two years, where his assignment was as Assistant Navigator on a Fast Attack Nuclear submarine. In the summer of 1984, he guided the submarine up into the Arctic Ocean to gather intelligence. Submerged for 64 days!

Patric now does a presentation on The History of American Submarining. Additionally, he has been a key Note Speaker for three Veterans' Day celebrations, and three Memorial Day Celebrations.